SPINNING IN THE '70s

Editor
P. R. Lord.

Associate Professor, School of Textiles,
North Carolina State University at Raleigh,
North Carolina, U.S.A.

MERROW

First published 1970

677.0282'2
SPI

ISBN 0 900 54101 6

Merrow Publishing Co. Ltd., 276, *Hempstead Road, Watford, Herts., England*

Printed in Great Britain at the St Ann's Press, Park Road, Altrincham

Preface

In April 1969 a course entitled "Spinning in the '70s" was held at the University of Manchester Institute of Science and Technology. Experts from several countries delivered lectures about aspects of yarn manufacture which might be expected to figure largely in the coming decade, and these lectures were presented to an international audience drawn from industry, research organisations and universities. The audience was given an opportunity to question the speakers and, because of their experience, the questions and answers formed a valuable part of the conference. This book has been written to provide a record of the proceedings.

At this point it is fitting to record grateful thanks not only to the speakers themselves, but also to their respective sponsoring organisations who gave willing consent for the authors to participate. Other experts, who were unable to present papers, made many helpful suggestions; thanks are given to them for their invaluable assistance.

At the time of the conference it was not possible to cover the topic as fully as originally intended, and additional material has been introduced into the book to remedy this. Furthermore, the course was an advanced one intended for those already well versed in the technology; additional material has been introduced, and the information edited in such a way as to render it of value to textile students generally.

Grateful acknowledgements are given to my former colleagues and students who have helped with the production of the book in a variety of ways; particular mention should be made of Mr. J. S. Taylor, who was co-organiser of the course mentioned, Dr. M. S. Sadasivam, Dr. N. Senturk, Mr. R. P. Cox, Mr. K. P. Mishra and Mr. P. P. Chandarana. Conference authors, their organisations and the titles of their papers are listed below, and this is intended as formal but grateful recognition of their original work on which much of this book has been based.

(1) Mr. H. Cripps of Shirley Institute;
    "A review of short-staple spinning methods".
(2) Messrs. S. L. Anderson and J. Ingham of Wira;
    "A review of long-staple spinning methods".
(3) Mr. D. C. Hossack of Filtrona Textile Products Ltd;
    "Tape yarns".
(4) Dr. P. Volans of Monsanto Chemicals Ltd;
    "Network yarns".
(5) Mr. R. Lyon of Shirley Institute;
    "Performance of break-spinners other than the drum type".
(6) Dr. P. A. Smith of Leeds University;
    "Break-spinning at Leeds University"
(7) Dr. P. R. Lord of U.M.I.S.T.;
    "Break-spinning at U.M.I.S.T.".
(8) Messrs. C. J. Copple and P. H. Challoner of T.M.M. (Research) Ltd;
    "Break-spinning of long-staple yarns".
(9) Mr. Z. Pospivil of V.U.B. (Czechoslovakia);
    "Processing yarns in the pilot plant of V.U.B. using the BD200 break-spinning machines".
(10) Mr. K. Susami of Toyo Rayon Co. Ltd. (Japan);
    "Break-spinning in Japan".
(11) Mr. J. Kasparek of V.U.B. (Czechoslovakia);
    "Characteristics of break-spun yarns".
(12) Dr. H. J. Selling of Vezelinstituut T.N.O. (Holland);
    "Twistless spinning".

Finally, an acknowledgement to my wife whose forbearance and common sense have helped in many ways.

P.R.L.
October, 1969

School of Textiles,
University of North Carolina,
Raleigh,
N.C. 27607,
U.S.A.

Contents

1

Spinning. An Introduction

This introductory chapter discusses the early history of spinning with the object of setting out the background to modern developments. The ring frame emerged from the ferment of ideas in the industrial revolution to become one of the most important machines in yarn production. It has technical and economic limitations, however, which restrict the scope for further major improvement. The possibilities of technological advancement in a number of directions are reviewed.

From the earliest times, man has clothed himself in fabrics of one sort or another. At first, he depended upon animal skins and furs. Then he learned to make crude materials by interweaving flexible strands, such as vines and creepers, into primitive forms of cloth. This was the beginning of textile manufacture, which has now grown into one of the world's great industries.

The production of textile fabrics by an interweaving process was possible only if suitable strands were available. The stems of plants, and strips of animal skin, possessed the strength and flexibility that enabled them to be woven into coarse materials.

As man became more civilised, he demanded more sophisticated fabrics for clothing and other purposes. Finer and more uniform strands were needed, and these were derived from a variety of sources. In China, for example, wonderfully fine continuous filaments were obtained by unwinding the cocoons of silkworms. Flexible strands were made by combining several of these filaments together, and the strands of silk were woven into fabrics of the finest quality. China became famous for her silks, which were carried by traders to every part of the civilised world.

A* 1

Silk, however, was expensive and in very short supply. Other sources of weavable strand were needed from which to make textiles cheap enough and serviceable enough for the common man. Such strands were obtained by the process that has become known as spinning

Short Fibres

Nature provides us with an immense variety of short filaments or fibres. Seed hairs, the leaf and stem strands of plants, and the hairs of animal coats are available to us in many forms. Some of these fibrous materials are less than an inch in length; others may form strands that are several feet long.

At some point in history, man discovered that he could convert these relatively short fibres into continuous strands of virtually any length he needed. First, he drew out the fibrous mass into loose strands or slivers, then by twisting the strands he locked the fibres together to form a strong, flexible, coherent strand or yarn. This process, spinning, has been in use for thousands of years, and it still provides us with much of the yarn needed by the textile industry.

At first, the materials made from spun yarns were uneven and coarse. But over the centuries, spinning techniques and skills became more refined. Finer fibres, notably cotton, came into use alongside the animal and bast fibres from which the early yarns were largely made. Until comparatively recent times, spinning was carried out mainly by hand, using only the most primitive equipment. Then, in Britain, spinning was caught up in the Industrial Revolution. The demand for finer fabrics continued to grow, and mechanisation of the spinning process was essential if the necessary yarn was to be produced. Cotton became the most important of all the textile fibres, providing materials that were cheap and serviceable; wool complemented cotton, yielding full, warm fabrics of the finest quality.

The textile industry developed rapidly during the eighteenth and nineteenth centuries. The processes involved in converting fibre into fabric became strangely isolated one from another, each manufacturer concentrating his attention upon his own particular stage of textile production. Thus, the cotton spinner was absorbed in spinning cotton, his end-product being a cotton yarn; the worsted spinner focussed his attention upon the production of worsted yarns, and so on. This resulted in the separate development of the various textile processes, each manufacturer observing a curious detachment with respect to the ultimate product, the fabric.

This segmented growth of the textile industry was detrimental to the overall development of the industry as a whole, but it had the advantage of concentrating the efforts of inventors and engineers on specific aspects of the industry. During the Industrial Revolution, a spate of ideas and inventions flowed from the minds of textile men. Cotton, in particular, benefited from this activity, and the history of the cotton industry in Britain forms a useful background to the development of spinning techniques.

MECHANISATION OF STAPLE FIBRE SPINNING

Mechanisation of the spinning process began with the distaff and the spindle. The downwards pull of the rotating spindle produced a yarn from the sliver on the distaff, and the yarn was wound on to the spindle. This method of spinning was in common use until about two centuries ago. The next development was the spinning wheel, in which a rotating wheel imparted the rotary movement to the spindle. In a further improvement, known as the Saxony Wheel, a foot treadle was used, freeing the operator's hands. Flyer spinning was introduced in the 16th century and is still in use for the production of worsted and bast fibre yarns. Fig. 1.2 shows the principles of flyer spinning.

Roller Drafting

Roller drafting was invented by John Wyatt or Lewis Paul, the latter being granted a patent for his roller drafting spinning machinery in 1738. For the first time, attenuation of the fibre strands had been mechanised. In 1770 James Hargreaves took out a patent for the Spinning Jenny; this consisted of a wooden framework with a movable carriage and a number of spindles driven by bands from a cylinder rotated by a handwheel. During its operation, predetermined lengths of rovings held between the spindles and the carriage were drafted by movement of the latter away from the former, and twist was inserted by rotation of the spindles. Thus, in the Spinning Jenny, the process of twisting while stretching was mechanised.

The adaptation of roller drafting was developed by Arkwright in 1769 in his patented Spinning Frame, which is generally acclaimed as the forerunner of the roller drafting spinning frame of the present day. The roving was drafted by means of three pairs of rollers which were dead weighted by a lever system. Twist was imparted by flyers which also wound the spun yarn on to the bobbin with the help of a series of hooks. This was a forerunner of the differential motions which gave a continuous and concurrent spinning and winding action. Water power was first used to drive Arkwright's spinning machine, which became known as a water frame.

Crompton's Mule

The drawing rollers of Arkwright's frame and the stretch and twist arrangement of Hargreaves' spinning jenny were combined in Crompton's mule of 1779. Because of its crude construction, however, the mule made heavy demands on skilled manual labour. Richard Roberts improved Crompton's mule, producing the self-acting mule. This machine spun yarn which was not subjected to winding-on tensions during the twisting process, and the tension upon it was not necessarily greater than that imposed by its own weight. For this reason, the mule was capable of spinning a weaker yarn than any other machine then known; it was pre-eminent in the production of the finest yarns. Moreover, the low spinning tension enabled the mule to spin a finer yarn from a given quality of raw material than any other machine. Mule-spun yarn, because of the peculiar nature of the spinning process, possessed certain characteristics which were not easily obtained with other later methods of spinning. Yarn produced by the mule was fuller, softer to handle, more regular and more hairy than yarn spun on the ring frame which was to succeed it.

Mule spinning was a discontinuous process; the drafting mechanism stopped as the spun yarn was wound on to the body of the spindle. The intermittent nature of mule spinning resulted in low productivities. The machine needed a large area of floor space; it was complicated and required highly-skilled labour. The combination of all these disadvantages far outweighed the advantage in yarn quality for most practical purposes.

Spinning Progress

These early days of the nineteenth century were marked by a great ferment of ideas; many of them failed to achieve any success, but they often stimulated subsequent development. A patent by Williams [1], for example, in 1807 described a device with many of the features of break spinning. The principles are shown in Fig. 1.1. Fibres carried on the wire of a surface A were to be removed by a rotating comb B, and the fibre assembly drawn away along the axis of the comb to be wound on to a package. Rotation of the comb was to insert twist. Whether this particular device worked or not is unknown, but it undoubtedly included the elements of break spinning (see Chapter 8). It did not achieve any practical success.

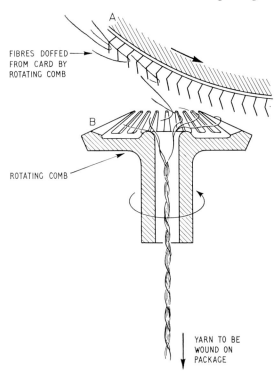

FIBRES DOFFED
FROM CARD BY
ROTATING COMB

ROTATING COMB

YARN TO BE
WOUND ON
PACKAGE

Fig. 1.1   Williams' spinning device of 1807.

In an attempt to dispense with the flyer, Danforth invented
the cap spinner (1828); this is still used today for spinning
worsted yarns. The basic principle is described in Chapter 3;
friction is used to give the differential motion required to
twist and wind concurrently.

In 1828, John Thorpe patented a device which served the
same purpose; it included a ring concentric with the spindle.
In 1844, Thorpe was granted a patent for a traveller similar

to that used in ring spinning today. Credit for the invention of
the modern traveller, however, must be given to Addison
and Stephens (1829) of New York and Jenks (1830) of
Pawtucket, Rhode Island. From that time onwards, the
ring frame system made steady headway; it was well
established by the end of the 19th century. Ring spinning
had the advantages of simplicity and high productivity;
these features, coupled with low operating costs, enabled the
ring frame gradually to replace the mule. Fig. 1.3 shows the
principle of the ring spinner.

During the last 50 years, ring spinning has attained a high
degree of efficiency. High draft systems have been developed
and it has become possible to attain given standards of yarn
regularity at very much higher levels of draft. When ring
frames were first introduced, relatively short lift, low speed
machines were employed. These were more productive than
mules and proved adequate under the conditions existing at
that time. Since then, the economics of spinning, particularly
of coarse count yarns, have demanded increasingly large
packages and high yarn delivery speeds. Improvements in
rings and travellers and the use of balloon control rings have
been important factors in attaining high spindle speeds.
Economies have been achieved by increasing the size of the
creel package and by the introduction of pneumatic under-
clearers and travelling cleaners. The modern ring frame is
a highly-developed spinning system. Over the last two
decades, however, labour costs have increased greatly, and
despite the progress made, spinning remains one of the most
expensive processes in yarn manufacture.

RING SPINNING

There are basic technical limitations in the ring frame
which restrict further increases in package size and production rates. An increase in package size substantially
reduces the cost of doffing and subsequent handling, and

this may be achieved by increasing ring diameter and/or spindle lift.

For a particular yarn count at a given spindle lift and speed, there is a minimum yarn spinning tension below which it is difficult to spin. At tensions lower than this, the

Fig. 1.2   The flyer principle.
Note: $\omega_f\text{-}\omega_s$ equals winding speed.

yarn balloon collapses, imposing limitations on the height of spindle lift that can be used. The use of balloon control rings or of "collapsed balloon" spindles overcomes some of the difficulties.

The use of very high spindle speeds may be limited by the following factors:—

(a) yarn delivery rate,
(b) yarn balloon,
(c) end-breakage rate,
(d) yarn strength,
(e) traveller velocity.

Yarn delivery rate is limited by the ability of the operator to make a satisfactory piecing when a yarn breakage occurs. The limiting speed for manual piecing is around 750 inches per minute when spinning coarse counts, and somewhat less for fine yarns. This limit may be raised by the use of automatic piecing mechanisms at the expense of increased capital charges.

With a given traveller, the yarn tension varies approximately as the square of the spindle speed. At low speeds the balloon would collapse, but at high speed the yarn tension increases; above a certain speed, the end breakage rate becomes excessive. The spindle speed at which this occurs depends to a large extent on yarn strength. Owing to the reduced yarn twist in the region between the lappet and the front roller nip, there is a reduction in yarn strength in this region. This imposes a limit on the spindle speed.

Traveller speed is one of the major limiting factors in high speed spinning. Until the middle of the present century, a maximum speed of about 70 ft./sec. was widely accepted. High traveller speeds produce frictional heating of the ring and traveller surfaces, causing traveller burns. This results eventually in traveller breakages, and there is therefore a limit to the ring diameters and package speeds which can be used. Ring damage may also occur, giving rise to peaks in yarn tension which lead to an increased number of end-breakages. The practical limit of the traveller speed depends particularly on the weight and shape of the traveller, the ring diameter and the contour of the ring flange. The commonly used C-section traveller makes only partial contact with the ring, and as it has a high centre of gravity, it tends to tilt.

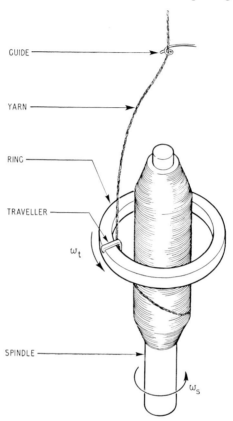

GUIDE

YARN

RING

TRAVELLER

ω_t

SPINDLE

ω_s

Fig. 1.3   Principle of the ring spinner. Note: ω_s-ω_t
equals winding speed.

The newer elliptical traveller has a low centre of gravity;
it presents a large bearing surface to the ring, with the result
that higher speeds can be used. Traveller speeds have been
further increased by the use of anti-wedge rings (introduced
in 1953) in which the bearing surface between ring and

traveller has been extended and matched to the ring profile. It is claimed that an anti-wedge elliptical traveller will permit speeds of over 100 ft./sec.; this can be increased to about 125 ft./sec. by using micro-etched ring surfaces and molybdenised travellers. The speeds quoted relate to a 2 in. diameter ring.

Cost Factors

The three important factors that decide the economics of spinning are labour, capital and power costs. In view of the rising cost of labour, it seems reasonable to reduce labour content at the expense of capital and power. This has led to increases in yarn package size and spindle speeds as labour costs have risen over the years.

Package sizes have increased because the cost of power needed to drive larger packages has decreased in relation to the cost of labour required to doff and rewind them. Reduction in the number of piecings and changes in machine utilisation are also factors. Because of technical limitations, spindle speeds must be decreased as package sizes are increased, and this affects the profitability of the operation. Furthermore, large packages necessitate the use of balloon control rings, which tend to make the operations of piecing and doffing more difficult and expensive. Balloon control rings also increase the hairiness of yarns.

Production per spindle hour has been increased by raising spindle speeds. Apart from the technical limitations mentioned earlier, the use of very high spindle speeds is limited also by economic considerations, as higher spindle speeds lead to higher power costs. According to DeBarr and Catling [2] the package power required per unit of production is approximately proportional to $D^{2.75} N^{1.5}$ (where D = ring diameter and N = spindle speed), to which other components must be added to arrive at the total for the frame. If the traveller speed were independent of ring size (it is not in reality, but the assumption may be made to simplify the argument), then $D \propto \frac{1}{N}$ and the cost of power per unit production would diminish slowly as the speed increased. This might seem to imply that high speed spindles should be used with very small diameter rings. Apart from the considerations already discussed, capital costs tend to rise ever more sharply with increasing speed, and labour costs for doffing and winding would increase under these circumstances. There is thus a balance to be struck, optimum conditions depending upon the financial environment. The costs of labour, capital and power are closely interrelated, and it is not possible to alter one without affecting the others.

In general, economics control the spinning process, and most ring frames are operated below the technical limit. For this reason there is little likelihood of a dramatic advance in ring spinning technique; speeds and package sizes will probably increase very slowly as labour costs continue to rise.

RECENT DEVELOPMENTS

Traditional fabrics were made from yarns spun from animal or vegetable fibres. With the rise of the chemical industry, it became possible to create man-made fibres from cellulose and other natural polymers, and then to make fibres from synthetic polymers. At first, man-made fibres were used mainly as continuous filaments; later they were chopped into staple fibre for spinning by traditional techniques used with natural fibres. More recently, interest has been concentrated upon the modification of filament yarns to give them special properties.

Continuous Filament Yarns

In the early days, filament yarns were used as a substitute for silk; these "artificial silks" had some characteristics similar to those of silk, e.g. fabrics made from them had a shiny lustre and a slippery handle. The resemblance was only superficial, however, and early "artificial silk" fabrics had characteristics which restricted their acceptance in the general textile field. Continuous filament yarns, in general, yielded fabrics which were smooth, lustrous and strong, but they lacked the warmth, handle and other desirable characteristics associated with fabrics made from yarns spun from staple fibres. Despite the increased strength and resistance to wear of fabrics from continuous filament yarns, these fabrics did not gain wide acceptance. In recent years, therefore, techniques have been developed for bulking continuous filament yarns in order to give their fabrics characteristics associated with staple fibre yarns.

The bulking of filament yarns gives them a much more acceptable appearance and a warmer feel. The texture of fabrics made from them has a resemblance to that of traditional fabrics which are familiar to the user, and bulked yarns have been widely accepted. They are very suitable for knitting, and the spectacular rise in the use of knitted fabrics has been such as to challenge the pre-eminence of the loom. The modified continuous filament yarn has acquired an ever-increasing proportion of the market, and in some areas there has been a massive swing from weaving to knitting. This is a significant factor in considering the future of staple yarns. There are differences in characteristics between bulked and staple yarns, and it is improbable that the demand for the latter will cease. An important difference lies in the extensibility of the yarn; when a non-stretch fabric is required, conventional yarns are generally preferred. The development of fibrillating yarns has introduced a new factor, however, yielding a product which has much of the character of staple yarns (see Chapter 5) and yet needs little or no twist. "Twist costs money" and fibrillating yarn may prove to be a formidable competitor in many textile fields.

Staple Fibre Yarns

Many staple yarns are made wholly from man-made

fibres, and many more from blends of natural and man-made fibres. Blending provides yarns which combine desirable characteristics of the constituent fibres, and the flexibility of the process is an important factor in its favour. There is little doubt that staple fibre will find a major outlet in blended yarns in years to come.

In the production of traditional yarn and fabric structures, new techniques are presenting new challenges. Sulzer weaving machines and air and water-jet looms, which are replacing many conventional looms, for example, require larger weft packages than an ordinary loom. In spinning, the ring frame will face competition from break, twistless and self-twist spinning methods, as discussed in succeeding chapters.

Non-Woven Fabrics

The end product in textile manufacture is the fabric, and fabrics may be made without yarn at all. Many advances have been made in the production of so-called non-woven materials, in which fibres are held together by adhesives, needle-punching, stitching or a combination of these. Paper could be regarded as the original adhesive-bonded fabric, and the cheapness of paper has enabled it to take markets from the textile industry, e.g. paper handkerchiefs, disposable garments, kitchen and other tissues. Industrial fabrics are made by using resin adhesives, and resin-bonded fabrics have also found uses in the carpet industry. Needle-punched fabrics are used as floor coverings, and the development of tufted carpets owes much to these new techniques. Needle-punched and stitch-bonded materials have made rapid progress in Eastern Europe. Stitch-bonding machines are capable of very high rates of production, but the cost of stitching yarns may be too high for the economic production of fine fabrics, even if sufficiently regular laps could be produced. Chemstrand has introduced a new spun bonded process in which the fibre adhesion occurs only where the fibres touch and the bond is not at all enlarged; this gives desirable fabric properties.

Fabrics produced by these novel techniques represent a corresponding fall in the output of fabrics made in the traditional manner. The effect is counterbalanced by the expanding population of the world and by the increasing demand per capita. There is no doubt, however, that the textile industry is undergoing fundamental changes which will affect all aspects of it to a greater or lesser degree. Apart from changes in the quantity of material required, there will be changes in the type of material wanted.

Finer Fabrics

Throughout his history, man has always demanded ever finer fabrics, with increasingly sophisticated standards of decoration. These trends are being strengthened by modern man's ability to control his immediate environment. The adoption of central heating and air conditioning has tended to reduce the importance of warmth in many garments, and to place a greater emphasis on weight and appearance. In consequence, there is an increasing demand for finer fabrics capable of displaying all manner of decorative effects. Such effects, in great diversity, may be obtained from an ever-widening range of machines.

It is often assumed that the lighter the fabric, the finer is the yarn required. Fine yarns are more expensive than coarser ones, however, and improvements in yarn evenness have reduced the need for doubling yarns to obtain the desired regularity. A singles yarn may now be used where a doubled one was formerly needed for the same type of fabric.

These pressures have stimulated a ferment of new ideas and a reappraisal of traditional beliefs. Future historians may regard the mid-twentieth century as a period which marked the beginning of a new revolution in the textile industry. The first one, based on mechanical ingenuity, formed part of the Industrial Revolution that changed the

modern world. The second one is part of the Technological
Revolution that is carrying us along so swiftly towards a
bewildering future.

2

Short-staple Spinning

by H. Cripps*

During post-war years, the challenge of imports, the loss of export markets and the shortage and increasing cost of labour made it essential that the U.K. short-staple spinning industry should increase productivity substantially if it were to survive. The chapter describes how this was achieved as a result of great technological advances in spinning machinery and re-deployment of labour. It is suggested that the output of short-staple yarns in the U.K. is likely to remain at its late 1960s level of a little over 500,000,000 lb per annum during the 1970s, but that there will be changes in the demand for various types of yarns. In general, there will be an increasing demand for the coarser yarns and blends of cotton and man-made fibre and a decreasing demand for finer yarns, especially those of combed quality. The most probable changes in the short-staple spinning process likely to arise during the next decade are discussed in the light of current developments and market trends.

PRODUCTION IN THE U.K.

Production of spun yarns in the U.K. has diminished steadily during the present century. 1,960M lb. of spun yarns were produced, for example, in 1912; 1,070M lb. in 1936; 640M lb. in 1960; 505M lb. in 1962. Simple extrapolation of the graph of falling output might seem to indicate that no spun yarn at all will be produced by the late 1970s.

During the 1960s, however, a re-equipment scheme was introduced in the U.K., and imports were restricted. This had the effect of reducing the downward trend of spun yarn production, and the graph began to level off. In 1969, output of spun yarns was about 500M lb., and it seems

* Conference author. The Cotton Silk and Man-made Fibres Research Association, U.K.

17

probable that this level of production will be maintained during the 1970s.

CHANGING DEMANDS

Although the annual output of spun yarns is likely to remain steady, there will be changes in the demand for various types and counts of yarn. There is likely to be a significant reduction, for example, in the demand for all combed yarns, for cotton carded yarns finer than 30 tex (20s c.c.), and for rayon yarns finer than 120 tex (5s c.c.). There will probably be little change in the demand for carded yarns coarser than 120 tex (5s c.c.), and for synthetic yarns and mixtures coarser than 30 tex (20s c.c.).

In general, the demand for fine yarns will decrease and the demand for coarse yarns will increase. There are several reasons for this. Spun yarns are better than they used to be; they are up to 30% stronger and considerably more regular. For many end uses, there is less need to double fine yarns to produce a sufficiently strong and regular product. The demand for combed yarns, for the same reason, is reduced.

Continuous filament yarns, normal and textured, are being used in increasing quantitites for certain end uses which were traditionally the province of fine spun staple yarn.

An example of these two factors at work may be seen in poplin shirting. Traditionally this used a twofold 80s c.c. yarn, which was later superseded by a singles 40s c.c. yarn. More recently, warp knitted shirts of continuous filament nylon have entered this market, and now account for about half the sales of shirts in the U.K.

Non-Woven Fabrics

Non-woven fabrics, during the 1960s, had little effect on the demand for spun yarns, even though some types of non-wovens require no yarn at all. The majority of non-woven fabrics were used as felts, interlinings, blankets and so on;

in general, they were not of the type that would replace fabrics made from spun yarns. Non-wovens have a high growth potential, and production is likely to increase from the 1969 level of about 30 million sq. yd. per year to about 180 million sq. yd. per year by the mid '70s. Even then, their share of fabric production in the U.K. will be only about 6% of the total, and the effect of non-wovens on spun yarns is not likely to be very significant during the '70s.

The rising demand for coarse rayon yarns comes mainly from their increasing use in carpets. Medium count yarns spun from man-made fibres and blends will be required for weaving and knitting. Cotton, like most natural fibres, will lose further ground to man-made fibres and yarns during the 1970s. More cotton, on its own and in blends, will be used for knitting.

Condenser Spinning

Condenser spinning uses waste fibre from the cotton system and also viscose rayon staple. The production of cotton waste is diminishing, as less cotton is being processed and there is a lower percentage of waste. Less combing is being done, and the amount of comber waste is diminishing. Also, the waste from the high production card is only about half of that from the low production card. All things considered, therefore, it is probable that condenser spinning will make increasing use of man-made fibres in future. Although cheap raw materials are used in condenser spinning, it is no longer a cheap process. The yarns produced have special properties; they are weak and can cause trouble in winding and weaving, but they are full and easily raised. If a modified form of break spinner becomes available, capable of producing condenser type yarns, it will have significant influence on the condenser spinning industry.

Future Trends

Table 2.1. shows the amounts of staple yarns produced in

DEMAND FOR SPUN YARNS (M. lb.)
in the U.K.

	Cotton		M.M. and Blends	
	1968	1975	1968	1975
Weaving	315	230	70	100
Knitting	27	40	29	48
Carpets	–	–	36	50
Sewing	14	11	3	5
Others	30	25	5	10
	386	306	143	213

Table 2.1

the U.K. in 1968, and their end uses. It also forecasts the end uses and weights of spun yarns for 1975. The amount of cotton staple used in weaving is likely to decrease appreciably by the mid '70s. On the other hand, the amount of man-made fibre used in weaving is likely to increase. In knitting, cotton spun yarns and man-made fibres and blends will be used increasingly. Carpets will probably increase the demand for staple yarns, which will be much coarser than the average yarn spun in 1968. There will thus be a significant decrease in the average yarn count. Sewing threads are unlikely to alter greatly, but it is probable that the use of man-made fibres and blends will increase at the expense of cotton.

The total output of spun yarns in 1968 (529M lb.) will, by 1975, have fallen only to 519M lb.

In the 1970s, machinery will work more intensively, and more shift working will be adopted, using the 4-shift system in which machines run for 160 hours per week. Runs will be longer, and the variety of yarn counts spun will be smaller. Intensive production will result in a reduction of the number of spindles from 3.8 million (1969) to about 1.8 million ring frame equivalent spindles. The adoption of break spinning will reduce the number still further; one break-spinning spindle is the equivalent of 2 or 3 ring-spinning spindles.

RECENT DEVELOPMENTS

Revolutionary changes in spinning technology took place during the 1950s and 1960s, following the post war boom. These changes were particularly marked in the U.K., incorporating as they did many of the developments that had been taking place elsewhere since the 1920s. During the 1950s, export markets were being lost in the U.K., labour was becoming scarcer and dearer, and heavy competition was being met from overseas. Higher productivity was essential if the textile industry was to meet the challenge. The most obvious and effective way of achieving higher productivity was to shorten the textile-making process by reducing the number of machines in the production line, to run the remaining machines faster, and to produce larger packages. The production of larger packages was necessary to reduce handling, so that the effects of productivity would not be offset by increased loads on the operative.

Shortened Process

When some processes are omitted in spinning, high drafts must be used in remaining processes and/or doublings must be sacrificed. During carding, fibres become hooked and the direction in which the hooked fibres are presented to each process is important. Although later drafting processes tend to reduce the hooks, they are never completely eliminated. The higher the draft, the greater is the need to present the fibres to the drafting system with their hooks trailing. The direction of the fibres is reversed at each packaging operation and, since most of the fibres leaving the card have trailing hooks, there should be an even number of packaging processes between the card and the ring frame. In other words, there should be an odd number of machines or processes. If this is the case, fibres will enter the drafting system of the ring frame (where the draft is normally highest) with their hooks trailing. Failure to present the fibres in the appropriate direction at the ring frame can result in a loss of strength of up to 10%. The most common line-up used for carded yarns during the 1960s was two drawframe processes and one speed frame process between the card and the ring frame.

Improved Machines

During the late 1940s and early 1950s, work at the Shirley Institute, Manchester, U.K. indicated that better-engineered machines were essential if product regularity was to be improved. In meeting the demands for improved product quality, machinery makers also satisfied the requirements for increasing the machine speeds. Although the speed of the ring frame had increased in the late '40s, the technological revolution really began in 1953 with the introduction of the Whitin Model J Comber. This machine operated at about 150 nips per minute, which was more than half as many again as was normal at that time.

In 1955, the Whitin "Even-draft" drawframe was introduced; this was capable of processing fibre at 300 ft. per minute, which was about twice the normal speed of drawframes at that time.

Other textile machinery makers, too, introduced new and improved machines. A drawframe which would process sliver at about 120 ft. per minute had 6 or perhaps 8 deliveries. To maintain rigidity, the number of deliveries had to be reduced to 4 as delivery speeds approached 400 ft. per minute. As speeds continued to increase, further reductions were made in the number of deliveries per frame. In 1963, Platt's Mercury drawframe was introduced; this had one delivery which processed sliver at 1500 ft. per minute. The very high processing speed of this drawframe was achieved by a combination of advances in textile engineering and technology.

In 1959, SACM introduced their high production card; other manufacturers produced new machines in the same field. Card parts were operated faster; cylinders and doffers were clothed with rigid or metallic wire which reduced card waste losses and eliminated the need for frequent stripping. New techniques were devised to overcome the problem of stripping a high speed doffer. SACM used their perforated doffer from which the web was stripped pneumatically. New lightweight balanced fly combs were designed to operate at frequencies of 50 cycles per second. The most common solution was to employ a roller take-off mechanism. New cards were expensive; in appearance, they were similar to existing cards and, in fact were not fundamentally different from them. The conversion of cards became an attractive alternative to buying new ones.

The removal of dust liberated by low production cards was essential if the health of card room operatives (in particular strippers and grinders) was not to be seriously impaired. The Shirley Pressure Point System was developed for low production carding and over 8,000 cards were fitted with this system. High production carding liberates considerably more dust than low production carding, and dust removal systems have now become an essential feature of the high production card. Further, more dust is now liberated at later processes as a result of the higher speeds, larger packages and, to some extent, the use of crushing rollers at the card. Attention must be given to this problem of dust liberation at later processes if another generation of byssinotics is to be avoided.

Bale Digesters

For some time, the blow room process has been a largely automatic sequence, only the initial bale feeding being done manually. Bale digesters can now do the initial feeding automatically. These devices are not new; they were shown by Trützschler in 1959 but it took almost a decade for them to establish a real foothold in the Lancashire textile industry.

Bale digesters may be of the saw-toothed beater or plucking variety. They deliver the fibre in a very open state and have been satisfactory for simple cotton blends; the maintenance of accurate blend proportions can be a problem, however, particularly when mixings include bales of different density and size. It is not uncommon for cotton spinners to use three or four varieties of cotton, which may be in bales of different sizes and densities. Also, in adopting bale digesters the opportunity of using very large mixings can be lost.

There are several ways of minimising the shortcomings of bale digesters; one is by pre-blending, another by employing the modern equivalent of stack mixings and another by use of simple mixings of only one type of bale. The technique of pre-blending has been used in the U.S.A. where bale digesters are reputed to provide the theoretical equivalent of 1,000 bale mixings. The Platt's Meminghan Blender, which is an example of a stack mixer, builds up layer after layer of fibre in sandwich style, and removes sections across the sandwich thickness. In contrast, the Trützschler Multi-point Mixer and the Hergath 6, 10 or 12 fold mixers feed fibre into vertical containers or hoppers which are topped up in sequence, and from which fibre is removed by a horizontal lattice.

Fibre Transport

From the blowing room, fibre may be carried to the cards either as laps or in loose form. Laps can be transported manually or automatically. Loose fibre may be carried pneumatically to a chute or hopper behind each card. The maintenance of acceptably low levels of medium and long term regularity may, however, present problems, particularly with chute feeding.

Combers

The production rates of combers have continued to increase and some are able to process cotton fibre at rates of up to 80 lb. per hr. Some are fitted with autolevelling draw boxes.

Speed Frames

Speed frame package sizes have been stable for the past few years at about 14 in. × 7 in. dia. for spinning coarse counts and 12 in. × 6 in. dia. for finer counts. Maximum spindle speeds are about 1200 rev./min. and 1800 rev./min. respectively. Some machine makers incorporate a positive bobbin drive as opposed to a cone drum drive, with the flyers closed at both ends. Several machinery makers offer speed frames which can be doffed without removing the flyers. As speed frame speeds and package sizes have increased, it has become necessary to increase the twist inserted into the roving. This has imposed a greater demand on the drafting system at the ring frame, with the result that roller weightings have to be increased appreciably.

Ring Frames

There have been no outstanding new developments in ring frames in recent years. Ring frames continue to be better engineered, and drafting systems improved or made more flexible. From time to time, new types of ring and new ring finishes appear. Battery driven trucks help the spinner to patrol, numerous ring frame autodoffers are available, and autopiecers have appeared. Nevertheless, it is difficult to avoid the conclusion that the ring frame has reached the limit of its development. It produces a yarn good enough for almost any end use, but the need to strike the optimum balance between the three major cost components in ring spinning (i.e. capital, labour and power) limits the speed of spinning that can profitably be used. The ring-frame process

B

is the most costly of any in yarn production. Indeed, it costs
more than all the other processes put together, accounting
for about 60% of the total cost of staple yarn production.

Since there is no likelihood of any significant reduction
in ring frame spinning costs, the time is ripe for a successor.
Break spinning has provided a technological break-through
which will have a tremendous impact on the industry in the
1970s. (See Chapter 8).

FUTURE DEVELOPMENTS

If simpler cotton blends are used or if pre-blending is
adopted, bale digesters are likely to be used increasingly in
the 1970s. If quite complex blends continue to be used, the
performance of bale digesters will have to be improved if
they are to make real headway. If bale digesters are widely
adopted, the more open state of the fibres will stimulate the
introduction of simpler and more effective methods of
opening and cleaning. Chute fed cards, or automatic
handling of laps will be more widely used, particularly if
card production rates increase. More and more man-made
fibres will be used during the 1970s. These will require
relatively simple opening lines, and cleaning will be un-
necessary. It will be essential to retain flexibility in the blow
room, however, when both cotton and man-made fibres are
used.

The tow-to-top conversion of man-made fibres requires no
opening, cleaning or carding. Production of tops from short
fibres of, say, $1\frac{1}{2}$ in. is not economic, except perhaps for small
coloured lots. It is unlikely that tow-to-top conversion yarns
will replace the normal short staple yarns. Tow-to-top yarns
are more likely to challenge the longer staple worsted yarns.

Production rates at the card of around 100 lb. per hour
have been achieved, and rates will continue to increase;
machinery makers forecast production rates of 200 lb. per
hr. These increasing rates of production at the card will lend

impetus to the chute or hopper feeding of cards. It is not inconceivable that card production rates may eventually approach those of the scutcher; if this happens the card could be mounted at the end of the opening line.

During the early '70s at least, the choice of feed to the card is likely to lie between automatically handled laps or chutes. Chutes are probably the more attractive, as they require no labour and there are no piecing problems. Lap feeds might appear to make for greater flexibility, but it is claimed that chute feeding can be equally flexible, and a change from one mixing to another can be achieved without undue waste of time or fibre.

Break Spinning

Break spinning demands very clean, nep-free cotton which is produced, for example, by tandem carding. Suitable fibre may be obtained in other ways, and it may well be that the '70s will see the introduction of improved opening and cleaning in the blowing room to meet the needs of break spinning. Here, the use of bale digesters would assist greatly, converting the raw material into well-opened small tufts at the start of the opening process. Alternatives could be to use high grade cottons, and to improve the efficiency of cleaning at the single card. Special cards, perhaps less complicated than those used in traditional cotton carding, are likely to be developed during the 1970s to deal with man-made fibres. The decrease in demand for combed yarns will probably continue, despite the common practice of blending combed cotton slivers with man-made fibres. It seems certain that other means of producing cotton sliver suitable for blending with man-made fibres will be sought to meet the increasing demands for blends.

Blending

The ultimate processing speed of sliver in a drawframe could be as high as 2,500 ft./min. but the basic drawframe process is unlikely to change. Development could take place, however, in two very important ancillary processes associated with the drawframe, i.e. blending and auto-levelling. The blending of cotton with man-made fibres, and of man-made fibres with man-made fibres is carried out both in the blowing room and at the drawframe. Break spinners can also blend fibres.

Neither blending at the drawframe nor in the blowing room is entirely satisfactory. The blending of cotton and man-made fibres during opening has the disadvantage that the cotton requires cleaning whereas the man-made fibre does not. This means that pre-cleaning of the cotton fibre is necessary. Also, the carding conditions for the fibres may be different; this may cause problems. On the other hand, some fibres help others through the carding process; a cotton/nylon blend, for example, cards more easily than 100% nylon. There are problems too, in the mixing of wastes, which are consequently of less value.

Blending at the drawframe requires that two or more different types of laps be made. The laps must be kept separate and carded separately. For some end uses, three passages of drawing are required, i.e. one more than usual. This can result in overdrawing, which reduces fibre cohesion in the sliver and can cause difficulty in later processes. Blending drawframes will probably be developed in the '70s, some of which may deal with fibres in ribbon or web form. A drawframe capable of intimate blending, for example, is fed from 16 cans to give 4 layers of 4 slivers to be drafted; there are 4 drafting systems, each of which is fed with 4 slivers, 4 webs emerging to provide a sandwich which goes through a further drafting system.

Autolevelling

Autolevelling has become necessary largely because of the fewer opportunities to double during the shorter processing sequence. Chute feeding at the card is a further factor in the increasing importance of this technique. Autolevelling is essentially a means of minimising yarn count variation and it can be carried out at the card or at the first or second passage drawframe. Thickness of sliver can be measured, or cans can be weighed. Mechanical, capacitance, pneumatic, hydraulic or photoelectric devices are used for measuring the linear density of the slivers entering the drafting system. In open loop autolevelling, the linear densities of the slivers are measured and corrections are made at a later stage in the process, the result of the correction not being measured. In the closed loop system, detection of the error in linear density is made after the drafting has occurred, and the correction is made before the slivers enter the drafting system. As the correction is made, the detector decides whether this correction is sufficient, or whether an over-correction has been made; this information is fed back to the control device. Sometimes a mixed system is used, employing elements from both types of basic device.

Autolevellers, even when they are working perfectly, reduce irregularity in certain wave bands only at the expense of increasing it in others. This, along with other considerations, has a bearing on the placing of autolevellers in a processing sequence.

During the 1970s, an increasing number of drawframes will have automatic can doffing and autolevelling, and special drawframes will be developed which are intended purely for blending.

Omission of a speed frame process is one of the attractions of some forms of break-spinning machine, and it seems likely that the future of the speed frame will be linked closely with that of the ring frame. The speeds and package sizes in the remaining speed frames will probably increase marginally during the 1970s.

Ring Frame

The ring frame is unlikely to be the subject of any

significant development in future years. It is already technologically possible to push it past its economic optimum speed, and machinery makers will clearly direct much of their attention to the development of break-spinning machines. Spindle speeds at the ring frame will perhaps continue to increase by about 2% per annum because the average spindle speed in the industry is a little less than the optimum. In any case the optimum speed will change as the balance of costs change, but the situation will be overtaken by developments in break spinning. Up to the mid '70s, break-spun yarns will probably replace about 15% of ring-spun yarns, but by the end of the '70s the figure could well be very much higher. It has been claimed that the differing characteristics of break-spun yarns, particularly their lower strength compared with ring-spun yarns, will prevent them from replacing more than 40% or 50% of ring-spun yarns. Developments in break spinning technology are almost certain to overcome present deficiencies in the yarns, and by the late '70s break-spun yarns will probably be capable of replacing any ring-spun yarn.

Two other systems of spinning may find a place in short staple spinning, namely the TNO twistless spinning and the CSIRO Zerotwist method, even though the latter has so far only been used for worsted yarns. Development of short staple spinning by these systems will probably be a feature of the late 1970s.

3

Long-staple Spinning

by S. L. Anderson* and J. Ingham*

The position in long-staple spinning is reviewed. The woollen system is under pressure and, as the production of man-made fibres increases and the available labour force decreases, it is likely to decline in favour of the semi-worsted system and possibly one or more of the newly-emerging systems. In the worsted system, the future is greatly affected by the economics of batch production. Lot sizes are likely to increase, but this is increasingly a luxury trade and there are doubts about re-equipping with high productivity machinery. Early advances may occur in subsidiary devices such as the Wira Autospinner, but new high production systems may eventually be adopted in some sections of the trade.

Introduction

Staple fibres are classified generally as long or short. Short staple fibres are usually taken to mean cotton or cotton-type materials of staple lengths below 5 cm. (see Chapter 2). Long staple fibres include a very wide range of lengths and character and they are commonly sub-classified into woollen, worsted and semi-worsted. The first section of this Chapter deals with the woollen system and the second with the worsted system. Semi-worsted fibres are discussed in Chapter 13.

WOOLLEN SPINNING

Woollen spinning is that process where, after carding, a web of wool or/and man-made fibres is split longitudinally,

* Conference author. Both authors are members of staff of Wira of Leeds, U.K.; Mr. Anderson is the Asst. Director (Research).

the individual ribbons of web then being drafted by a factor less than 1.5 and spun into yarn.

60% of the woollen yarns produced in the U.K. at the close of the '60s was made on the mule frame and 40% by the ring frame. 80% of the yarn produced was used for weaving and 20% for carpets.

Pressures which will influence woollen spinning in the '70s include the following:—

1. The increasing production of man-made fibres and relatively static wool fibre production.
2. Emergence of the semi-worsted system which is predominantly suitable for man-made fibres, since the high coefficient of variation of fibre length of woollen blends renders them unsuitable for roller drafting.
3. Shortage of manpower, causing a retreat from labour intensive processes such as mule spinning.

The three chief contenders for woollen spinning in the '70s are break spinning, ring spinning and mule spinning. Break spinning of long staple man-made fibre is likely to be possible by the '70s and to account for a significant amount of the comparatively coarse yarn for carpets by 1975. The production of woollen weaving yarns will decline, but it will still be significant. As yarns for weaving are of fine counts, it is probable that they will still be spun by mules and ring frames. Ring frames may gradually take over from mules in this area.

These predictions are qualitative extrapolations from existing trends and cannot take account of really novel developments. In woollen processing, it is possible to contemplate, for example, a device which would consolidate and strengthen the slubbing direct from the rubbing aprons at the end of the card. This would eliminate the spinning process entirely; yarn would be wound directly onto packages, providing a continuous process for the conversion of fibre into yarn.

WORSTED SPINNING

Fibres processed on the worsted system range from botany wools of about 5 cm. mean fibre length up to crossbreds of about 10 cm. mean fibre length, with diameters ranging from about 19 to 40 microns. The discussion which follows includes also man-made fibres which are processed on the worsted system.

The Late 1960s

The trend of machinery usage through the '70s is uncertain, depending as it does upon trends in methods of garment production and the rate of development of radically new methods of spinning. Manufacturers are reluctant to buy new machinery until they can convince themselves that they have made the right choice for their business. During this period, there is scope for modification of existing

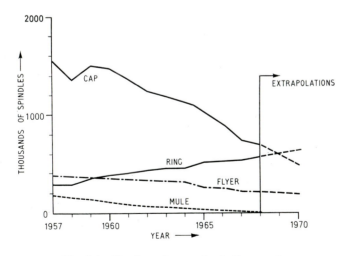

Fig. 3.1   Number of worsted spindles running.

B*

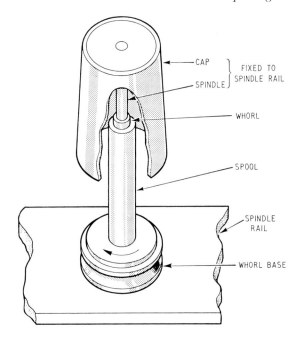

Fig. 3.2   Cap spindle and spool.

machinery. An example of this is the introduction of the
Wira Autospinner, a device for dealing automatically with a
yarn break in cap spinning.

   There are some 200 worsted spinning firms of various sizes
in the U.K.; of these, about one quarter are members of a
larger group. These firms produce a variety of types of yarn,
but for the present purpose they may be sub-divided into
simple groupings such as makers of weaving yarns, hosiery
yarns etc.

   Fig. 3.1, based on data from the Wool Industry Bureau of
Statistics, shows the number of spindles operating in the
period 1957 to 1968. Four methods of spinning are included,

viz., cap, ring, flyer and mule. At the beginning of the 1960s, there were about $2\frac{1}{2}$ million spindles; by the end of the decade, the figure had fallen to about $1\frac{1}{2}$ million. Originally, cap spinning was predominant, but the situation changed rapidly; by the late 1960s there were about $\frac{3}{4}$ million cap spindles in use, representing only half the total number of spindles operating in the industry. Flyer spinning has been decreasing too and by 1969 there were only $\frac{1}{4}$ million in use, representing one sixth of the total. Mule spinning had almost disappeared. Ring spinning, on the other hand, has been increasing and by 1969 accounted for about one third of the total number of spindles.

Cap Spinning

The cap spinner shown in Fig. 3.2 is the traditional method of spinning yarns; it is used with wool to which about 3% of oil has been added prior to combing. The use of oil is a traditional technique handed down by our forefathers; their reasons for using it are not completely understood. Oil has long been recognized as a fibre lubricant, and it undoubtedly brings about some slight reduction in the inter-fibre coefficient of friction. It also plays a major part in minimizing the generation of static electricity, the free ions left over from scouring rendering the oil a conductor of electricity. The oil systems of processing can be used without humidification, whereas humidification is essential in the spinning of dry combed wools. (When anti-static agents are used, a r.h. of about 60% is required; in the absence of anti-static agent, a r.h. of 80% is necessary.)

In cap spinning, there is often a temporary collapse of the balloon. The yarn touches the shoulder of the cap, and the oil lubricates the yarn in motion round the cap, particularly when the bobbin is empty. This reduces friction, enabling spinning to continue. In the case of a dry combed yarn, it is possible that the yarn will not recover from the collapse, and it may break. The presence of the oil also

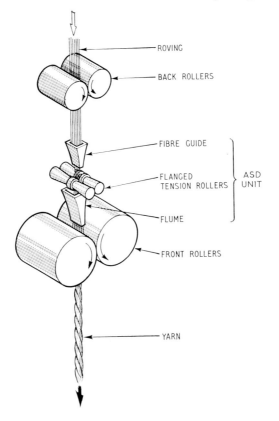

ROVING

BACK ROLLERS

FIBRE GUIDE

FLANGED
TENSION ROLLERS

ASD
UNIT

FLUME

FRONT ROLLERS

YARN

Fig. 3.3   Ambler Superdraft system.

produces a sideways adhesion between the fibres; this is useful in some spinning conditions near the limit.

The Ambler Superdraft system is a British system which was used originally on cap frames. It is now applied also to ring frames, and can deal with drafts up to 100:1 (see Fig. 3.3).

OIL		DRY
Weaving	Hand knitting	Hosiery
CAP (30g) $\frac{3}{4}$ million RING (250g) (A.S.D.) 50%	FLYER (110 to 150g) $\frac{1}{4}$ million 17%	RING (250g) $\frac{1}{2}$ million 33%

Fig. 3.4   Details of spinning systems.

Package sizes are important. The cap system uses 30 g. (1 oz.) spools whereas the ring system can produce 250 g. packages (except where the counts are fine, when small rings must be used with 30 g. spools). Flyer systems produce 100–150 g. packages. Spindle speeds are of the order of 6,000 to 7,500 rev./min. for both cap and ring frames and 3,000 to 4,000 rev./min. for flyer frames.

Yarn production on the worsted system in the U.K. is about 90 million kg. per annum. Excluding the relatively small amount of worsted carpet yarn, this production is divided almost equally between weaving and knitting yarns. The latter are divided into about two-thirds hosiery yarn (i.e. machine knitting) and one-third hand knitting yarn of thick count.

In principle, man-made fibres may be processed on any of the long staple machinery; wool systems, on the other hand, are divided into oil processing and dry processing as shown in Fig. 3.4. Most of the weaving yarns are made on the oil system, using cap spinning or Ambler Superdraft ring frames spinning large packages. The flyer system, which is also an oil system, is used to produce hand knitting yarns, whereas hosiery yarns are produced mainly from dry combed tops on ring frames. In the latter case, apron-type drafting is usual but some Ambler Superdraft frames are used. It is usual to spin on to large packages.

Production of yarns for hosiery and hand-knitting is divided almost equally between wool and man-made fibres. In the case of yarns for woven fabrics, the proportions are about 85% wool and 15% man-made fibres.

Most weaving yarns in the U.K., are made on the cap system, using small packages and oiled tops. In other countries, large package ring spinning and dry-combed materials are the rule.

Re-equipment

The re-equipment undertaken by a worsted spinner depends on the nature of his business. If operating large package ring frames, he is interested in the development of new machinery beyond the ring frame. If he is operating cap frames, he must decide whether to introduce ring frames or to hold on as long as possible in anticipation of new machinery being developed.

There is also the longer term problem of the extent to which worsted yarn will be replaced by texturised filament yarn. It has been suggested, in this connection, that there may not be any future for the staple spinner at all. The estimated trends of world consumption of apparel fibres provide useful information in this respect. Fig. 3.5, based on I.C.I. data, indicates the production and estimated production for the 20th century. From 1969 to the end of the century, it is estimated that overall consumption will treble, with wool remaining at about the same level as in 1969. The balance is made up by an enormous increase in synthetics. The latter is not divided into continuous filament and staple, but it is reasonable to suppose that if wool is still in widespread use there will be a demand for staple man-made fibres. There will thus be a need for "long staple" processing machinery.

It seems probable that wool, in the 1970s, will be used as a luxury fibre in speciality fabrics. This is worth bearing in mind in relation to the question of the size of production lots.

In addition to the increasing competition from continuous filaments, the worsted spinner faces the prospect of a probable swing from woven to knitted garments. In choosing new

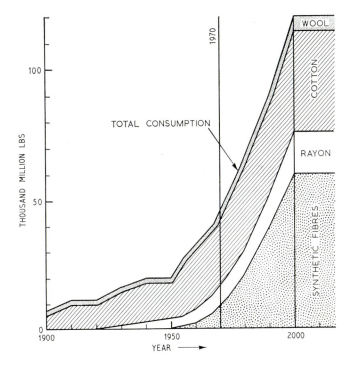

Fig. 3.5   Estimated world consumption of apparel fibres.

machinery, the hosiery spinner has a problem which is simpler than that of the weaver. He is operating in an expanding market and is likely to be dealing in large lots. Under these circumstances, his interests must be in large package high speed production with as much automation as possible.

The manufacturer of weaving yarns has a complicated problem, one of the most important factors being labour. The Bradford Raper drawing system produces up to about 2,500 kg. per week on a single shift. For low draft spinning, some five to six drawing operatives are required; with Ambler Superdraft spinning, which uses thicker roving, only two are needed. Cap spinning frames require 8 operatives to produce 38 tex (24s worsted) yarn, whereas a modern ring system using 250 g. packages would require about 4 operatives for a similar yarn at the same rate of production. Cap spinning thus uses 100% more labour than ring spinning for the coarser counts and up to 50% more for the finer counts. If labour costs alone are considered, there is everything to be gained by changing over from caps to rings. But other factors must be taken into account, such as the sizes of lots processed for woven fabrics.

Lot Sizes

In 1965, Liddy of CSIRO made an analysis of lot sizes at a number of firms and found the average to be about 250 kg. The maximum weight was 2,500 kg., but some 70% of the lots were less than average; 33% were less than 100 kg., and as many as 17% were less than 50 kg. More recent data from two British mills spinning dyed tops showed that 75% of the yarn by weight was in lots greater than 50 kg., but 75% of the lots by number were less than this. Some were less than 5 kg. This situation arises because the high quality end of the trade deals in exclusive designs in small quantities. The technique of blending tops of different colour is predominantly a British practice; though expensive, it is done for effect purposes. Small lots can be avoided only if larger lots of undyed yarn are split into smaller batches for dyeing, and the fabric designs are made less exclusive.

Lot sizes are important with respect to the capacity of spinning frames. A modern 200 spindle ring frame will produce about 50 kg. per doff, and with Ambler Superdrafting it would creel 300 kg. This type of frame, obviously, is not very suitable for small lots of less than 50 kg.

Cap spinning frames are usually of 200 spindles which creel 50 kg. and produce 12 kg. per doff. Frames of this type are more suitable for the small lot trade, but even these are inefficient for lots of the order of 5 kg.

In a Wira forecast of the trends in lot sizes, estimates were made for counts above and below 18 tex. In the case of medium and coarse counts, the forecast indicates a movement away from small lots. In the fine count range, the trend is similar but less emphatic, with some suggestion of no change. Factors taken into account in making this forecast included the disproportionately high cost of small lots, the reduction in variety required in the fabric, and the possible development of new techniques for achieving variety in the fabric (such as differential dyeing).

If this forecast is correct, there will be some alleviation of the small package problem. There is, however, another factor to be considered. It is predicted that yarn counts will become finer to meet the demand for light-weight fabrics stimulated by the introduction of domestic central-heating, and the increasing use of the motor car. In the worsted trade, fine counts produced on the present system are synonymous with small packages. The dilemma, therefore, is not resolved.

The advent of automatic winders and the weaver's preference for singles knots instead of twofold knots are factors which affect package size. The automatic winding of singles yarns makes small spinning packages far less disadvantageous than they used to be. Adherence to the use of

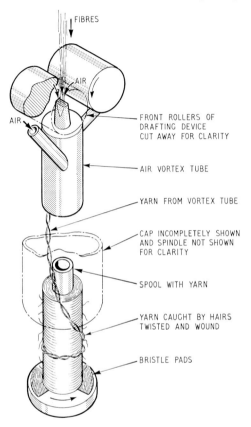

FIBRES

AIR

AIR

FRONT ROLLERS OF
DRAFTING DEVICE
CUT AWAY FOR CLARITY

AIR VORTEX TUBE

YARN FROM VORTEX TUBE

CAP INCOMPLETELY SHOWN
AND SPINDLE NOT SHOWN
FOR CLARITY

SPOOL WITH YARN

YARN CAUGHT BY HAIRS
TWISTED AND WOUND

BRISTLE PADS

Fig. 3.6   The Wira Autospinner (not to scale).

oil is something of a nuisance, however, as it tends to impede
the operation of the knotters and yarn clearers.

Spinners of weaving yarns who are considering re-
equipment of their twisting and winding sections are likely
to leave changes in their spinning machinery for as long as
possible. This situation is conducive to the introduction of

labour-saving modifications to existing spinning frames, provided that they are not too costly. It is against this background that Wira produced the Autospinner, a device attached to cap frames which reduces the work load of piecing broken ends.

Wira Autospinner

The Wira Autospinner is a simple, low cost device which automatically joins a yarn end to the bobbin during spinning, thus reducing the amount of supervision needed.

When a break occurs during spinning, untwisted fibre is delivered by the drafting device and the means of twisting has been disconnected. To piece up again, it is necessary to introduce twist to the fibres emerging from the drafting device. This is usually done by reconnecting these fibres to the broken yarn end which is pulled back from the bobbin. In the Autospinner, an auxiliary pneumatic twister is introduced so that under all circumstances twisted yarn is delivered. The reconnection with the yarn package is a separate operation.

The twisting element is an air vortex tube so arranged that an axial port operates at sub-atmospheric pressure. This port is in close proximity to the fibre delivery of the drafting system and the fibres are inhaled into the vortex tube. Air entering through tangentially disposed ports creates a vortex within the tube and inserts twist into the fibre assembly entering through the axial port. This twist runs back to the drafting system. The twisted fibre strand leaves through the end of the tube opposite to the fibre entry as shown in Fig. 3.6.

The free end of the twisted strand migrates freely downwards until it is caught by fibres protruding from the bobbin. If the bobbin is empty, it contacts a bristle pad attached to the base of the spindle. During this time, some twist is able to leak out of the free end of the new yarn but sufficient is retained to give it adequate strength. When the end meets the fibres from the bobbin or the bristle pad it is caught and the end is "licked" round the bobbin. From then on, the normal process of twist and wind commences. The spindle now inserts the true twist and the vortex tube merely inserts a modicum of false twist.

When a frame has such a system installed for each spindle, it is possible to break out one or many ends in any combination and the system will automatically repair them straight away. This should provide a means of increasing the machine efficiency to a considerable degree.

FUTURE DEVELOPMENTS

A number of novel techniques may come to fruition in the 1970s. Break spinning of short fibres was being exploited commercially by 1969. The possibility of break spinning long staple fibres is discussed elsewhere.

There are obvious advantages in a continuous process in which yarn is produced directly from raw staple fibres. In the case of wool, difficulties are created by the necessity for removing the grease, suint and vegetable impurities. It is possible that sheep may be kept in pens to prevent contamination of the fleece, but it will still be necessary to remove grease and suint.

Break Spinning in Liquids

Break spinning in liquids is a possible solution to the problem, as the spinning fluid could also serve as cleaning agent. Early attempts to spin wool in this way were unsuccessful, as entanglement of the individual fibres occurring in the suspension prevented their alignment, but a discovery at Wira goes some way towards solving the problem. If the viscosity of the liquid medium is increased sufficiently, fibre entanglement in the suspension can be prevented. In theory, therefore, a liquid break spinning process is possible in which a suspension of textile fibres in a liquid is introduced continuously into a centrifuge, a yarn having real twist being withdrawn from the suspension.

Fig. 3.7 illustrates the basic principles of a proposed device to make rudimentary yarns from wool. It comprises a reservoir containing liquid into which the input fibres are fed by a chute; even distribution of fibres in the liquid is ensured by a paddle. The reservoir is connected to the base of a centrifuge driven at high speed by a belt, and the suspension of fibres in the liquid is fed to the centrifuge by a pump. Centrifugal force makes the fibres align themselves along the axis, enabling the spun yarn to be drawn off continuously by nip rollers. The side wall of the centrifuge

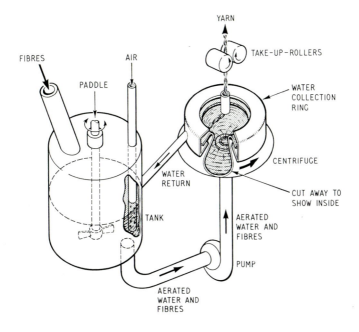

Fig. 3.7 A water spinner.

pot is curved inwards to prevent liquid from being thrown out of the top. An overflow pipe is provided through which liquid leaving the pot flows to an annular trough. Liquid from the trough is recirculated to the reservoir. A mixture of glycerine and water was found to have a viscosity sufficiently high to prevent fibre entanglement. It is necessary that the effective density of the fibres being spun should be less than that of the liquid medium; provision is therefore made to aerate the suspension so that small bubbles of air adhere to the fibres. This is done by injecting air into the reservoir through orifices in an air supply pipe. Rudimentary yarn was produced by this method during the late 1960s.

Self-twist Yarn

The development of self-twist yarn by the Australian C.S.I.R.O., described in British Patents [3] will be an important feature of spinning in the '70s. Self-twist yarn is, in effect, a twofold yarn in which there are alternate lengths of Z and S twist. Two singles yarns from two adjacent drafting heads pass separately through intermittent false twist tubes; they are then combined together to be wound onto a cheese. Since the twists are intermittent, the two strands self-twist themselves to make a fully useable yarn. Machines of this type are already (1969) in use in Australia.

Speeds of production are very high, probably up to 300 yd./min. This is an exciting development in spinning; it is likely to become a serious competitor to alternative spinning techniques (See Chapter 7).

4

Textured Yarn Processes

by P. R. Lord

Texturing is a relatively new field of textile processing; in two decades it has become of prime importance in the area of yarn production. Advances in the chemical industry stimulated corresponding advances in textile technology, resulting in a range of new machines, techniques and products. The new products opened up new markets which stimulated further progress to a point where the limits of development appear to be in sight. Devices typical of the variety of new machines are described.

In the early 1950s, nylon and the polyester fibres consolidated their position as commercially-important textile fibres. The continuous filament yarns of immediate post-war years had characteristics different from natural or regenerated fibre yarns then in use. Fabrics made from the synthetic filament yarns had attractive and unusual properties, notably superior wear and easy-care characteristics; they could be washed easily, and drip-dried. But they also possessed less desirable features which restricted their textile application. They were smooth and slippery to the touch, and felt clammy when worn next to the skin. They did not possess the warmth and comfort of fabrics made from natural fibre yarns.

The superiority of "traditional" yarns in this respect was due, in large measure, to the fact that they were spun from short staple fibres. Yarns made in this way were fuller and fluffier than those derived, like the synthetic fibre yarns, from continuous filaments. Spun yarns were bulky and light, with innumerable pockets of air entrapped between the short fibres. This air was primarily responsible for the heat-insulation characteristics of spun yarns, and the fabrics made from them. Also, perspiration could escape through the interstices of the yarn.

It was a natural step for synthetic fibre manufacturers to produce synthetic staple fibres by cutting or breaking the continuous filaments. Synthetic staple fibre could be spun into bulky yarns by techniques used for cotton, wool and other natural staple fibres, providing yarns with greatly improved handle and warmth, which yet retained the unique characteristics associated with synthetic fibres.

Texturising

During the 1950s, new techniques were developed for the modification of continuous filament synthetic fibres in such

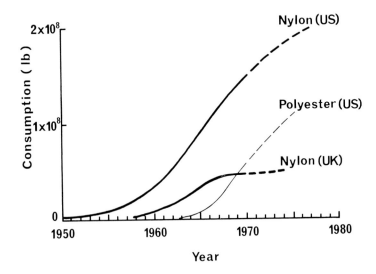

Fig. 4.1   The growth of demand for nylon and polyester fibres.

a way as to provide bulkier and more comfortable yarns without the need for cutting the filaments into staple fibres. Instead, the filaments were bent, crimped, curled or looped in various ways to create bulkier yarns possessing many of the characteristics associated with spun yarns. Processes of this type became known as texturising.

During the 1960s, texturised nylon, polyester and other synthetic fibres made remarkable progress (see Fig. 4.1) and established themselves in many important textile applications.

In the 1970s, it seems inevitable that the rising graph of texturised filament production must begin to level off, but there is no doubt that yarns of this type will continue to play an important role in the textile industry.

Warmth; Comfort

Texturising gives yarns a soft and woolly feel, and increases the warmth and comfort of fabrics. The loops and crimps entrap a multitude of small pockets of air. If air is still, it is an excellent insulator, and the fibres in a texturised yarn reduce air movement to a minimum. The fibres themselves conduct heat more readily than static air, and the warmth of a fabric is related directly to the amount of entrapped air. The bulkier and softer the yarn, the warmer it will be. The filaments of synthetic fibre play only a minor role in controlling the warmth of the fabric; the static air provides insulation, the filaments preventing air movement and holding the fabric together.

Mechanical and Physical Properties

Warmth is only one of the desirable characteristics of a textile material. Yarns and fabrics must also be flexible, which means that the yarn should be of fairly low linear density and constructed from fine components. Ordinary staple yarns are satisfactory in this respect, but their mechanical flexibility is restricted by their structure. Flexibility depends on the extensibility of the outermost

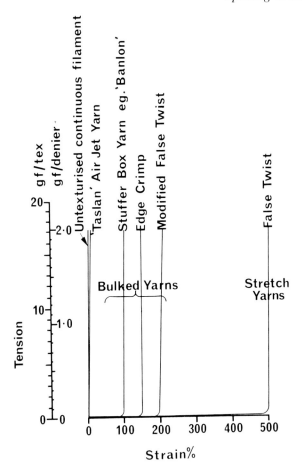

Fig. 4.2   Graph showing extensions to crimp-removed condition.

fibres of the yarn. A straight fibre is much less extensible than a coiled, looped or crimped fibre (see Chapter 7; Fig. 7.1); the extensibility of such fibres is controlled by a combination of bending and torsional stiffness determined by the geometrical shape of the fibre in the yarn.

Bending and torsional stiffnesses are functions of the linear density of the fibre; a fine fibre is more flexible than a coarse one. A yarn made of many looped, coiled or crimped fine fibres, loosely assembled so as not to restrict one another, would thus be flexible and very extensible. The extent of these properties will depend opon the geometric configurations of the fibres making up the yarn, their relative disposition and the extent to which they restrict one another. The balance of characteristics, including the softness of the yarn, thus depends on the manner of texturising. Other things being equal, the softer a yarn, the greater is its covering power and the more desirable its handle. In general, an increase in the bulkiness of a yarn results in greater warmth, softness, flexibility and extensibility. An untexturised continuous filament yarn, with a minimum of bulk, is deficient in these characteristics. Texturised yarns possess them to a degree that depends upon their physical structure (see Fig. 4.2).

The thermosetting polymers from which most texturised yarns are made are tough and strong; the yarns therefore have good abrasion resistance and durability. These characteristics are carried forward into the fabrics, which also have good pill and crease resistance, good dimensional stability and excellent washing and drying properties. Synthetic fibres, as a rule, do not absorb moisture as well as natural fibres but the entrapped air holds moisture and bulked yarns are reasonably comfortable in this respect. They acquire static electric charges more readily, but special finishes may be used to minimise this tendency.

Texturised yarns are wound on to large packages, providing long knot-free lengths of a uniform product which lends itself admirably to knitting. The increased use of texturised polymer filaments has proceeded side by side with a rapid increase in machine knitting, and each development has helped the other. Texturised yarns and machine knitted fabrics, for example, are both capable of being produced at high speed. The knitting process provides fabric of high flexibility and extensibility; it is essentially a loop through loop process, and the yarn itself is flexible and extensible. In some ways, yarn and fabric complement one another; the high cover factor of the yarn, for example, tends to offset the poorer cover factor of the fabric.

Classification

Texturised yarns are commonly classified as follows:–

(i)   stretch yarns,   ⎫ as produced on false
(ii) modified stretch yarns, ⎬ twist machines.
(iii) bulked yarns.

Stretch yarns have high extensibility and good recovery, but only moderate bulk in comparison with the other two categories. They are used mainly in stretch fabrics which are made up into many domestic goods and garments. They are produced mainly by false twist type machines.

Modified stretch yarns are, in fact, stretch yarns which have been subjected to a further treatment, usually heat treatment, e.g. in the partly strained condition. This modifies and stabilises the characteristics of the yarn. The additional process is commonly integrated into the yarn texturing machine. A typical treatment consists of over-feeding a stretch yarn into a heated zone; this acts like a stuffer box, giving the yarn greater bulk and lower stretch. Yarns of this type give good stitch clarity and smoothness to knitted fabric and they are, in consequence, widely used for garment manufacture.

Bulked yarns have moderate stretch, being used in applications where bulk is more important than extensibility, e.g. in carpets, upholstery, warm garments and hosiery. They are produced by stuffer-box, air-jet, and various other types of crimp producing devices. Typical yarn structures are shown in Fig. 4.3.

STRETCH YARNS

Batch Process

One of the earliest methods of producing a stretch yarn was to insert a high twist by using a normal uptwister, then to heat set the yarn on the package and untwist. These yarns had residual torque and it was normal to ply two or more together to give a torque-balanced final product. The twist level used was high and varied between 114 t.p.i. for a 15 denier (2 tex) yarn to 47 t.p.i. for a 200 denier (23 tex) yarn. This gave a twist factor varying between about 6 and 9

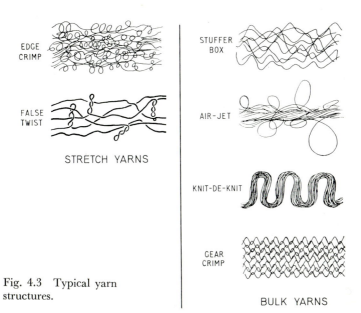

EDGE CRIMP

FALSE TWIST

STRETCH YARNS

STUFFER BOX

AIR-JET

KNIT-DE-KNIT

GEAR CRIMP

BULK YARNS

Fig. 4.3 Typical yarn structures.

as shown in Fig. 4.4, which was considerably higher than the twist factor normally used in staple yarns. When the yarn was set and subsequently untwisted to a given level, the torque in the filaments caused them to form into loops. This gave a bulky stretch yarn with some residual torque, and it was common practice to double such yarns, with yarns twisted in the opposite direction. The ply twist was generally a very low S twist, so that a clear twill line could be obtained with the normal right hand twill. The Helanca system is based on this technique, but includes a greater number of operations; the bulk of the resulting yarns is increased up to three times its original value and the elasticity is such that extensions of up to 500% can be obtained with the finer yarns. This method is essentially a batch process incorporating several operations on ordinary uptwisters at speeds of

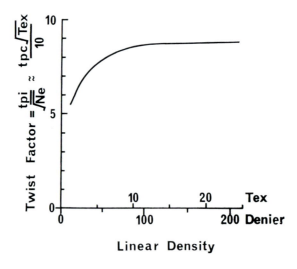

Fig. 4.4   Twist levels used in stretch yarns.

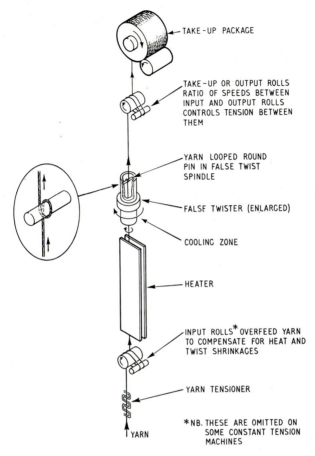

Fig. 4.5 A false-twist machine.

some 10,000 rev./min.; production speeds are, therefore, low and continuous processes involving much higher speeds were rapidly introduced.

Continuous Process

A diagram of a typical continuous process is shown in

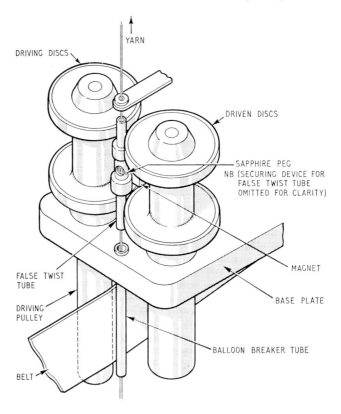

Fig. 4.6   Typical magnetic false-twist spindle.

Fig. 4.5. The heart of the process is the false twist spindle, which has become progressively smaller and has operated at ever-increasing speeds as the process has developed. At the end of the '60s speeds of 600,000 rev./min. were achieved and the barrel of the false twist spindle had been reduced to about $\frac{1}{8}$ in. diameter (see Fig. 4.6). The spindles in devices of this type run in magnetic bearings. They dissipate a relatively large amount of energy in a small space and tend to become hot. To operate in a magnetic bearing, the spindles must be constructed of magnetic material; this prevents the use of light alloys which might have made higher speeds possible. Rotation of the spindle in a magnetic field stimulates eddy currents, causing additional heating, and the design of spindles to minimise eddy currents may become an important factor in the future development of the process.

The spindles are driven by tyred wheels which place a further limitation on the speeds which can be achieved. If a 10:1 drive ratio is used, for example, a $1\frac{1}{4}$ in. driving disc would have to rotate at some 60,000 rev./min.; at such speeds, the tyre polymer may creep, causing the tyres to grow in diameter. The speed and diameter of the drive rollers are thus limited. Creep can be restrained by suitable keying to the drive wheels, permitting an increase in the operating speed. The relative radius of curvature between spindle and drive roller is very small and in consequence the Hertzian stresses are high. As a result of this, pitting of the tyre surface may occur after a time, and this imposes a limit on the smallness of the diameter of the drive portion of the spindle. These factors, taken together, impose a technological limit on the speeds which may be used in practice, and it seems unlikely that speeds will increase appreciably in the future.

The diagram in Fig. 4.5 has been drawn to show important elements in the design, but it cannot be shown in proportion. The space allowed for cooling, for example, is inadequate; it is probably more difficult to cool the yarns rapidly than to heat them. It is obvious that precautions must be taken to avoid leaving a high power heater on whilst the yarn is stationary or moving slowly, to prevent overheating. On the other hand, if cooling is inadequate, the yarn will not be set before untwisting. The untwisting zone is not above the false twist spindle as might be expected; it is at the spindle, because twist from below passes with the yarn over the pin

C

and cancels the opposite twist above. There is thus no twist above the spindle.

The yarn tension in the working zone is controlled by the relative roll speeds and the temperature. The yarns have residual torque and may be supplied either as torque yarns (in which the user alternates his yarn in the fabric to achieve balance) or as doubled torque-free yarns. A 60 denier (7 tex) yarn having 78 t.p.i. inserted at 600,000 rev./min. can be produced at 640 ft./min. (7,700 inches/min.). If it were possible to twist a 200 denier (23 tex) yarn on such a machine at such a speed, the yarn would be produced at nearly 13,000 inches/min., which may be compared with other forms of yarn making machines (e.g. self twist—5000

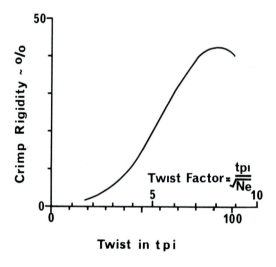

Fig. 4.7   Typical crimp/rigidity curve.

inches/min; break spinning—2,000 inches/min. for coarser yarns). As the twist level is increased, up to a point, the bulk of the yarn increases (see Fig. 4.7); this means that increase in bulk is obtained at the expense of productivity. Too great a twist or too high a heater temperature will reduce the strength of the yarn and a compromise has to be made between the strength on the one hand and adequate bulk and proper setting on the other. Generally, the twist levels in Fig. 4.4 give a reasonable compromise; a substantial increase above these levels could reduce the strength quite rapidly. A normally accepted tenacity is 3.5 gf/denier (30 gf/tex).

Tubeless System

It is possible to eliminate the false twist tube completely, and to operate directly on the yarn surface. To do this, it is necessary to have surfaces travelling at high speed in opposite directions. In theory, a cylindrical body being rolled in this way will merely rotate and will not change the position of its axis; in practice, it is necessary to have a means of stabilising it. In theory, also, the yarn is perfectly regular and the normal forces between the surfaces and the yarn can be maintained; in practice, it is necessary to allow for variations. One way of doing this is to thread the yarn through the bores of two counter-rotating rubber-lined cylinders, as shown in Fig. 4.8. The introduction of a disc rotating in a different plane can supply the oppositely-moving surface. Such a system is capable of inserting twist at very high speeds, but it has not been widely used. This is partly because the rotational speed is not easy to control, partly because the surface of the yarn is abraded, and partly because a combination of bending and torsion is believed to be better than torsion alone. Any change in yarn diameter will undoubtedly cause a change in twist, unless the speed of the twisting element is altered. Also, the rubbing of a yarn over a pin, as in a normal false twister, could produce a bulking effect somewhat similar to that obtained in the edge crimp process (to be described later). Nevertheless, a commercial machine, the Fujiloft FL 8, is in production and it is claimed that a twist insertion rate equivalent to a spindle speed of 3,375,000 rev./min. is obtained when processing 20 denier (2.4 tex) yarn; at 100 t.p.i. this would give a take-off rate of 33,750 inches/min. When processing 70 denier yarn, the equivalent speed would drop to 1,800,000 rev./min. and the take-off rate would be about 24,000 inches/min.

Edge-Crimp Texturiser

Another device for producing stretch yarns is the edge crimp texturiser. In its simplest form, this operates by running the filaments over an edge; the rubbing of the compression zone of the yarn bent over this edge causes molecular disorientation, giving the yarn an asymmetrical molecular structure. When relaxed and heated, the disorientated molecular zone shrinks, causing the filament to curl. In more sophisticated edge crimp machines, the yarn is processed hot, and is cooled after passing over the crimping edge (see Fig. 4.9). The amount of curl may be

Fig. 4.8 Principle of the Fujiloft friction twisting machine.

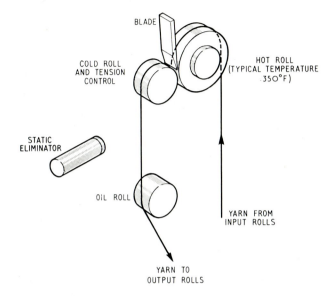

Fig. 4.9 The edge-crimp machine as used in making Agilon.

considerable, and the yarn tends to form into coils whose helices reverse in direction at periodic intervals. This alternating filament "twist" is balanced, and the yarns are therefore similarly balanced; they have no residual torque. This is a distinct advantage. Often, the full effect of edge crimping is not developed until the fabric is made and subjected to dry heat at a later stage. The crimp frequency (number of coils per unit length of uncrimped filament) is inversely proportional to (tex $^{\frac{1}{2}}$ × radius of coil)—N.B. The crimp frequency increases with a fall in linear density of the yarn; this frequency gives a quantity comparable to the spindle speed in a false twist machine. In practice, a machine

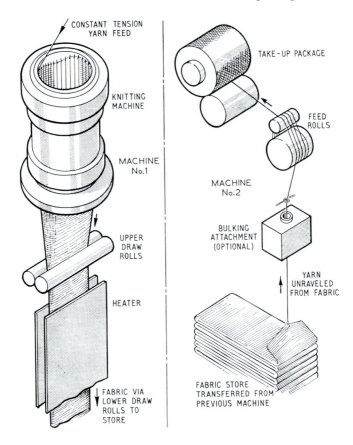

Fig. 4.10   Diagram of Knit-de-Knit process.

can operate from 90 to 140 yds./min. (3,200 to 5,000 inches/ min.) when producing 15 denier monofilament nylon. The crimp is a function of the type of yarn, local temperature, yarn tensions, angle of yarn deformation round the edge and the state of the edge itself. Careful control is needed to maintain the crimp frequency and the characteristics of the yarn produced.

BULKED YARNS

A number of methods exist for producing bulked yarns, including knit-de-knit, stuffer box, air-jet and twist-texturing processes.

Knit-de-Knit

The knit-de-knit machine is virtually a series of knitting machines producing a tubular fabric which is heat set; the yarn is then disassembled from this fabric. Normally, this takes place in two separate operations, as shown in Fig. 4.10, and on the face of it there is no reason why it could not be a continuous process. Occasional tuck backs occur, however, which cannot be unravelled, and this fact alone may prevent the use of a truly continuous process. The cylinders of the crimping machines rotate at up to 800 rev./min., and each course contains about 40 in. of yarn, i.e. the production rate is up to 32,000 inches/min (about 900 yds./min.). The bulk coners, which disassemble the yarn, wind it on to a package at up to 850 yds./min. (30,000 in./min.). The entire process requires about 900 watts/head, which is quite economical at the speeds involved.

Stuffer-box

The stuffer-box system, as its name implies, involves compressing the filaments into a confined heated space, as shown in Fig. 4.11. The filaments, being unable to support load as struts, collapse. As more filament is forced into the stuffer box, sharp crimps are created in the collapsed filaments, which are set as they are heated and then cooled. The speeds achieved by these machines can be as high as 650 yd./min. (23,000 inches/min.), but with very heavy

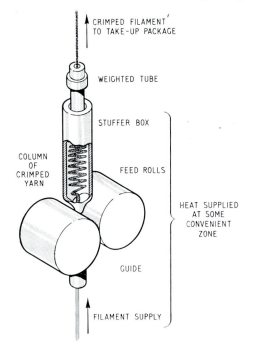

CRIMPED FILAMENT
TO TAKE-UP PACKAGE

WEIGHTED TUBE

STUFFER BOX

COLUMN
OF
CRIMPED
YARN

FEED ROLLS

HEAT SUPPLIED
AT SOME
CONVENIENT
ZONE

GUIDE

FILAMENT SUPPLY

Fig. 4.11   Typical stuffer-box device.

yarns the linear production rate drops (although the mass production rate does not).

The knit-de-knit and stuffer box machines are both capable of dealing with a wide range of linear densities of yarn. A typical range is from 7 to 5,000 denier (0.8 to 560 tex); the heavier yarns are often used for carpets. A stuffer-box system (see Fig. 4.11) is also used to produce yarns for garments; a typical output speed is 1,200 ft./min. to (14,400 inches/min).. The degreee of bulking (up to about 300%), elasticity and handle may be varied to give a wide range of products.

Air-Texturing

Air textured yarns are made by overfeeding filaments through a confined zone of highly energetic air turbulence. The excess lengths of filament are converted into random loops, which are locked into the structure as the yarn passes into a tension zone. This provides a yarn which resembles spun yarn; it is bulkier than untexturised filament yarn with low extensibility compared with many other texturised yarns.

The air texturing process does not normally include heat setting, but steam may be used instead of compressed air. Wray [4] has carried out experiments in which neither steam nor air is used; the loops are formed by other means and then allowed to intermingle. In the standard air texturing process, the passage of air over the cylindrical yarn feed needle creates a continuing series of tiny but energetic air vortices of alternating senses. These impart alternating twists to the filaments passing through, and because the filaments are relaxed, they form into loops. If the needle is offset in the air venturi passage, an overall rotational movement is created; if a pretwisted yarn is used, it is important that the overall motion should be such as temporarily to untwist the yarn. The speeds which can be achieved depend on the rate of loop formation; this in turn depends on the air pressure used and the design of the venturi-needle system. Bearing in mind that the cost of compressed air is high, there is obviously a limit other than the technological one, but speeds in excess of 600 ft./min. (7,200 inches/min.) have been reported.

Twist Texturing

The twist texturing machine provides a relatively new approach. In this device, two ends of yarn are twisted together, and set by a heating and cooling cycle; they are then untwisted into two separate strands of texturised yarns. The twist, in this case, is not inserted by a twisting head as

c*

in a conventional machine; the two ends are twisted together
by a specified amount before starting, and this twist is made
to run back relative to the yarn so that it is retained in the
system. The amount of twist is determined by inserting,
into one strand, a bobbin with a specified number of turns
wound on it, This bobbin is emptied over-end, so that the
turns on the bobbin are converted into turns in the strand.
These strands self twist before entering the heater, only to be
separated at a later stage (see Fig. 4.12). The machines
work most economically in the 15 to 70 denier range (2 to
8 tex), differing from most other forms of twisting machine
in that the speed is controlled by the heat setting cycle time,
and is independent of yarn twist. This implies that finer
yarn can be processed faster, as it can be heated and cooled

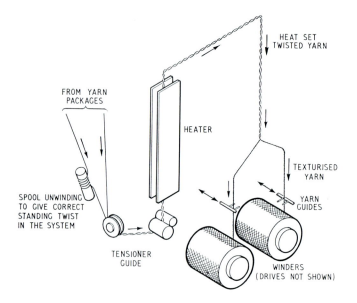

Fig. 4.12 Principle of twist texturing.

more rapidly. In fact, a 15 denier yarn may be produced at 1,400 ft./min. (18,000 inches/min.) and 70 denier yarn at 1,000 ft./min. (12,000 inches/min); speeds of up to 1,800 ft./min. have been quoted. The limit is set by heat transfer considerations and improvements in production rate will almost certainly take place.

Future Prospects

Many types of texturising devices have thus made rapid progress since the mid-twentieth century; some make use of mechanical twisting devices, some use indirect twisting devices and others crimping. The mechanical twist devices have carried the philosophy of "the smaller, the faster" almost to its ultimate limit; there are few other industries which can boast of using speeds approaching a million rev./min. commercially. Speeds will no doubt increase still further, but it is difficult to see another major leap forward in productivity from these machines unless the friction twist devices overtake them and set new standards.

In the field of bulked yarn machines, some of the devices impart loops or crimp by non-mechanical techniques, and very high production speeds become possible. There are high hopes that conjugate fibres (in which one fibre component shrinks relative to the other) will lead to producer-textured yarns which will be competitive with throwster-textured yarns. The question of capital costs must be considered, and it seems likely that eventually a technique such as twist texturising may lead the field, especially for the production of finer yarns. For coarser yarns, such as those used in the carpet industry, the stuffer-box and knit-de-knit processes vie for the highest production rates. Production rate, however, is only one of the factors to be considered; the types and qualities of yarns required to meet changing demands will have a major influence on the types of texturised yarn produced in the years ahead.

5

Network Yarns

by P. Volans*

Since the 1960s a number of technologies have been developed for producing feedstock for the textiles industry from oriented polymer films. These rely on the ability of some highly-oriented films to break down spontaneously into two-dimensional assemblies of fibres called *split film* products.

A method has now been developed for producing a three-dimensional assembly of fine interconnected fibres in the form of a network yarn. A polymer foam is produced which, after drawing to a high degree, may be fibrillated to a yarn at up to 1000 ft/min. Examination of the structure shows that fibres are derived from the cell walls in the foam. These fibres are very fine and flexible and exhibit very few free ends. The yarn has considerable strength without twist and produces fabrics showing good drape, handle and wear properties.

Introduction

For thousands of years, man has been making textiles by assembling a mass of fibres into continuous strands or yarns, and then interlacing these yarns to form a fabric. Until comparatively recent times, the fibres available were restricted to those provided by nature. But during the last half-century or so, man has learned to make fibres by extruding synthetic polymers, and we now have a range of synthetic fibres available to the textile industry.

The development of the synthetic fibre industry has done more than provide us with new types of fibre. It has also brought new thinking into the whole field of textile production, and we have seen radically new textile techniques

* Conference author. Monsanto Chemicals Ltd., Newport, Mon., U.K.

appearing in recent years. One interesting example of these has been the introduction of the so-called network yarns in which a fibrous structure is created direct from synthetic polymer, i.e. without going through the expensive processes of extruding fibres and then spinning them to provide a yarn.

The development of network yarns has stemmed from research which began in the 1930s. The patent literature at that time indicated a very real interest in the production of yarns from polymers by direct routes. Interest centred largely on the drawing of sheets of polymer to increase strength in the direction of draw, with simultaneous weakening across the direction of draw. This effect can bring about the breakdown of a polymer sheet into interconnected fibres aligned in the direction of draw.

These experiments, however, were ahead of their time. The polymers then available were not suitable for the establishment of a commercial process, and it was not until about 1954 that the idea was resurrected and used for making PVC fibres from sheets. Events during the late 1950s were to open the way to the production of commercially useful materials by techniques of this sort.

Stereospecific Polymerisation

By 1956, Karl Ziegler [5] in Germany and, independently of him, Phillips Petroleum and Standard Oil in the U.S.A., had developed new catalyst systems which permitted ethylene to be polymerised under relatively mild conditions. Instead of the 5000 atmospheres or so previously used, only a few hundred atmospheres pressure was needed, and the products differed from conventional polyethylene. The polymer was no longer branched, it was of high density and highly crystalline. Ziegler's work was followed up by Giuilio Natta [6]. Using catalysts based on the Ziegler system, Natta developed his well-known techniques of stereospecific polymerisation, introducing into polymers a degree

DRAWN   SHEET   FIBRILLATES

RELAXED   SHEET   GIVES   TWO-DIMENSIONAL   NETWORK

Fig. 5.1   Production of network yarns. Method 1.

of crystallinity which had not been known before. Natta's work led directly to the commercial production of poly-propylene plastics and synthetic fibres.

The production of highly-crystalline polyethylene and polypropylene stimulated renewed interest in the development of fibrous yarns from drawn film. Both polymers became available in commercial quantities and were eminently suitable for conversion into film.

Fibrillation; Split Film

When highly drawn, these films developed high tenacity in the direction of draw, and became very weak across the direction of draw, with the result that fibrillation occurred spontaneously. Fibrillation took the form of a multitude of parallel slits in the sheet, which made the material appear as if it consisted of a large number of fibres. The Danish inventor O. B. Rasmussen [7], one of the pioneers in this field, was renowned for the originality and scope of his inventiveness; his ideas ranged from the mechanical working of a film through ultrasonic disintegration to its disruption by the explosion of silver azide which was incorporated before drawing in the film. Fibrous materials and sheets of fibres were produced very cheaply by methods such as these. The products were, in general, rather heterogeneous and coarse; they became known as split film materials.

An oriented sheet will break down across the direction of draw to form a series of continuous filaments with a degree of inter-connection as shown in Fig. 5.1. Such materials can be twisted into strings and twines. The fibres derived from films are rectangular in cross-section and those derived from a fibrillation process vary in size according to the degree of working. Fibres of this type have made only a limited impact on the textile market, mainly because of their coarseness.

It is interesting to note that twisted tape, as used in rope manufacture, will undergo some degree of fibrillation. The fibrils are coarse, but they serve to bind the rope together very effectively. It is difficult to separate the tapes once they have been twisted, as the fibrils migrate and interlock in a manner similar to the fibres in a normal twisted staple yarn.

Slit Film

Market trends caused a swing away from split fibres during the early 1960s. In the mid '60s, however, there was a rise in the prices of natural fibres such as hemp and sisal, and interest was stimulated in alternative materials with more stable prices. Although more expensive per pound weight, the high-tenacity drawn polyolefins were able to compete with natural products on a strength/cost basis. With the successful introduction of binder twine and later of ropes made from polyolefins, attention was concentrated on slit film, rather than split film. Slit film is made by cutting film into narrow ribbons, which are used for making various fabric structures. The tapes became narrower as development proceeded, until eventually it was possible to produce fine structures as in the "Barfilex" filament process (see Chapter 6). With the exception of the last product, these materials are generally coarse, and have been used largely for sacking, carpet backing and similar applications.

Despite the success of slit and split film in uses such as these, it is apparent that real success in the textile industry must lie in the production of finer, more uniform products. The fine fibrillation of film has been studied by a number of workers, including J. E. Ford [8]; reports from Japan indicate that it is possible to produce fine fibres from a wide range of polymers, including nylon. These fibres may be as fine as 10 denier, and promising carpet yarns and fabric yarns have been made.

Significant progress has also been made in slitting technology. A fairly uniform staple fibre was produced initially by a high speed slitting process. This was superseded by the pattern slitting of a film to yield a uniform two-dimensional network of fibres which could be cut into narrow sheets and then be twisted into yarns. Control of network slitting has been refined by Plasticisers Ltd. to the point where uniform nets of 5 denier filaments are produced by mechanical slitters. The process may be carried further by introducing a crimping stage.

Yarns of this nature will probably be used for carpet tufting; the crimped fibrils give good cover and anchorage of the material is better than could be otherwise obtained. These yarns have much in common with staple yarns; strength in the crosswise direction is low, but strength is high along the length of the yarn.

UNDRAWN FOAM

DRAWN FOAM FIBRILLATES

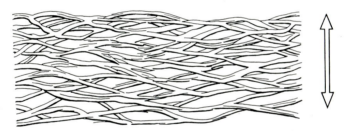

RELAXED STRAND GIVES THREE-DIMENSIONAL NETWORK

Fig. 5.2   Production of network yarns. Method 2.

NETWORK YARNS

At the close of the '60s, the penetration of split and slit film products into the textile field was limited by the coarseness of the fibres available. The introduction of network yarns, however, makes use of fibrillation to provide a unique three-dimensional structure which opens up new prospects for this type of material. The component fibre elements of these yarns are of the order of a few denier and they are combined into a structure resembling a three-

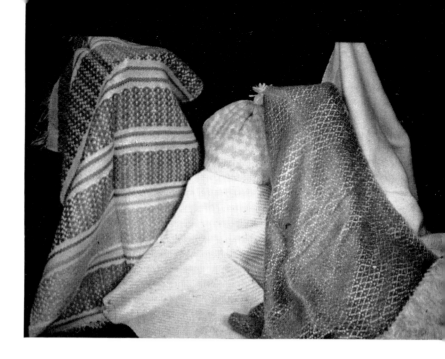

Fig. 5.3 Some typical network yarn fabrics—*Monsanto Chemicals Ltd.*

dimensional version of wire netting. Hence the name, network yarns.

Fibrillation is an essential feature of the network process because of the scale on which it operates. In the mid '60s, Baxter and Gilbert of Monsanto Chemicals Ltd. conceived the idea that a three-dimensional array of inter-connected films could be drawn; after fibrillation this would give rise to an inter-connected three-dimensional network of very fine fibres resembling a yarn. They also realised that a form of three-dimensional film array is to be found in the structure of a foamed polymer; they demonstrated that by drawing polystyrene foam some 6 to 8 fold, a structure was created which could be fibrillated to give a flexible collection of polystyrene fibres with very few free ends. Most of the fibres were interconnected three-dimensionally, as the product was derived from the thin walls of the small cells;

all the fibres were fine and small. Fig. 5.2 shows the essential steps in the process.

Polystyrene is of little interest for this purpose; it is very sensitive to solvents, and has little intrinsic strength. Development of network yarns by Changani and Volans [9] has been concerned largely with high density polyethylene and polypropylene. The first essential is to produce a stable foam of uniform structure in a form which can be drawn at an elevated temperature. A suitable foam may be drawn to such a degree that the films within the internal structure of the foam are capable of fibrillating. Fibrillation may be brought about in various ways.

Continuous Sequence

The three simple processes used in producing network yarns may be carried out in continuous sequence. The polymer is commonly extruded to produce a foam. A buffer zone is used to accommodate any mismatch between components in the process line. Material from this buffer zone is fed to a draw chamber held at a suitable temperature (depending upon the polymer used), where it is drawn to a linear draw ratio of up to 12.

The emerging drawn foamed film is passed through a fibrillator and wound on to a bobbin at the end of the line. A short, continuous line of this sort is capable of producing a single strand at up to 100 ft./min. The strand, after drawing, may emerge at up to about 1000 ft./min. This is at least an order of magnitude higher than the production rate which can be achieved with commercial staple spinning machinery.

It is possible to make a self-coloured drawn foam strand, and an attractive lustre is derived from the multiple reflection of the oriented films within the drawn material (see Fig. 5.3). The drawn foam strand may be converted into a variety of products which have a range of properties differing from those of slit film. Drawn foam strand has a softness and a sheen completely different from slit film.

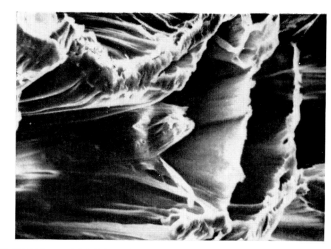

Fig. 5.4 The foam structure. A scanning electron micrograph.

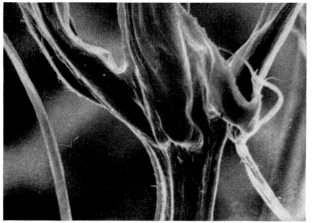

Fig. 5.5 A network fibre junction. A scanning electron micrograph.

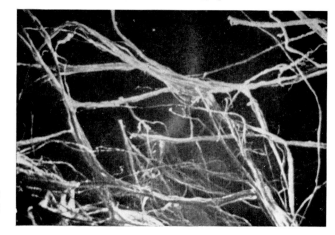

Fig. 5.6 The network structure. A scanning electron micrograph.

A uniform foam structure is necessary to ensure uniform distribution of fibres in the drawn yarn. The cells vary in size, and the fineness of the cell structures must be controlled to provide a desired network structure. Seen through the microscope, the cell structure consists of films joined at triple points (see Fig. 5.4), with less frequent multiple point junctions. These junctions are preserved in the final structure as shown in Fig. 5.5. The residual cell structure is well illustrated by pictures taken with the aid of a scanning-electron microscope (see Fig. 5.6).

After drawing, all the cell walls are contracted across the draw, resulting in some puckering, but the original junctions are still preserved. In the fibrillation process, development of cracks in the cell walls leads to the formation of individual fibres. At this stage of the process, the drawn strand is broken down into the network yarn with its fine three dimensional structure. The nature of the network structure may be seen by opening up the mass of fibres, as shown in Fig. 5.7.

Fibrils

The fibrils occur in a variety of sizes. A statistical analysis of the dimensions of the fibrils is displayed in three dimensional form in Fig. 5.8. A photograph of a cross-section is included so that the true cross-sectional shape of the fibrils may be seen. In general, each fibril is flat and thin, with a very high cover factor and good flexibility. This results in a yarn with many of the characteristics required for normal textile applications.

The fibrils are all interconnected and the absence of obvious ends is an unusual feature. The yarn could be used without twist in a manner similar to the T.N.O. twistless yarn. The crosswise strength is low, but the fibres have more than enough coherence to withstand the fabric-making processes, and the yarn has high strength in the draw direction (i.e. along the yarn axis). If the yarn is twisted,

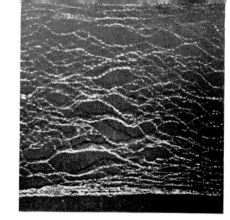

Fig. 5.7 *Above:* Bulked network. *Left:* Network yarn extended to show structure. *Below:* Network yarn.

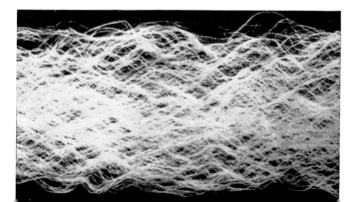

the network junctions act in the same way as migrating fibres. It seems probable that twist would be inserted only where certain fabric effects were desired. Unlike continuous filament yarns, these network yarns have bulk; like continuous filament yarns, however, they have no free ends. They resemble staple yarns, but are not hairy. They are related to split film yarns in that the individual filaments are derived from fine sheets by a splitting technique.

Properties

Continuous filament yarns are generally stronger than staple yarns of the same material. Network yarns with zero twist have a tenacity in the region of 2 gf/denier (18 gf/tex), the actual figure depending on the method of production. A twisted yarn of similar material may have a tenacity of up to 45 gf/tex. There is thus a considerable range of tenacities available for any particular type of network yarn.

The behaviour of these yarns under twist is similar to that of staple yarns; the strength increases with twist up to about 6 t.p.i. and then decays as the yarn becomes over-twisted.

It is possible to change the dimensions of the films within the foam, and in this way affect the behaviour of the yarn. Fig. 5.9 shows three polyethylene foam products of decreasing cell size; there is an increase in tenacity of the drawn foam strand as the cell size is decreased.

The tenacity of a network yarn cannot equal that of the corresponding simple filament yarn; in the network yarn, a higher proportion of the material does not resist the load. In the case of polypropylene there is a similar relationship between drawn foam and drawn film; on fibrillation of these structures, there is a further decrease in tenacity (see Fig. 5.10). The extension at break is affected similarly by differences in yarn structure; the higher the draw ratio, the lower is the extension at break (see Fig. 5.11).

Some of these network products have been subjected to

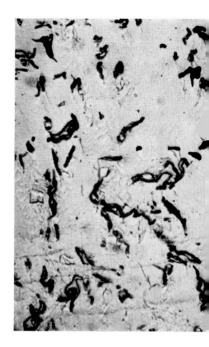

Fig. 5.8 *Right:* High-density polyethylene network yarn. Cross-section. *Below:* Theoretical cross-section of yarn.

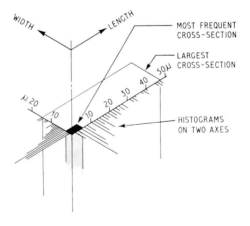

conventional textile processes, and a number of fabrics have been woven on an experimental scale. The drape and handle of these materials were very good, but crease recovery was poor. Martindale figures show that the wear properties of fabrics made from non-twisted yarns were good. The wear properties of fabrics from twisted yarns were even better (see Table 5.1).

Many problems remain to be solved in the field of network yarns but it is apparent that the process offers a potentially cheap route to a wide range of useful materials. The network technique will be particularly useful for producing coarse yarns; it is as easy to create a fine structure in a coarse yarn as in a fine one. Adequate strengths and wear properties can be achieved, and the handle of the materials is acceptable for many purposes. It remains to be seen whether network yarns made from these polymers can achieve a wide acceptance or whether additional fibrillating polymers will be developed. Whatever the outcome, it seems likely that network yarn will provide a useful addition to the variety of yarns available to the textile manufacturer.

Yarn	HDPE	Twisted HDPE	Texturised HDPE	P P
Denier	1960	1430	1960	2320
Tex	220	160	220	220
Twist	nil	2 t.p.i.	nil	nil
Weave	plain	twill	plain	twill
Some abrasion after	2,500 cycles	2,500 cycles	2,500 cycles	2,500 cycles
Failure after	42,000 cycles	60,000 cycles	37,000 cycles	50,000 cycles

N.B. HDPE = High density polyethylene
P P   = Polypropylene

Table 5.1   Martindale wear behaviour of fabrics from network yarns.

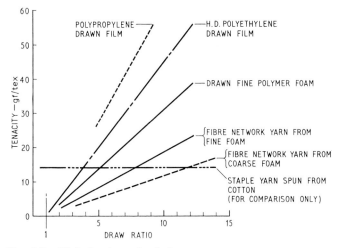

Fig. 5.9   High-density polyethylene.

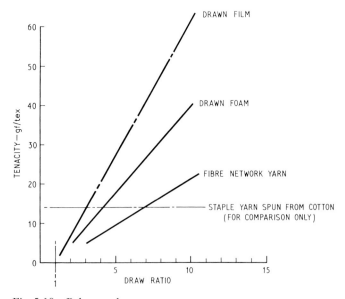

Fig. 5.10   Polypropylene.

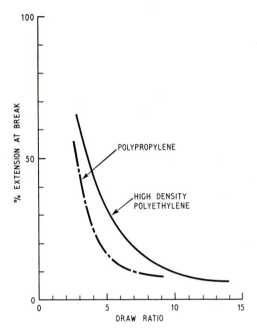

Fig. 5.11 Network yarns. Extension at break.

6

Tape Yarns

by **D. C. Hossack**[*]

This chapter describes the four main methods of tape manufacture;
(1) continuous chilled cast sheet, (2) discontinuous blown sheet, (3)
continuous extruded flat monofilament, (4) continuous drawn sheet
which is slit *in situ* during subsequent processes such as beaming or
weaving.

The methods are compared and their relative merits listed. The
applications of tape products are described, particularly in packaging
of various types, tufted carpet backing, scrims and other industrial cloth.
Polyolefin tapes are replacing jute in many applications, and the
relative advantages and disadvantages of the materials are outlined.
The 'Barfilex' process which produces yarns similar in properties to
conventional continuous filament yarns is described. This process is
compared with the mechanical fibrillation process, and their advantages
and disadvantages are discussed. The chapter ends by listing the
possible future trends in that part of the textile industry which uses
tapes and yarns made by the novel method described.

MELT SPINNING

Tape yarns are produced by melt spinning, the plant
being similar to that used in the production of melt-spun
filament yarns.

A typical melt spinning plant consists of a vertical extruder
or melt grid system, where polymer chips are heated above
their melting point to form a melt pool. The molten polymer
is then fed into a beam, which distributes it to a series of
spinning pumps. The pumps meter the melt and force it
through the spinneret.

[*] Conference author. Director, Filtrona Textile Products Ltd.,
Bletchley, Bucks., U.K.

The system is pressurised; in the case of a vertical extruder, the pressure is of the order of 80 atmospheres. This pressure is maintained by having a variable speed drive to the screw, which is actuated by a pressure sensing device located in the melt. In the case of polyester, the extrudate is spun into air; the filaments are accelerated rapidly, the ratio of the linear speed of wind-up to that at the spinneret being of the order of 40 to 1.

The undrawn filament is taken to a drawframe, where it is cold or hot drawn before being wound onto bobbins or crimped and cut into staple fibre.

A melt spinning process such as this is, in the main, discontinuous. A melt spinning process used for producing tape yarns, on the other hand, is continuous. There are at least four methods of production.

1. Continuously chilled cast sheet which is slit during the tape manufacturing process.
2. Discontinuously blown sheet which is slit during the tape manufacturing process.
3. Continuously extruded flat monofilaments.
4. Drawn sheet which is later slit in situ.

1. CONTINUOUSLY CHILLED CAST SHEET

The first stage of the production line is a horizontal extruder, the screw having a length/diameter ratio of about 24:1. The screw is divided into three sections; the first quarter of its length is used as a feed zone, the second quarter is a compression zone (which is necessary due to the difference in bulk density between the granules and the molten polymer) and the remaining half of the screw acts as a metering zone. The barrel is heated, its temperature being gradually raised along its length; in the case of polypropylene, the melt pool is at about 250°C. The melt is extruded through a heated slit die and cooled immediately

to form a sheet which might be, for example, 600 mm. wide
and 150 μ thick.

Drawing

The sheet moves about 5 times faster than the melt through
the die, giving a draw down ratio of about 5:1. It is then split
into separate tapes which are drawn. The draw ratio which
varies with the type of polymer used, is one of the variables
which determine the physical properties, particularly the
extension of the finished tape. In the case of polypropylene,
the draw ratio would normally be in the range 7:1 to 13:1.

The increase in length is accompanied by a decrease in
cross-sectional area. The width and thickness of the drawn
tape are proportional to the original undrawn width and
thickness divided by the square root of the draw ratio. As
there is no drawing in the transverse direction, the tape
tends to fibrillate (split lengthwise) in subsequent processing;
such tapes are said to be mono-axially drawn.

During drawing, the undrawn tapes pass round a multi-
roller draw stand, through an oven and on to a second draw
stand. The linear speed of the first draw stand is just
sufficient to produce tension in the sheet. The speed of the
second draw stand is varied according to the draw ratio
desired; for example, it might be about 9 times the speed
of the first draw stand.

The temperature of the first oven is about 160°C. After
drawing, the tapes are passed through a second oven at
about 140°C, and then through a third draw stand running
about 7% slower than the second draw stand. This allows
the tapes to relax, and lowers their residual shrinkage to
about 4% (which relates to the free shrinkage when tested
in air at 130°C for 4 mins.). The speed of the tape at the
wind-up varies from line to line and from producer to
producer.

Three basic factors limit the speed and production rate
of this process. First, molten material passing through a

small orifice has a maximum speed beyond which shear failure occurs. Second, the maximum rate of drawing depends to a large extent on maintaining the temperature at the draw point. Third, operatives must deal with tapes moving at speeds of up to 200 metres a minute.

Present day tape lines run at wind-up speeds of about 150 metres per minute. Higher speeds are possible, but they cause deterioration of the physical properties of the tape, so that the product is useless for sophisticated applications such as carpet backing. One effect of high speed is to produce a significant variation along the length of the tape and between bobbins. Difficulties may also arise in winding, which demands great skill. Winding is the stage which yields most waste and it is here that a profit can easily be turned into a loss. Weft packages weigh usually between 12 and 20 lb.; warp packages have a weight limit of about 20 lb. because of difficulties associated with side unwinding in a creel.

2. DISCONTINUOUSLY BLOWN SHEET

The discontinuous process is very similar to the above, but the film is extruded and then reeled; the sheets are then taken to a drawing plant. Advantages claimed for this process include more flexibility, higher drawing speeds and low waste. In making 20 lb. cheeses, however, the weight of the sheet reel will have to be 1800 lb.; this alone rules out the process for production of carpet backings.

3. CONTINUOUSLY EXTRUDED FLAT MONOFILAMENT

The melt is extruded through a series of narrow slits to form numerous undrawn tapes. Subsequent processes are similar to those already described.

4. DRAWN SHEET SLIT IN SITU

The fourth method is radically different from those described above. If tape yarns are to compete on a cost basis, their width/thickness ratio must be fully utilised in the final product. For example, to produce a cloth which has a high cover/weight ratio, the tape must be assembled in the fabric completely flat and untwisted. This is comparatively easy to achieve in the warp direction, but is much more difficult in the weft direction. A completely flat tape is not necessary in both directions, as the cover can be derived entirely from the warp, the weft serving merely to hold the assembly together. To ensure that the warp is completely flat, special unrolling creels and beamers are required. An installation of this type has a capital cost in excess of £12,500 ($31,000 approx.) and it occupies a very large floor area. If tape weaving is to become of general use, therefore, an alternative method of warp preparation is necessary.

In this connection, the warp sheet process is likely to gain ground during the early '70s. The process may be divided into two distinct parts; manufacture of the sheet, and conversion of the sheet into tape.

Extrusion

The first process in sheet manufacture is extrusion, using an extruder designed to produce a sheet at least 1 metre wide and of controlled thickness. Extruders of the Rototruder type are commonly used, in which the screw is vertical whilst the barrel, which is compounded with the annular die, rotates around it. This technique produces the accurate gauge control essential in this process.

Slitting and Drawing

The lay-flat tube, about 500 mm. wide, is slit continuously to the required width. It is then fed to a frame consisting of a series of heated feed rollers followed by a series of cooling rollers. Between these two groups is a pair of heated draw rollers, whose distance apart may be varied between about 2 and 75 mm. The limitation of the draw zone is necessary in order to ensure that drawing takes place evenly across the whole width of the sheet. No decrease in the width of the sheet is allowed to occur, the thickness thus being reduced in proportion to the draw ratio. The drawn sheet is wound on to a reel which is mounted in the place of the normal beam on a loom, warp knitting machine etc. Tapes are formed by passing the sheet through a slitting device at the back rest. This consists of a series of blades, appropriately spaced, formed into a block which takes the place of the back rest, or is compounded with it. Alternatively, the sheet may be slit at the front of a beamer, the beams then being made in the usual manner. Tapes produced in this way cannot be considered as monoaxially drawn, as there is no decrease in the transverse direction. A degree of transverse molecular orientation is introduced, which decreases the tenacity of the tape. Polypropylene tape drawn in hot air has a tenacity of about 5.5 gf/denier (49.5 gf/tex); on a slit warp sheet, all other conditions being the same, the tenacity would be about 5 gf/denier (45 gf/tex). On the other hand, the extension of the slit warp sheet is higher. These products are usually replacements for jute, which has a tenacity of about 1.6 gf/denier (14 gf/tex). The drop in tenacity of the slit warp sheet is not, therefore, very significant.

APPLICATIONS

Tape yarns are used increasingly in packaging, bags, sacks and bale wrappers. They provide base fabrics in open woven form, scrims, underlays for needle felts and similar products. They are used also as base fabrics in close woven form, and as decoration (such as wall coverings). Horticultural uses include vegetable bags, greenhouse shades, protection for growing bulbs etc.

D

Polyethylene does not rot, which gives it an advantage over jute in sacking applications, especially in tropical countries. Also, it does not absorb moisture. On the other hand, polyethylene sacks have disadvantages; they are very slippery, may be difficult to stack and suffer degradation due to the effects of sunlight. In carpet backing, polypropylene tape has several advantages over jute. It is more uniform; the tufting machine operates more efficiently with less needle damage; the carpet is more uniform and wastage is reduced. Also, in subsequent hot aqueous treatments, such as piece dyeing, polypropylene does not absorb water or dyestuff; it costs less to dry than jute, and dyeing is more efficient.

Competition With Jute

In the '70s, it is likely that the advantages of polyethylene tapes over traditional fibres, including jute, cotton or flax in their coarser forms, will stimulate increasing use of the synthetic material. Political upheavals in jute-growing regions tend to destroy confidence in overseas markets, and lost markets are not easily recaptured. The 1968/69 jute crop was poor, and many consumers were forced to use synthetic materials instead. In the past, the jute industry has withstood competition from synthetic materials largely through its price advantage; this has now been minimised through devaluation and the imposition of export duties, particularly in Pakistan. In addition, the Montecatini licence agreements come to an end in 1971, and there will almost certainly be an increase in the number and size of polymer plants, with prices falling as competition grows. The prices of tape should be stable during the early '70s, contrasting with the violent fluctuations which characterise the price of jute.

Carpets

The future of synthetic tape yarns will be linked directly with their use in carpet backing. The production of tufted carpets in the United Kingdom in 1967 was about 50 million sq. yds., and by 1970 at least half the U.K. production was using polypropylene backing. This represents a production of about 6½ million lb. per annum of polypropylene yarn, the figure being further increased to about 10 million lb. by exports to E.F.T.A., the Commonwealth and other countries. During the '70s synthetic tapes will continue to make headway in this field.

Conventional Dimensions

The high width/thickness ratio of tape may be regarded as one of its advantages, but it also mitigates against its wider use. Manufacturers are often conservative in their acceptance of new materials, and tend to mistrust tape because it does not have the familiar circular cross section. For this reason, German manufacturers produce a very wide, thin tape which folds readily into a superficially conventional form.

Much experimental work has been carried out in attempts to make yarns of conventional dimensions via the tape technique. Two processes are used commercially. In the first, tape is split mechanically; in the second, a sheet die is used in which there are a number of coarse spinnerets instead of a single wide slit.

In mechanical fibrillation, tape made in the usual manner is split longitudinally by one of various devices, such as pin rollers or oscillating fine saw teeth. These yarns exhibit a web-like structure when opened out.

"Barfilex" Process

Yarn produced by means of a bank of coarse spinnerets has a closer resemblance to a conventional continuous filament yarn. The "Barfilex" process, which uses this technique, is in operation in the United States, the United Kingdom, and Western Europe. In this process, a horizontal extruder feeds a beam which forms an extension of the barrel. Attached to the beam are branches which house the spinnerets. Conventional gear pumps are not used; the melt is moved forward by the screw. The compact beams are heated electrically. The filaments are drawn, wind-up speeds of up to 400 metres per minute being achieved in what is a true melt draw process.

Production costs for these two processes are similar, but it is difficult to compare the properties of the yarns. Mechanically fibrillated yarns, due to their web-like structure, do not always have the same number of filaments in a cross section, and the denier of the fibres varies. Furthermore, there is no fibrillation in the transverse direction; the thickness of the parent tape therefore determines one dimension of the filaments, and this limits the denier of the yarn. Commercial fibrillated yarns are commonly 1,000 denier or greater. On the other hand, the "Barfilex" process forms a yarn made of discrete filaments, with physical properties similar to those of conventionally-produced continuous filament yarns. Tenacity is usually about 6 gf/denier (54 gf/tex) and the extension may vary between 10% and 22% according to the processing conditions. The maximum shrinkage attainable is about 4%. A disadvantage of the process is that the yarns as wound on to the package are completely flat; they do not even contain a producer twist. It seems likely, therefore, that some degree of twist must be put in before they can be woven as warp; there seems to be little difficulty in using them as weft.

Both of the above methods are likely to achieve greater prominence during the early '70s, capturing markets now held by jute, cotton and viscose spun yarns. They will be used especially in woven carpet backing, in the weft of the conventional carpet, and in industrial fabrics of all kinds. Both types of yarn will find a range of such applications, but the "Barfilex" process would seem to offer the greatest potential. "Barfilex" yarns are of conventional dimensions; they have a familiar appearance, with discrete filaments; they can be processed by conventional technology. In addition, "Barfilex" yarns may be crimped and cut to staple fibre.

Acceptable polyester fibres may be produced by a modified form of "Barfilex" process, and it is to be expected that a significant amount of polyester fibre will be made by this means in the '70s.

7

Twistless and Self-twist Yarns

by H. J. Selling* and P. R. Lord

Twist is commonly regarded as an essential feature of a textile yarn; in fact, its main function is to hold the fibres together whilst they are assembled into fabric. Work at T.N.O. has shown that a temporary adhesive will serve the same purpose, and that woven fabrics do not suffer from the lack of twist.

Alternating twist may be used as an alternative to normal twist; as it is not necessary to rotate yarn packages to insert twist, very high production rates are possible. CSIRO have demonstrated that a strand with alternating twist can be locked by self-twisting with similar strands, and useful yarns may be produced at very high production rates. An assessment of this process is made.

INTRODUCTION

Until comparatively recent times, a textile fabric was regarded as a sheet of material made by interlacing yarns, the yarns themselves being made from a multitude of fibres twisted together to form a coherent strand. With the coming of man-made fibres, continuous filament yarns brought new concepts of yarn structure, but the idea persisted that true twist was necessary to hold the filaments together. In recent years, the texturising of filament yarns has become an established process, and there has been a further move away

* Conference author. Director, Fibre Research Institute TNO, Delft, Holland.

from traditional ideas of yarn structure. The function of twist, even in staple yarns, has come under critical review.

When warp and weft are woven to form a fabric, the fibres are held together by the intersecting yarns. Twist is not a necessary requirement for fabric strength. Indeed, it would be anticipated that fabric strengths could be improved if warp and weft consisted of perfectly parallel fibre assemblies. The main purpose of twist is to hold the yarn together during the assembly of yarn into fabric.

Recognition of this fact has stimulated research into new methods of holding fibres together into yarns without using true twist. One method of doing this is to entangle fibres to such a degree that they interlock. This is, in effect, the condenser spinning technique, in which a strip of web has alternating twist applied to it by rubbing tapes. These tapes consolidate the structure by external pressure and twist applied to the yarn. The web from which the yarn is made contains many non-straight fibres which are almost randomly oriented. Consolidation of the web causes many of these fibres to interlock and the strand produced can be used as a yarn. These yarns exhibit special characteristics; the lack of fibre alignment and straightness makes them weak, soft and full. These characteristics can be turned to advantage where cover is more important than strength, and condenser yarns have played a useful role in the textile trade for many years. They are, however, excluded from markets where a strong, lean yarn is required to give a strong, smooth fabric. To make such yarns it is necessary to improve fibre straightness and orientation, but improvement in these respects diminishes the interlocking of the fibres in condenser spinning.

New Techniques

Two new techniques of producing yarns without true twist are considered in this chapter. The first section is concerned with so-called *twistless yarns* produced, for

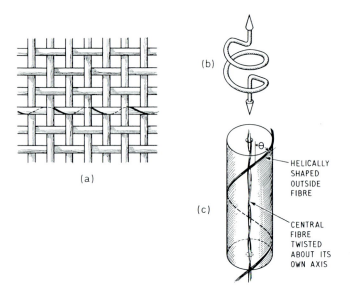

Fig. 7.1   (a) The yarn in a fabric. (b) Fibres in a twisted yarn.

example, by using temporary adhesives to hold together untwisted strands of fibre until the fabric has been made. The adhesive is then removed, the fibres being held together by forces arising from the interweaving of the strands. This type of technique is being studied in several countries, notably at the Fibre Research Institute T.N.O. in Holland.

The second section deals with the so-called *self-twist yarns* such as those produced experimentally in Australia. Intermittent false twist is inserted into each of two strands which then self-twist themselves to lock the structure into a stable system. Self-twist yarns are likely to become of commercial value during the 1970s.

TWISTLESS SPINNING

The approach used by the Fibre Research Institute T.N.O., Holland, was to consider the requirements of the real end-product, the fabric, rather than the yarn. A study was made, for example, of the effects of twist when the yarn is assembled into fabric.

Fig. 7.1(a) shows the outline of a fibre in one of the constituent yarns of a plain weave.

Ignoring the effects of fibre migration within the yarn, it may be assumed that the fibre will be gripped at the intersections of warp and weft. If the twist factor is high, the fibre will tend to behave as a helical spring similar to that in Fig. 7.1(b); such a system has a low stiffness along the axis of the helix, and this is controlled mainly by the torsional rigidity of the fibre. A straight fibre lying parallel to the axis of the yarn will be relatively stiff. A normal twisted yarn contains fibres whose helix angles vary from zero to θ as indicated in Fig. 7.1(c); as the components vary in stiffness, the axial load is not evenly distributed amongst them. If the fibres are parallel, this difficulty will not be encountered and the load-carrying capacity is improved. Since the breaking tenacity of the fibre is a fixed quantity, the permissible axial load will vary as the twist factor is altered. The larger the twist factor, the weaker the yarn; therefore, if coherence of the strand is no longer important (because the coherence results from fabric structure), the less the twist, the better. In theory, therefore, twistless yarns should yield better fabric strength.

The absence of twist would have other effects. A high twist yarn tends to make the fabric harsh, and a zero twist yarn would be expected to produce a softer feel. Also, twist scatters the light, dulling the colour of a dyed fabric, and reducing gloss and luminosity. A twistless fabric would be more brilliant, with a better colour factor than a conventional one.

D*

Tests were made to check these theories. A twistless yarn was made by using scaffolding threads of calcium alginate with a normal cotton yarn, the combination being untwisted until the cotton strand was twistless and held together by the alginate thread. Small pieces of fabric were made from these yarns, the alginate then being dissolved away. The fabrics were tested, and their strength and stretch properties assessed. Results were sufficiently encouraging to stimulate further research in the hope of finding a commercially viable technique in place of the expensive alginate process, e.g. the use of adhesives.

Tek-ja Process

Experiments in twistless spinning have been carried out for many years, providing a background to the research carried out by T.N.O. As far as is known, the first machine for making twistless yarns, developed by Fibrebond Laboratories Inc., U.S.A. [10], was based on a patent of Beardsley Lawrence. This was the basis of the so-called Tek-ja process.

An outline of the Tek-ja process is shown in Fig. 7.2. A roving was drafted in the conventional manner and was then pressed on to a roller carrying a thin film of adhesive. Whilst in contact with the adhesive roller, the fibres were subjected to the action of rubbing rollers which moved in reciprocal fashion along their axes. This condensed the fibres, impregnated them with adhesives and gave the yarn a round cross-section. The yarn was then dried and wound on to a package.

The production rate was claimed to be some three or four times greater than that of a traditional spinner, and on this basis it would be comparable to break spinning. The costs of production are not known, but these would depend in the main upon the price of adhesive, the amount needed, the cost of drying the yarn and the cost of the machine. It is probable that there were difficulties in drying the yarn

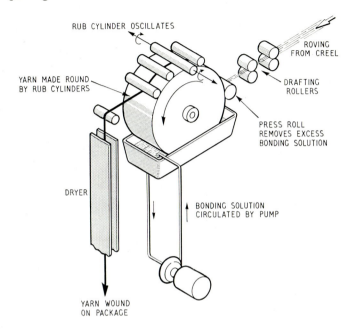

RUB CYLINDER OSCILLATES

YARN MADE ROUND
BY RUB CYLINDERS

ROVING
FROM CREEL

DRAFTING
ROLLERS

PRESS ROLL
REMOVES EXCESS
BONDING SOLUTION

DRYER

BONDING SOLUTION
CIRCULATED BY PUMP

YARN WOUND
ON PACKAGE

Fig. 7.2   The Tek-Ja process for making a 'no-twist' yarn.

sufficiently quickly. Also, the strength of the wet slubbing would be low, creating problems in operating the process under high speed conditions. It was not found possible to apply more than 8% starch; in consequence, the yarn was suitable only for weft. It is doubtful if the process proved commercially operable.

T.N.O. Experiments

At T.N.O., a different approach was made to the problem. It was decided that false twist should be inserted to give temporary strength to the wet fibre assembly on its way to the final package. The package would then be dried as a

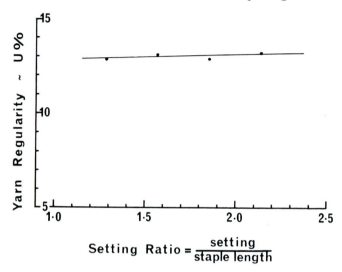

Fig. 7.3

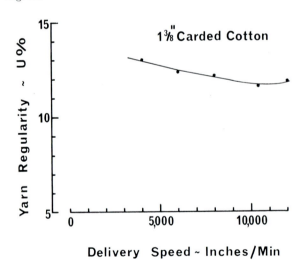

Fig. 7.4   The drafting of scoured cotton in the wet state. $1\frac{3}{8}$ inch carded cotton.

whole instead of attempting to dry the running yarn. Difficulty was experienced, however, in drafting the fibres in a normal system at speeds greater than 3,000 inches/min., and an alternative was sought.

In a normal drafting system, forces are applied in a direction perpendicular to the fibre stream through the drafting rollers or aprons (i.e. the weighting). The surface motion of these elements is thus transmitted to the fibres with the intention of keeping the floating fibres under control. The extent to which this is successful depends on the magnitude of the weighting and the coefficients of friction between one fibre and another, and between the fibres and the surface of the drafting elements. It was considered that if the cohesive forces could come largely from within the fibre assembly, smaller external forces would be required. Further, if interfibre properties were made more uniform, fibre control would be easier and there would be less need for a close tolerance to the setting of the drafting rollers. The roving was therefore boiled in an alkaline solution to remove fatty substances, and used in the wet state. Good fibre control was obtained and the drafting system became independent of the setting, as shown in Fig. 7.3. In consequence, it was possible to draft fibres whose staple length was less than half of the setting. This implies that the same machine can be used for a range of staple fibres.

The regularity of the product improved with speed up to some 10,000 inches/min., as shown in Fig. 7.4. If the rest of the system could work at this rate, it would be equivalent to a twisting device operating well in excess of 100,000 twists/minute.

Application of Inactive Adhesive

In practice, it was not possible to dry the running yarn at these speeds. If an active adhesive was used, the layers of yarn on the spool stuck together, making the yarn unusable. An attempt was made, therefore, to wind the

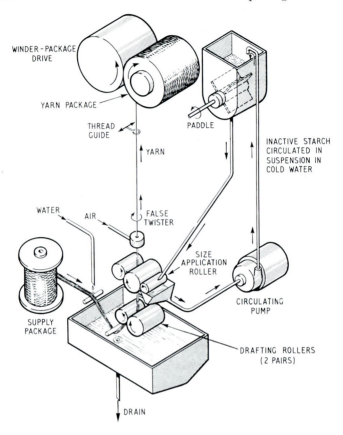

Fig. 7.5   T.N.O. twistless-spinning machine.

twistless yarn on to the package and then activate the adhesive. Adhesive was applied to the fibre strand before winding, in such a way that subsequent activation would make the fibres in one strand adhere to one another without adhering to the fibres in adjacent strands—at least, not to any significant extent. The adhesive had to be inactive during

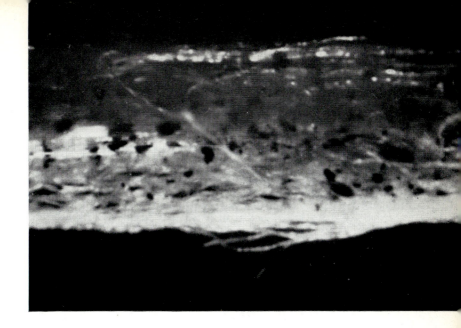

Fig. 7.6   Particles of size in twistless yarn.

application and to be distributed efficiently inside the strand itself. Powdered potato starch, a cheap and effective adhesive, was held in suspension in cold water, in which it remained inactive. Suspension was maintained by continuous circulation, and the particles of inactive starch were applied by a system of press rollers as shown in Fig. 7.5. Very good dispersion of size particles was obtained; Fig. 7.6 shows the particles after they have been swollen in a subsequent process. Starch could be applied in this way at speeds up to 6,000 inches/min., and it is probable that higher speeds still could be achieved. (When spinning flax, which contains pectin, this stage can be omitted.)

False Twist

A false twister of the air vortex type (see Fig. 7.7) was used to give temporary strength to the strand during its transit from the front rollers of the drafting device to the

take up package. The air inlet holes of the air vortex
twister were slightly inclined in order to help the strand on
its way; absence of twist in this zone means that the strand
is very weak. Air was supplied at a pressure of about
$\frac{1}{2}$ atmosphere; the central bore was 1 to 2 mm. diameter
depending on the yarn count being produced. The technique
proved very effective, the only difficulty being that minute
particles of starch would eventually accumulate and affect
the airflow. Fig. 7.8 shows a laboratory machine.

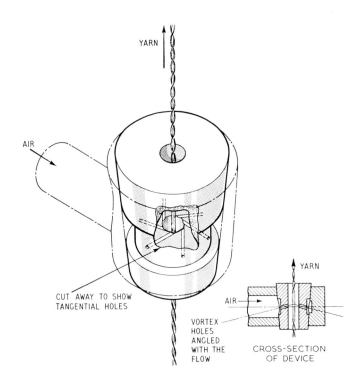

Fig. 7.7   Air-vortex false-twist device.

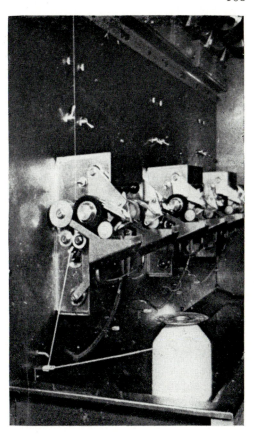

Fig. 7.8 T.N.O. machine for producing twistless yarn.

After the strand had been wound on to the bobbin, the package was removed and steamed for an hour at 110°C. During that time, the starch was activated, producing adhesive films which spread along the fibres as the particles swelled. The package was then dried in an oven at about 100°C, the final package being firm and solid. There was some adhesion between adjacent yarns, which helped to make the package solid without causing trouble in unwinding.

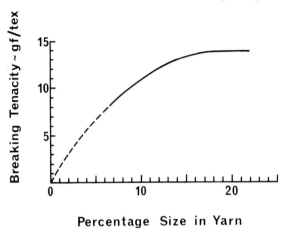

Fig. 7.9   The effect of starch in twistless yarns.

Yarn Characteristics

The finished yarn had a flat cross-section and was, in consequence, more flexible than a normal yarn containing the same amount of size. As size content affects the stiffness and strength (see Fig. 7.9) adjustments had to be made to provide for the differing needs of warp and weft yarns. The ranges of size concentration found to be suitable for a cotton weft and warp were 9%–12% and 12%–15% respectively. These gave mean tenacities of about 11 gf/tex for the weft and about 12.5 gf/tex for the warp; these tenacities were adequate for weaving.

The yarns were assessed in a wear-resistance tester designed to simulate the action in weaving, and it was found that resistance to wear increased markedly with the starch content in the yarn. Average values were about 1,000 cycles for a weft yarn and 1,500 cycles for a warp yarn; the required limits were 200 and 400 respectively. The minimum recorded values for twistless yarns were about 50% greater than these limits.

FIBRE LOSS IN COTTON SHEETS DUE TO WASHING AND USE

Yarns	Linear Density (tex)		Threads/Inch		Fabric Weight		Strength gf/tex		% Loss in Weight/Cycle	
	Warp	Weft	Warp	Weft	g./m.²	oz./yd.²	Warp	Weft	Wash Only	Wash and use
Normal										
Twisted	28	30	66	63	159	7.1	12.8	13.1	0.08	0.10
Twistless	30	30	58	51	139	6.2	10.4	10.0	0.10	0.13
Twistless	20	20	76	68	124	5.6	15.3	16.3	0.07	0.08

Table 7.1

Simplicity and high productivity are only two of the advantages inherent in this technique. Some of the costly processes now carried out on fabric could with advantage be carried out on the yarn before assembly. Yarn could be dyed, for example, when wet, thus saving an expensive drying operation. Yarn could be mercerised before being assembled into fabric. Resination of separate fibres rather than fabric might reduce the loss of strength associated with that process; it might be possible to incorporate a resination phase in an integrated process.

Laundering

It was anticipated that repeated washing might adversely affect fabrics made from twistless yarns. Table 7.1 shows results of washing tests which were carried out. As twistless yarns were bulkier than conventional ring yarns, either the yarn count had to be made finer or the number of threads per inch in the warp and weft reduced to obtain a true comparison. In both cases, the fabric weight was reduced; when the number of threads per inch was reduced, there was a considerable loss in fabric strength. None of these changes, however, had an appreciable effect on the percentage fibre loss in use; in fact, by using finer yarns, the percentage loss rate was reduced and the absolute loss rate remained about the same. It is possible, therefore, to make

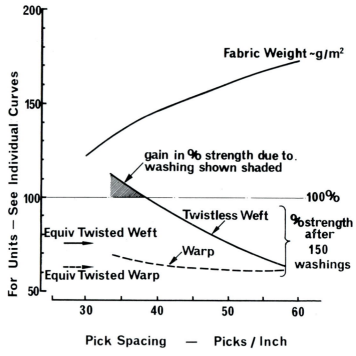

Fig. 7.10   Fabrics from twistless yarns.
            Warp: 40 ends/cm. 30s c.c. (20 tex) twisted cotton yarn.
            Weft: various pick spacings. 20s c.c. (30 tex) twistless cotton
            yarns.

lighter sheetings which will perform as well, and will
incidentally bring considerable savings in laundry costs.
   A further test was made in which the sett of the cloth
was kept constant and the pick spacing was varied over a
wide range. As the pick spacing was altered to give a more
open structure, the weftwise extensibility dropped markedly
(probably due to the changes in yarn crimp) and the fabric
weight decreased. Surprisingly, the percentage strength
after 150 washings did not change as much as had been

feared (see Fig. 7.10); in fact, at about 35 picks/inch, the strength was improved by washing despite some fibre loss. At first, it was thought that this was a mistake, but further tests confirmed that it was not so. The increased strength was in fact caused by shrinkage of almost 1%, which had the effect of binding the fibre in the fabric structure. In a fabric with a spun warp and twistless weft, at 35 picks/inch, the weftwise tensile strength of the fabric was 7.1 gf/tex whereas at 58 picks/inch it was 17 gf/tex; the warpwise strength varied between 12.5 to 14.2 gf/tex. This illustrates how the normal pressure exerted by the warp threads affects the weftwise strength of the fabric.

The results of this experimental work have confirmed that twist is not essential so far as the fabric is concerned; it is necessary only in the intervening processes, and it may be replaced effectively by temporary adhesion. The machine used for drafting fibres and inserting the adhesive is not complicated, and it is reasonable to assume, therefore, that twistless yarns could be made cheaply and at a very high production rate. If wet processes normally applied to a fabric could be applied to the yarn, the avoidance of drying stages would be a further factor in reducing costs.

SELF-TWIST YARNS

By the late 1960s, self-twist yarns were being produced in pilot plants under mill conditions in Australia; production was under the supervision of C.S.I.R.O., who hold a number of patents on the subject.

It has long been known that two strands, each twisted in the same direction, and placed together, will self-twist to form a stable structure. The technique is similar to the ancient one used in farming, twisted lengths of straw, or "bonds", being used for binding sheaves of straw. In making the bonds, one man uses a "wimbole" or crank to insert twist, whilst another man holds the bond in one hand and feeds discrete lengths of straw to the open end with the other. For storage purposes, the bonds are bent double and allowed to self twist to form a stable structure similar to that shown in Fig. 7.11.

Alternating twist is another technique which has long been known for producing self-twist strands. The twist is set by using adhesives, by intermingling fibres or by thermosetting them to provide stability. Perhaps the oldest example of this is condenser spinning.

The C.S.I.R.O. patent [3] combines elements of both these basic ideas, alternating twist in one strand being combined with the alternating twist in another strand to bring about self-twist as shown in Fig. 7.12. The alternating twist in the single strand is a false twist; it would be unable to survive on its own unless stabilised by some means such as one of those outlined above. When the two strands self-twist, the yarn itself acquires an alternating twist; this locks the fibres effectively in the component strands. As the strands themselves are self-twisted, there is little or no residual torque in any lengthwise portion of the complete system. Provided there is no internal slippage, the yarn so formed will not become untwisted. If, however, one strand is able to slip relative to the other, it may become untwisted.

**Twist in Strand Opposite
To Twist Of Body**

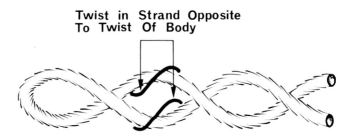

Fig. 7.11   Simple self-twist.

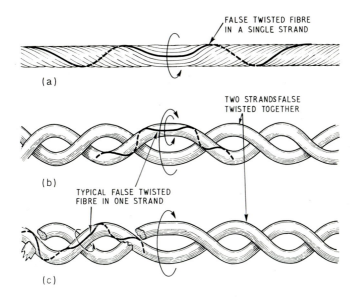

FALSE TWISTED FIBRE
IN A SINGLE STRAND

(a)

TWO STRANDS FALSE
TWISTED TOGETHER

(b)

TYPICAL FALSE TWISTED
FIBRE IN ONE STRAND

(c)

Fig. 7.12   Elements of a self-twist yarn.

Theoretical Considerations

A self-twist yarn may be studied by considering a strand laid on a smooth cylinder in the same way that one strand would be laid on the other in the yarn. A diagram of this is shown in Fig. 7.13. In particular, consider the part BD and let the forces acting on this element which arise from the continuations of the strand be T_1 and T_2. Also, let the external force required to balance these be T_r. Each of these can be resolved into horizontal and vertical components which can be denoted by the suffixes H and V respectively. The element of strand is wrapped around the cylinder as is

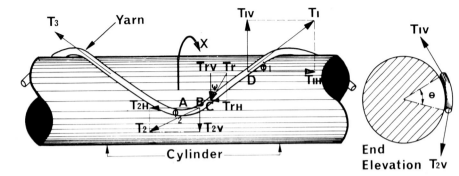

Fig. 7.13   Yarn on a smooth cylinder.

shown in the end elevation; there is therefore a capstan
effect and

$$T_{1V} = T_{2V} e^{\mu\Theta} \quad \text{..............Eq. 7.1.}$$

where μ is the coefficient of friction and θ is the angle of
wrap in radians.

Dealing with the vertical components, $T_{rV} = T_{1V} - T_{2V}$
therefore

$$T_{rV} = T_{2V}(e^{\mu\Theta} - 1)$$

$$= T_2 \, \text{Sin} \, \varnothing_2 \, (e^{\mu\Theta} - 1) \quad \text{..............Eq. 7.2}$$

At point A the angle $\varnothing_2 = 0$, therefore $T_{rV} = 0$.

This implies that there could be no tension build up along
the strand; the whole system would be unstable and unlikely
to retain the ply twist. It was specified that the cylinder be
smooth, but in practice one strand is twisted about the other
and neither is smooth. Indeed fibres projecting from one
strand can interlock with the other strand, and junctions so
formed will not obey the classical theories of friction. Such a
junction may be the starting point of a tension build up;
instead of $T_2 \, \text{Sin} \, \varnothing_2$, therefore, let a value T_j be inserted.
T_j is assumed to be independent of the radial pressure acting

on the strand; it is therefore unaffected by any angle of wrap. Also, let the forces due to other such junctions in other places be ignored because, as the tension builds up with the angle wrap, these other junctions will become of decreasing importance. It is the first junction that is the most important.

$$T_{rv} = T_j(e^{\mu\Theta} - 1) \quad \text{............... Eq. 7.3}$$

This is an approximation, but it still remains true that T_{rv} can no longer be reduced to zero by altering $\varnothing$; a build up of tension occurs which is ever more rapid until it reaches its limiting value somewhere along the length of the strand. The tension in the strands provides radial forces which help the yarn to cohere and, in consequence, to bear an axial load. It must be stressed, however, that the forces generated by the initial interlocking of the fibres play a crucial part in starting the build-up of tension along the strand. Because of this, it is much easier to make a twistless yarn from hairy strands than from smooth ones. If two twisted strands are merely pressed together, it is rare for a bond of sufficient strength to be formed. If, however, there is a twist loss, i.e. one strand rotates relative to the other, then a projecting hair from one might be licked-in by the other; the capstan effect would multiply the load which could be borne by the bond so formed, i.e.

$$T_f = e^{\mu\beta} T_b \quad \text{...................Eq. 7.4}$$

where T_f = final strength of the bond
μ = coefficient of friction
β = angle of wrap of hair about the strand
T_b = strength of original bond.

Another possibility is that fibres making up the constituent strands may migrate amongst one another. If, however, the strand is itself round and twisted at the point where the bond is required (as in Fig. 7.12(c)), then it is unlikely that such migration will occur. If the strands are flat, it is more likely that elements will react to provide a bond which is independent of the hairiness. Also, non-round fibres can provide such a bond because they do not slip over one another so readily.

Hair connections seem to be an important locking mechanism which might involve some twist loss, leading to an extension of the no twist zone; it is, in fact, found that a self-twist yarn usually consists of consecutive portions of S twist, O twist, Z twist, O twist etc. In hand-made yarns, the zero twist portions varied in length between $\frac{1}{2}$ in. and 4 in. according to the initial twist inserted and the nature of the strands.

Twist affects the colour and lustre of a fabric; it would be expected, therefore, that a fabric made from a simple self-twist yarn would show periodic differences in appearance, with undesirable patterning. It has been proposed that one self-twist yarn should be self-twisted with another to minimise this effect. Another solution would be to double the yarns in the conventional matter, but this might be a more costly operation.

Phasing

The load-carrying capacity of the complete structure is given by the summation of the elements i.e.

load-carrying capacity $= \Sigma \ T_{rH} = \Sigma(T_{rv} \ Tan\Psi)$............Eq. 7.5

and this represents the total of all the axial components of the frictional forces occurring in a given cross section. It will be noted that T_{rv} is a minimum when $\varnothing_2 = 0$ and the strength of the structure at A (Fig. 7.13) will thus be a minimum. This would apply equally to an assembly of twisted strands or to one of twisted fibres, providing no external forces were brought to bear. Thus, if the zero-twist portions of the fibres within the strands and of the strands themselves were to coincide (as in Fig. 7.12(b)), there would be weak points in the yarn. If the staple length of the fibres were inadequate to bridge the zero-portion, then these points would be very weak indeed. A solution is to move the zero-twist portions of

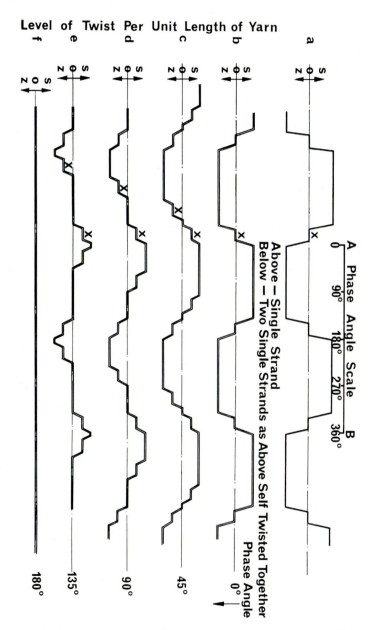

Fig. 7.14 Approximate self-twist of two yarns each containing alternating twist.

the strand relative to the zero-twist portions of the ply as in Fig. 7.12(c). This so-called phasing is important because it affects the self-twisting characteristics.

Fig. 7.14 shows some twist diagrams in a formalised way; (a) shows the twist structure of a single strand, and two of these are to be self-twisted with various phase relationships between them. In (b), the two strands are in phase and the zero twist positions for both the strand and the final yarn coincide. As the phasing is altered to minimise local weaknesses, the twist pattern changes as shown in diagrams (c) to (f). These diagrams are theoretical. In practice, the twist would not exist in such steps, as it would tend to run to the zero-twist portion and the real curves would be smoothed. In the last case, there is no self-twist at all. Clearly, there is a limit to the relative phase angle that can be used; in the case depicted, this limit is not much greater than 90°. The zero-twist portions of the strands occur at the parts marked x. If the staple is short, the yarn strength will depend solely on the self-twist in the complete assembly, which is reduced in the zones concerned. In consequence, there is an advantage in using longer staples so that an appreciable number

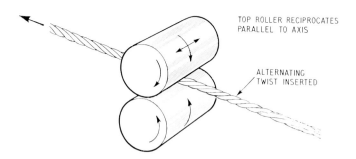

Fig. 7.15   Alternative means of inserting alternating twist in a strand.

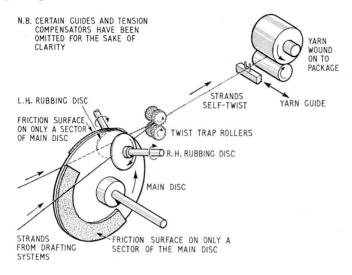

N.B. CERTAIN GUIDES AND TENSION
COMPENSATORS HAVE BEEN
OMITTED FOR THE SAKE OF
CLARITY

YARN
WOUND
ON TO
PACKAGE

L.H. RUBBING DISC

STRANDS
SELF-TWIST

YARN GUIDE

FRICTION SURFACE
ON ONLY A SECTOR
OF MAIN DISC

TWIST TRAP ROLLERS

R.H. RUBBING DISC

MAIN DISC

STRANDS
FROM DRAFTING
SYSTEMS

FRICTION SURFACE ON ONLY A
SECTOR OF THE MAIN DISC

Fig. 7.16   C.S.I.R.O. self-twist device.

of fibres have portions trapped in the high-twist zones. For
this reason, the method would seem to be more applicable
to long than to short staple fibres. It is possible, however, to
self-twist yarns having different amplitudes and patterns
of alternating twist; the case cited should be treated as
merely an example.

Henshaw Device

A machine for manufacturing self-twist yarn has been
described by Henshaw [3], the required twist being
obtained by reciprocating rollers similar to those shown in
Fig. 7.15, or by an intermittent rubbing device which
operates alternately on each of the two strands. These two
strands are gripped by a pair of fluted rollers immediately
they leave the twisting device. The rollers serve two purposes;

(i) they prevent twist loss after rubbing ceases and (ii) they bring the strands together so that they may self-twist. A diagram of one of the devices is shown in Fig. 7.16. When a friction surface on the main disc approaches a rubbing disc, which is also surfaced with a friction material, the yarn between the surfaces is twisted and the twist is trapped by the toothed rollers as the yarn advances. During this time, twist of the opposite sense is accumulated upstream, and this is later able to pass the twist trap whilst the rubbing surfaces are out of contact. A similar process continues on both sides of the main disc but, for the reasons already outlined, these are out of phase. The two strands are brought together at the toothed rollers by a vee shaped groove in their surfaces, and the yarn is then allowed to self-twist before winding. The whole operation is continuous and rapid.

In his patent, Henshaw claims that with a 100° phase angle and a $9\frac{1}{2}$ in. long twist cycle (the distance AB in Fig. 7.14) he was able to produce a 60 tex wool yarn at 138 yards/min. (5000 inches/minute approximately). The yarn was made from 60–64s quality Noble combing wool and its strength was 5 gf/tex with a regularity of 13.3 U% and a mean extension to break of 11%. On average, 77 turns were inserted in each $4\frac{3}{4}$ in. of strand between twist changeovers, i.e. 16 t.p.i. When self twisted, it is estimated that the twist levels in the ply might have been between ±5 t.p.i.

Hand-Twisting Experiments

Tests made by hand-twisting woollen strands showed that with a zero phase relationship between the strands, and with 75 turns inserted into each strand length of $4\frac{3}{4}$ in., the ply twist in the resultant yarn was about 20 turns in a length of about 4 in. The zero-twist portion of the yarn was about $\frac{1}{2}$ in. long and the $9\frac{1}{2}$ in. cycle length had reduced to about $8\frac{1}{2}$ in. because of the twisting. Hence each strand started with twists of ±16 t.p.i., but after self-twisting each strand had about ±12 t.p.i., and the ply twist was about ±5 t.p.i. These levels seemed to be quite constant over the lengths mentioned and the change from S to Z (or vice versa) was fairly rapid. The yarns were stable in the sense that they did not become disassembled in use, but they were not stable in another sense. As tension was applied in the region of the twist changeover zone, the amount of twist varied in an elastic manner by up to 10% of the total; the greater the tension, the lower became the ply twist. The reason for this can be seen by referring to Fig. 7.13; the resultant of T_1 and T_3 will cause A to move in the direction X, which is such as to unwind the ply. The S and Z portions of the yarn looked considerably different from one another because of the differing light reflections, and this would affect any fabric made from it. It might be possible to obtain a deliberate patterning effect, but the tension untwist behaviour and the difficulties of accurate relative placings of the strands could make this impracticable. A random variation might be interesting, but it is more likely that the twist variations would have to be disguised by some means or other.

Other attempts to make phased yarns by hand were more difficult; but it was found that if the zero-twist portion of the strand was very short and the phase angle large, there were appreciable lengths of yarn without ply twist. Within these lengths, the strands tended to snarl when the tension was relaxed, and periodic knot-like faults appeared along the length of the yarn. This difficulty could be avoided by deliberately extending the zero-twist zone of each strand sufficiently to overlap; the twist could be seen to exist in steps as suggested in Fig. 7.14 (c).

Twist Transfer from Strand to Ply

Because of the high twist in each component strand, the yarns had a harsh feel which may preclude them from uses where a soft handle is important. This seemed to merit a preliminary investigation as to why so little twist should be transferred from strand to ply. Consider the torsion of a cylinder made of isotropic material, i.e. as if made of metal or some such substance,

Let τ = torque

C = modulus of torsional rigidity

D = diameter of cylinder

J = polar 2nd moment of area

n = number of twists per unit length

suffices p, s & 1, refer to ply, initial and final strands respectively

$$\tau = C J n = \frac{\pi D^4}{32} C n$$

The torque existing in two similar cylinders $= 2 \times \frac{\pi D^4}{32} C n$

If these two cylinders are placed in contact with one another so that their axes are parallel, the value of J will change. By the parallel axis theorem:

$$J_p = \frac{\pi D^4}{32} + \frac{\pi D^2}{4} \cdot \left(\frac{D}{2}\right)^2 \text{ for each}$$

$$= 3 \frac{\pi D^4}{32} \text{ for each}$$

$$= 2 \times \frac{3\pi D^4}{32} \text{ for the pair}$$

Under stable self-twist conditions $\tau_p = \tau_s$

and $2 \frac{\pi D^4}{32} C n_s = 2 \times \frac{3\pi D^4}{32} C n_p$

$\therefore$ $n_s = 3 n_p$

but $n_1 - n_s = n_p$

whence $n_p = \frac{n_1}{4}$

i.e. only 25% of the initial twist in the strand will be transferred to the ply.

This, however, assumes that the yarns do not squash, and

are perfectly elastic and isotropic, which is not the case. If, for example, the yarns were to squash such that their centres were brought to $\frac{D}{2}$ units apart then $\frac{n_p}{n_1} = \frac{2}{5}$ i.e. 40% of the twist would be transferred; if the centre distance were further reduced to $\frac{D}{4}$, **47%** of the twist would be transferred. However, the tighter the strand twist, the less is the chance of the strands squashing together. It would seem, therefore, that percentage twist transfer will be dependent on the nature and twist level of the component strands. Strands of highly-crimped fibre are likely to behave better than sleek compact ones.

From the foregoing it would seem that this is a very promising approach which is likely to be used for twisting long crimped staple fibres into the equivalent of fairly hard-twisted yarns resembling worsted yarns. The production rate of 5000 inches/min. is very high compared with rates using traditional techniques. Even if it were necessary to double the self-twisted yarns to disguise twist variations, the output rate would still be many times that of traditional equipment.

Future Prospects

In the long term, the success of the self-twisting device will depend on how it performs in service. The outcome of mill trials held in Australia at the close of the '60s will indicate what prospects lie ahead. If the economics prove favourable, adoption of the self-twist machine would bring revolutionary changes to the textile industry, and might affect the balance of consumption between competing fibres. At the output rates contemplated, it would be uneconomic to work in small lots, and this might reduce the variety of yarns available. The price gap between production and "custom made" lots would widen, the latter becoming almost wholly a luxury trade.

E

8

An Introduction to Break Spinning

by P. R. Lord

Break spinning (or open-end spinning) is on the verge of major commercial acceptance. This chapter introduces the reader to break spinning, which is described in considerable detail. Different types of break spinner are reviewed.

Introduction

The process of yarn manufacture may be divided into a number of operations, including drafting, twisting and winding. These may or may not be concurrent.

In drafting, the supply material is stretched to make any element of the supply longer and thinner; to make very fine yarns, considerable drafting is needed. Fibres tend to move in bunches during drafting, and it is necessary to control fibre movement if a yarn of good regularity is to be produced. Over the years, drafting techniques have changed. In early devices, such as the spinning jenny, fibres were drafted against twist; the twist applied forces to the fibres which helped to control them during the drafting operation. In these early techniques, drafting and twisting could not be separated.

Later, with the advent of roller drafting, it became possible to separate drafting and twisting, but it was usual to combine the twisting and winding functions. Conventional modern machines still operate in this way. In the ring frame, for example, the package is rotated to insert twist *and* to wind the new yarn on to the bobbin. Commercial machines do not exist in which the operations of drafting, twisting and winding are entirely separate. The linking of these operations restricts the performance of the spinning machine. In particular, rotation of the yarn package to insert twist imposes a number of limitations, e.g.:—

1. The power needed to rotate the yarn package is higher than that needed simply to insert twist;
2. The yarn package is limited in size, as it must be confined within a yarn balloon;
3. The package speed is limited by mechanical considerations, by the development of high yarn tensions, and by excessive power consumption.

In break spinning, these operations are not linked in the same way; in particular, winding and twisting are quite separate. Breaks are made in the flow of fibres, and there is a so-called "open end" to the yarn being made. It is from these two concepts that the alternative names of "break spinning "and "open-end spinning" are derived. The basic principle is that fibres travel separately across the break, and become attached to the open end of the yarn; this is then twisted to insert true twist, which converts the newly-assembled aggregate of fibres into yarn as indicated in Fig. 8.1. A third alternative name for the process is "free

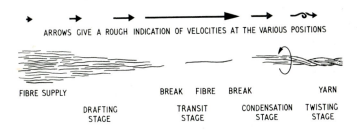

ARROWS GIVE A ROUGH INDICATION OF VELOCITIES AT THE VARIOUS POSITIONS

| FIBRE SUPPLY | BREAK | FIBRE | BREAK | YARN |

| DRAFTING STAGE | TRANSIT STAGE | CONDENSATION STAGE | TWISTING STAGE |

Fig. 8.1   The basic principle of break spinning.

fibre spinning", the derivation of the name being self-evident. Isolation of the twisting operation makes it possible, at least in theory, to insert twist merely by rotating the open end. Small objects can be rotated faster than larger objects, and the small open end of yarn makes very high speed operation possible. Also, a comparatively small amount of power is needed to rotate a small object, and break spinning is thus a potentially cheap process. Break spinning offers a further advantage in that the package size is no longer limited by the spinning unit; the limit is imposed by the winder, and larger yarn packages can thus be made.

In general, therefore, break spinning makes possible higher speeds and productivities; the increased size of yarn packages permits of reductions in the cost of doffing and winding, and there is the theoretical possibility that power costs per unit production may be cut. Reduction of power costs, however, depends upon the design of the machine and the speed at which it operates. If it is operated at very high speed, the power cost per unit production could be greater than that of a conventional machine. Nevertheless, it is apparent that break spinning creates a new pattern of costs, in which labour cost becomes less important in relation to capital and power costs. This is significant at a time when labour becomes ever more expensive and recruitment more difficult.

STAGES IN BREAK SPINNING

Conventional spinning systems include the three operations of drafting, twisting and winding, the entire sequence of operations being linked by a fibre transport system. In break spinning, other stages are introduced. Breaks must be created in the fibre flow, necessitating the use of a very high draft ratio in the first stage. Ideally, the flow should be reduced to single fibres passing into the spinner in line astern. Under these conditions it would not be possible for any force or torque to be transmitted upstream; the open end would be free to rotate and insert true twist into the yarn.

In practice, it is possible to relax this requirement as long as the fibres are in open order, and do not make contact with one another to any significant extent. Nevertheless, it is still a requirement that torque should not be transmitted upstream, and it is still necessary to have a draft ratio in the first stage much higher than that used in conventional drafting. For example, if the material fed to the drafting system contains, say, 30,000 fibres, then the initial draft ratio would have to approach 30,000:1. If the machine were spinning a yarn of 50 tex (12s c.c.) at 15 twists/inch and 30,000 twists per min., the yarn withdrawal rate would be some 2,000 inches/min. If it is assumed that the linear density of the fibres is 0.2 tex, and that the fibres enter the spinner in single file, then by the principle of conservation of mass flow, the speed of the entering fibres would be

$$\frac{50}{0.2} \times 2,000 = 500,000 \text{ inches/min. (700 ft./sec.).}$$ Thus it can

be seen that the initial supply of fibres must be reduced to a fast moving thin stream which is later converted to a slower and thicker stream; this is then twisted to form yarn. The implication is that there must be a very high initial draft ratio followed by a so-called condensation stage which can be represented by a fractional draft ratio. The product of these two ratios gives the overall draft ratio, which is the same as that used in conventional spinning. In the case cited, the initial draft ratio was 30,000:1, the condensation "draft"

ratio was $\frac{1}{250}$:1 and the overall draft ratio was $30,000 \times \frac{1}{250} =$

120:1. Had the fibres travelled into the spinner two by two,

then the draft ratios would have been 15,000:1 and $\frac{1}{125}$ and

120:1 respectively.

The stages in break spinning may be set out as follows:—

1. Initial drafting
2. Fibre transport
3. Fibre condensation
4. Twist insertion
5. Winding of the yarn.

1. Initial Drafting

So much has been written about twist insertion units that it has tended to obscure the overall picture, especially the importance of the drafting stage. Break spinning requires that there should be breaks in the fibre flow, and it is necessary to have a very thin stream of fibres to make this possible. Very high fibre speeds are therefore needed. As break spinning devices are by nature high speed machines, operating speeds are even higher than they might otherwise have been.

Consider first the possibility of using a conventional drafting system without other aids, and let the case already cited be used to illustrate the points. If fibres are to be delivered at some 500,000 inches/min. and the front rollers are, say, 1 in. diameter, then these front rollers would have to rotate at about 160,000 rev./min. If the count were reduced to, say, 24s c.c. and the same twist factor were used, about 21 twists/inch would be required; the yarn withdrawal rate should be about 1,400 inches/min., the linear speed of the fibres entering the spinner about 180,000 inches/min. and the front roller speed about 57,000 rev./min. For a coarse count, say 6s c.c., the front roller speed would have to be about 450,000 rev./min. Thus, over a wide range of counts, front roller speeds would be excessive and under these onerous conditions the front rollers would still have to deal with single fibres. In experiments carried out at Leeds University, speeds between 100 and 3,000 rev./min. were used, but it was found that at higher speeds, the airflow caused by rotation of the front rollers disturbed the fibre flow, making spinning increasingly difficult. It is clear, therefore, that an unmodified, conventional drafting system cannot be used.

Air Flow

Another possibility is to use an air flow to pull fibres from an advancing fringe controlled by a single pair of nip rollers. In this case, the rollers can rotate at a slower speed, the drafting occurring as individual fibres are pulled from the fringe by the airstream. To do this, the air velocity must be in excess of the fibre velocity required. In the ideal case where fibres travel singly, the air velocity needed to spin the 12s c.c. yarn would be in excess of 700 ft./sec., i.e. it would have to approach the velocity of sound, and this would cause difficulties. With the coarser count, supersonic speeds in excess of some 2,000 ft./sec. would be needed. Thus, to deal with the range of counts mentioned, the air speeds would be greater than values ranging from 250 to 2,000 ft./sec. Furthermore, fibres would have to be removed singly from the nip of the supply rollers. Taking the maximum surface of speed of these rollers as, say, $12\frac{1}{2}$ ft./sec., the nip would have a fringe containing between 20 and 160 fibres. It is relatively easy to remove single fibres from a fringe of 20 fibres; it is more difficult to remove them from a fringe of 160 fibres, unless they are evenly spread across the nip without entanglement. At lower roller speeds, the problem becomes more difficult.

Fortunately, the requirement that fibres must travel singly can be relaxed. For instance, if the fibres could travel in a stream of 10 fibres thick (i.e. the fibre flux $=10$), the foregoing air and fibre velocities could be reduced by a factor of ten, bringing the system into the realms of possibility. A combination of roller and air drafting such as those described has been found to be a practical proposition; it is dealt with more fully in Chapter 10.

Large-Diameter Roller

Another possibility is to use a larger roller to carry the fibres forward. If, instead of a 1 in. diameter roller a 3 in. one were used, and if a fibre flux of 3 were permissible, the range of roller speeds would vary from 6,300 rev./min. for the 24s c.c. to 50,000 rev./min. for 6s c.c. Even bearing in mind that the permissible fibre flux might be larger than 3, the higher speed is still excessive, and the amount of power consumed merely by rotating the roller would be considerable. This power is approximately proportional to $D^{3.8}N^{2.6}$, and for a constant surface speed, the power requirement would increase as $D^{1.2}$. There is thus a disincentive to make the roller too large; on the other hand, it is necessary in practice for it to be large enough to do its job properly. For example, there is the possibility of lapping the roller. For short staple of the order of $1\frac{1}{2}$ in., lapping may be prevented by using a roller considerably greater than $\frac{1}{2}$ in. diameter; this presents no difficulty. With long staple of, say 6 in., the diameter would have to be considerably greater than 2 in. Taking into account the possibility of two fibres becoming attached to one another, then the diameters would have to be at least 1 in. and 4 in. respectively. Hence the size of the front rollers depends on the staple to be handled.

Rotor

So far, it has been implied that two rollers are required; this is not necessarily so, as the second roller merely ensures adhesion of the fibre to the drafting roller surface. As the second roller also consumes power, which may be considerable at the speeds concerned, there is every reason to consider other means of securing the desired adhesion. One

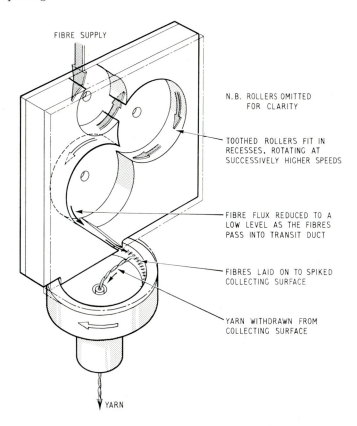

FIBRE SUPPLY

N.B. ROLLERS OMITTED
FOR CLARITY

TOOTHED ROLLERS FIT IN
RECESSES, ROTATING AT
SUCCESSIVELY HIGHER SPEEDS

FIBRE FLUX REDUCED TO A
LOW LEVEL AS THE FIBRES
PASS INTO TRANSIT DUCT

FIBRES LAID ON TO SPIKED
COLLECTING SURFACE

YARN WITHDRAWN FROM
COLLECTING SURFACE

YARN

Fig. 8.2   A Meimberg-type break spinner.

technique is to use a rotor with toothed surface. Meimberg [11] proposed such a system, as shown in Fig. 8.2. Czech workers have used a similar arrangement in the BD 200 machine; Fig. 8.3 shows the principle of the mechanism. The thinning rotor speed is about 8,000 rev./min., and the power consumed by it is about one quarter of the total. The thinning

E*

rotor is 64 mm. in diameter ($2\frac{1}{2}$ in.) and the yarn count range recommended is between 15 and 50 tex; the fibre flux would thus seem to vary between 1 and 9. The fibre flux entering the rotor varies between about $\frac{1}{4}$ and $2\frac{1}{4}$. The advancing fibre fringe is partly disintegrated by pneumatic means and the difference in fluxes suggests that the teeth not only tear at the fringe but provide an airflow which is later augmented to carry and accelerate the fibres once they are removed. The extent to which this involves the fibres becoming hooked round the teeth is unknown.

The fibre flux at this stage is important. Edberg [12] showed that a flux much greater than 3 is likely to lead to fibre entanglements, although experiments described in

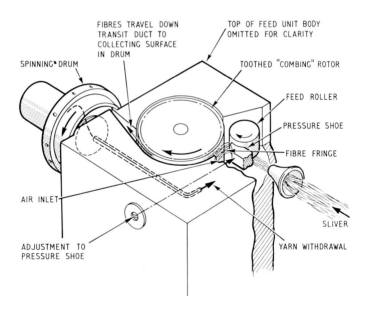

Fig. 8.3   Break spinner of a type similar to the VUB machine.

Chapter 10 suggest that, with care, this can be improved upon. Krause [13] has shown that as the flux goes down from $5\frac{1}{2}$ to about $\frac{1}{2}$, the observed standard deviation alters from 3.5 to 0.76. The regularity index provides a good measure of the evenness of the fibre flow; the regularity index of the yarn should be the same as that of the supply, providing no further irregularity is introduced. The results shown in Table 10.7* indicate the importance of attaining a low fibre flux; the thinner the stream at this point, the better. This, in turn, indicates that the surface velocity of the carrier should be as high as possible, whether it is a toothed surface or an airflow or a combination of both. Fortunately, many break-spinning devices introduce multiple doubling at a later stage, which extinguishes many of the irregularities introduced by using relatively slow-moving media to carry the fibres. A reasonable size of opening device can thus be used.

Stripping from Card

The foregoing methods have been or may be used commercially, but there is a further technique which has been used in conjunction with break spinning only in an experimental way. There is a practical limit to the size of the rotor or roller carrying fibres just before they enter the spinning unit, and this is related to the power consumed. A basic assumption is made that a special device is required to get the fibres in the state required, whereas it might in fact be possible to utilise a previous process. A survey of the stages prior to spinning indicates that the main cylinder of the card is one place where the fibres are sufficiently open. In earlier or later processes the flux density is too high. The fibres on the doffer are too dense to be useful, and the action of doffing the web creates an undesirable number of hooks and entanglements in the web. On the surface of the main cylinder the fibres are reasonably well ordered and, if continuously stripped, the surface will normally contain very few fibres; unfortunately, by stripping in this way, the

* See page 204

carding action is reduced. By double carding and taking fibres from the second cylinder, it should be possible to obtain a good supply of fibre. Experiments carried out in this connection are described in Chapter 9; results were better than might have been expected.

2. Fibre Transport

The most practical system of transport is to carry the fibres in an airstream, and this method is almost universally used. It is possible that water may be used in certain circumstances, but little information is available about this technique.

3. Fibre Condensation

Fibres arrive at the spinner at high velocity and a low fibre flux, and leave at a much lower velocity and higher fibre flux. This process, called condensation, involves a fractional draft ratio. For instance, if the fibre flux of the approaching stream is unity (as in the theoretical ideal), then the fractional draft ratio will be (No. of fibres in the yarn cross section) –1, i.e. for a 50 tex yarn (12s c.c.) made of 0.2 tex fibres there will be a ratio of $\frac{1}{250}$. If the fractional draft is caused by *telescopic condensation*, the increase in linear density* will be accompanied by a corresponding drop in velocity. In the case mentioned at the beginning of this chapter, the velocity would have to change from about 700 ft./sec. to about 3 ft/sec. in a few milliseconds, which could involve a deceleration of the order of 1,000 g (where

---

* Fibre flux is defined as the number of fibres in the flow cross-section.

$$\frac{\text{Linear density of yarn or other assembly}}{\text{Linear density of the average fibre}}$$

is the equivalent of fibre flux when the fibres are converted into a yarn or other fibre assembly.

g $=32$ ft./sec.^{2}). If the fibre flux at entry were increased tenfold (i.e. the highest flux suggested), then the deceleration would still be of the order of 100 g. The resulting force applied to the fibre in this deceleration phase could vary between 1 and 100 mgf; if applied to the leading end of the fibre, this would probably cause it to buckle. During the telescoping action, many fibres are likely to suffer this buckling, and resulting entanglements would be very difficult to remove. A minority of fibres which are decelerated by forces applied to their trailing ends would tend to straighten. Condensation implies that the fibre stream becomes more dense as deceleration proceeds, and it is more likely that the force will be applied somewhere along the length of the fibre. It is probable, therefore, that there will be a degree of buckling in most fibres. Furthermore, it is unlikely that all the telescopic elements will behave in the same way; some fibres will be decelerated more sharply than others, and some will buckle more than others. In general, therefore, considerable positional disorder would be anticipated using this method of condensation. Buckling would mean that the fibre extent, as assembled in the yarn, would be poor; the yarn would tend to be weak and bulky. The positional disorder would create irregularity in the yarn. Telescopic condensation, so far as these factors are concerned, has little to recommend it.

Layering

The converse of deceleration, i.e. acceleration, would seem to be desirable, but acceleration appears to be incompatible with the required changes in linear density. However, by *layering* one very thin layer upon another it is possible to build up a thickness sufficient for the purpose required. Acceleration may play a useful part in the process; it may reduce the thickness of the layers, but this can be countered by increasing the number of layers. It is possible for a collecting surface to move at a greater surface velocity than that of the arriving fibres, thus accelerating the fibres as they land on the surface. The first portion of the fibre to arrive is accelerated; if the fibres are reasonably straight when they arrive, the leading ends will be accelerated and this will tend to straighten them. To make the system work at high speed, the collecting surface must be cylindrical; this enables the concurrent operations of laying on the fibres and taking off the fibre assembly to proceed at their different velocities. In other words, there is a differential action in which it is theoretically possible for the fibre supply device, the collecting surface and the newly-removed fibre assembly all to rotate at different speeds (see Fig. 8.4). In successful designs, the fibre supply device is usually stationary. At this stage, the fibre assembly is about to be converted into yarn by insertion of twist.

Advantages of this technique of condensation include:—

1. There is no undesirable deceleration involved; on the contrary, there may be a beneficial acceleration which tends to straighten fibres.

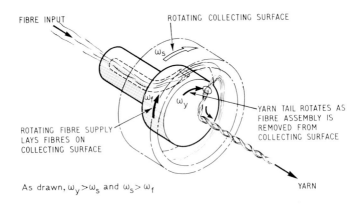

FIBRE INPUT

ROTATING COLLECTING SURFACE

ω_s

ω_f ω_y

YARN TAIL ROTATES AS FIBRE ASSEMBLY IS REMOVED FROM COLLECTING SURFACE

ROTATING FIBRE SUPPLY LAYS FIBRES ON COLLECTING SURFACE

As drawn, $\omega_y > \omega_s$ and $\omega_s > \omega_f$

YARN

Fig. 8.4   Differential device to give layering.

2. There is a beneficial levelling action caused by multiple doubling resulting from the many layers involved.

This technique is considered further in Chapters 10 and 12.

In all the practical break spinning devices developed during the 1960s, fibres were carried in an air stream. It is therefore difficult to consider practical aspects of the transport or condensation stages without reference to the twist insertion stage.

4. Twist Insertion

There are several comprehensive surveys of break spinning methods [14, 15, 16, 17] which describe devices of many types. These may be classified in various ways. One method, for example, is to classify break spinning systems by considering the forces involved, but this is often more difficult than it appears. For instance, the well-known Barker device (Fig. 8.5(a)) might be classified as a mechanical system, as mechanical forces are a major factor in its operation. One of the main reasons for the failure of this device, however, was the pneumatic forces caused by high-speed rotation of the rollers. Likewise, the air-vortex tube might be classified as a pneumatic system, but electrostatic and friction forces also play a large part. In practice, all workable systems appear to fall into the category of aero-mechanical systems in which electrostatic forces may occasionally be involved.

Axial/Spiral Systems

Break spinning systems may be classified according to the way in which the fibres approach the assembly zone. To some extent, this depends on the condensation system. For example, the Pavek system shown in Fig. 8.5(e) collects fibres by means of conically-disposed needles, the yarn being

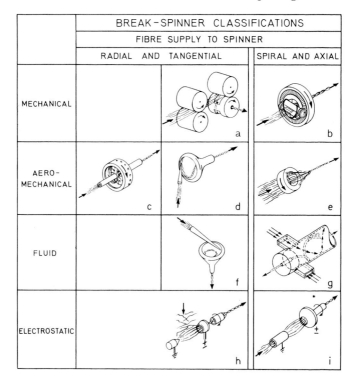

Fig. 8.5

withdrawn from the apex of the needle basket. The fibre flow is parallel to the axis of rotation, and the twisting element need not be very large; this could be advantageous in permitting high speeds. The Pavek system could be classified as being of the axial type. The vortex system in Fig. 8.5(g), on the other hand, might be classified as a spiral type. The drum spinning system has a circular collecting surface and fibres may approach the surface in a variety of ways. In practice, drum spinning systems can be classified into radial and tangential types.

Radial/Tangential Systems

In the radial system, the *radius* of the collecting surface must be larger than the staple length of the fibres. If this is not the case, twist will run back through the fibre supply system; there will not be a break, and false twist rather than true twist will be inserted. In the tangential system, the *circumference* must be considerably greater than the staple length, or end breaks and poor yarn will result. In the axial and spiral systems, on the other hand, there is no obvious direct relationship between spinning limits and staple length.

There is thus a significant difference between the radial/ tangential and axial systems. In the former, size is dependent on the staple length, whereas in the latter it is not. Bearing in mind the size/speed relationships, with radial or tangential systems working on long staple, the drums or rollers are likely to be large and the operational speed low by break-spinning standards. In this respect, the axial or spiral systems appear to have an advantage. In practice, however, this advantage has not become apparent, probably because of the difficulty of preserving fibre order and straightness in these systems. Successful radial and tangential systems employ a layering type of condensation, whereas the axial and spiral systems involve a considerable proportion of telescopic condensation. During the 1960's the latter were not able to produce yarn of a quality suitable for commercial success.

Forces

In the horizontal classifications shown in Fig. 8.5, the different forces involved may vary by several orders of magnitude. Electrostatic forces are very weak and mechanical forces can be very strong. For this reason, it is unlikely that electrostatic forces will be used on their own. Lord & Jejurikar [18] found that as the relative velocity of the fibre and the electrostatic field increased, the meagre electrostatic force diminished. Thus, electrostatic forces may be used only as an adjunct to one or more of the other forces. This does not mean that electrostatic forces are of no value; under certain circumstances, they can be very useful indeed.

Fluids

Of the fluids available, water and air are obvious choices for use in break spinning. Air is the fluid most commonly used. In devices where the collecting surface is stationary, an element of telescopic condensation is inevitable; yarns will be weaker, fuller and less regular than those made by devices which use only the layering mode of condensation. For this reason, it would be expected that such a device would compete best in the condenser spinning field. Even in the air vortex spinner, some layering takes place because the points at which the fibres assemble on the yarn oscillate along the length of the yarn. This is considered more fully in Chapter 9.

Mechanical Devices

Two examples of a mechanical device have been described. The axial/mechanical device shown in Fig. 8.5(b) was proposed by Speak and Sedgwick in the last century, and the tangential/mechanical device shown in Fig. 8.5(a) by Barker in about 1930. In the latter machine, a pair of rollers with a raised portion gives an intermittent nip; this periodically draws fibres from the back rollers. In one of the front rollers, a passage connects the periphery (on to which the fibres are laid) with an axial hole. If a seed or priming yarn is introduced into the axial hole, it is drawn in, the end lying on the roller periphery. When a tuft of fibres is withdrawn from the advancing fringe of the back rollers, it is laid on the end of the yarn. A slight withdrawal of the yarn will draw the tuft with it, and the next tuft will be laid on the end of the former tuft. At the same time, rotation of the roller will have inserted one turn of twist to convert the new portion into yarn. The process continues in this way.

Considerable development work has been carried out on devices similar to the latter, particularly by S.R.R.L. in America. The Barker device [19] tends to throw fibres from the collecting surface even at fairly modest speeds, due to the combined action of the pneumatic and centrifugal forces. Kyame and Copeland [20] and others at S.R.R.L. used a suction grid on the surface of one of the rollers, which enabled higher speeds to be used. The project was abandoned eventually, as the speed could not be increased sufficiently, and the device became too complex. This work showed clearly, however, that mechanical forces alone cannot be used at high speeds, and pneumatic forces must be taken into account. It is probable that devices like that of Speak and Sedgwick must have suffered similar difficulties. In any event, the latter is only of historic interest; a cumbersome device of this sort could not meet the needs of today.

It seems, therefore, that the aero-mechanical type of break spinner offers the greatest prospect of commercial success. It will probably have a tangential fibre supply, taking full advantage of the layering form of condensation. This is not to say that axial/spiral devices will not be developed; these too might have an important part to play.

9

Electrostatic and Air Vortex Spinners

by R. Lyon*

Methods of break spinning using either an air vortex or an electrostatic field to manipulate the fibres are outlined. Several patented devices have been examined and their performance is described. The examples selected illustrate the operational characteristics and the attractive features of each technique. Changes were made to improve spinning performance; the nature of these changes and the reasons for them are explained. Data are given about the range of fibres which could be spun and the limitations of yarns produced. Attention is drawn to problems which must be overcome before these methods could be used commercially for spinning in the '70s.

Introduction

The Shirley Institute undertook a fundamental study of break spinning in 1964. The purpose of this work was to survey the field generally, and to investigate the potentialities and limitations of break spinning as they applied to the spinning of fibres of cotton staple length. In particular, the methods disclosed in patents were examined, and yarns that could be made from them were assessed. It was not within the terms of reference to develop any of the processes.

Altogether, some 87 patents were examined and the devices described were classified into groups according to the operating principles. Three of these were of real interest; (1) the drum method, which is discussed in Chapter 10, (2) the

* Conference author. Cotton Silk & Man-made Fibres Research Association, Didsbury, U.K.

electrostatic method, and (3) the air vortex method. Neither of the latter two systems is in commercial use, but if certain practical problems could be overcome they may be developed to the stage of being commercially viable.

ELECTROSTATIC SPINNERS

These devices belong to the axial-assembly group, in which fibres are fed, assembled and twisted more or less along the axis of the device. The fibres are withdrawn in approximately the same order as they are presented to the device. In one system of this type, the fibres are dispersed in an air stream and are then condensed and brought to the apex of a conical collector before being withdrawn along the axis. This technique may be adapted in several ways; collectors may, for example, pump their own air and draw in the fibres by virtue of their rotation, or they may be surrounded by jackets from which the air is extracted (perhaps through a porous wall). Many of the techniques, for a variety of reasons, are not practical propositions. One that shows great possibilities, however, is the electrostatic spinner. In this device the collector takes the form of an electrostatic field between two electrodes.

One of the earliest devices of this sort was patented by Oglesby; it is shown in Fig. 9.1. The fibres are fed to the two electrodes through a tube of varying cross section; the top electrode is hemispherical and the other ring-shaped. An air flow carries the fibres into the electrostatic field which tends to straighten and align them, and twist is inserted by a rotating mechanical device which grips the forming yarn end. In earlier models, Shirley Institute used as twister a glass tube bent into the form of a helix to provide mechanical grip on the yarn; it inserted twist and yet permitted the yarn to be easily withdrawn. Later, a more positive gripper was used; this was spring-loaded and nipped the yarn.

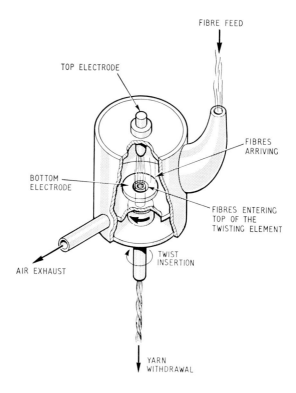

FIBRE FEED

TOP ELECTRODE

FIBRES
ARRIVING

BOTTOM
ELECTRODE

FIBRES ENTERING
TOP OF THE
TWISTING ELEMENT

AIR EXHAUST

TWIST
INSERTION

YARN
WITHDRAWAL

Fig. 9.1   Shirley/Oglesby electrostatic spinner.

Electrode Spacing; Field Strength

Preliminary experiments were carried out to test the effect
on fibre alignment of electrode spacing and field strength,
and to determine how fibres behaved in the airflow. With
wide electrode spacings, fibres tended to jump from one
electrode to the other as they became charged alternately
positive and negative. It was necessary to bring the electrodes
to within one fibre length of each other to minimise this

oscillation of fibres; even so, oscillation persisted with the shorter fibres.

Fibre alignment was more rapid at the higher field strengths. Good alignment of a few fibres could be obtained at a field strength as low as 2 kV per cm.; as the number of fibres in a transverse section reached that needed to spin yarn, it became necessary to increase the field strength to some 7 kV per cm. This applied when the machine was

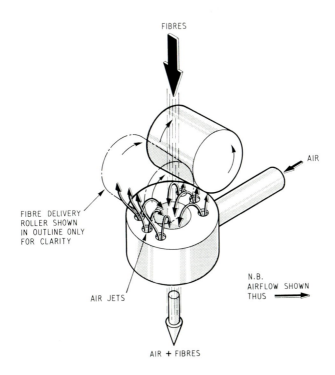

Fig. 9.2 Air-jet ring.

stationary; when the machine was running, it was not possible to secure good fibre alignment.

When the electrical field strength was increased above a certain level, there was a strong tendency for discharge to take place. Corona discharge increased progressively as the field strength built up, limiting the voltage which could be used. Shirley Institute used field strengths up to about 20 kV. per cm. but, in general, it was found that about 10 kV. per cm. provided a satisfactory compromise. In conjunction with the corona discharges, there was an "electric wind" which caused difficulty by driving fibres towards one of the electrodes. Also, trouble was caused by electrostatic charges which developed on the "Perspex" walls of the container. Clumps of fibre tended to collect on the walls of any insulator in the electric fields associated with these charge concentrations.

The electrodes were moved closer to the feed roller in an attempt to overcome these problems, but the air flow around the feed rollers, caused by their rapid movement, interfered with fibre alignment. The effect of the air flow was minimised by means of a compressed air ring, as shown in Fig. 9.2. Air was blown from the ring towards the rollers; the flow eventually turned inwards towards the axis of the ring, providing the air-flow pattern required in this zone. By varying the air pressure in the ring, it was possible to control the speed at which fibres were drawn off the rollers. This simple device worked over a wide range of air flows.

Airflow Problem

The introduction of mechanical forces (i.e. airflow), which were necessary to assist the electrostatic forces, highlights one of the main problems. At low air velocities, fibres tended to drift towards the negative electrode; at higher air velocities, applied to counteract this tendency, fibres were blown away from the electrode, the electrical forces being too small to control them. Also, at the higher

Fig. 9.3   Shirley/Arshinov electrostatic spinner.

FIBRE SUPPLY
THROUGH TOP ELECTRODE
↓

↑
BOTTOM ELECTRODE

Fig. 9.4   Fibres in a stationary Shirley/Arshinov spinner.

velocities, the fibres were in the region of high field strength
for too short a time for much alignment to take place. This
was a feature of all electrostatic devices tested at Shirley
Institute; it was necessary in virtually all cases to use a
mechanical method of controlling the fibres, as the electrical
forces were inadequate. Fairly satisfactory fibre control was
obtained with the compressed air ring, and fibres could be
moved into the electric field at different velocities. This
enabled an investigation to be made of fibre trajectories,
and of a wide range of fibre velocities. None of the arrange-
ments tested gave a satisfactory compromise between fibre

alignment and fibre control. With insufficient control, many fibres drifted to one of the electrodes or moved out of the field. This happened to many of the fibres in the Oglesby device; they passed through the field without becoming incorporated into the yarn. This experience highlighted the conflict between the mechanical forces applied to the fibres and the electrical restraining forces. Usually, entanglement and the forces arising from interfibre friction, together with the air drag, overcame the alignment forces.

An interesting and successful variation of this method was patented by Arschinov [21] (Fig. 9.3). The fibres are fed down a cylindrical tube which leads to the centre of one of two electrodes. The second electrode is in the form of a ring, and fibres enter the system along the axis. The mechanical air-drag forces operate along the axis of the electrostatic forces, this arrangement providing a better control of the fibre before the air carries it out of the field.

Shirley Institute Device

Fig. 9.4 shows a close-up of the device made at Shirley Institute. When the device was stationary, as shown in Fig. 9.4, fibre alignment was fairly good. When the device began to spin, however, fibre alignment was adversely affected, as shown in Fig. 9.5. During spinning, fibres tended to wander on the charged surfaces, and the system became unstable. Fibres were drawn into a conical mass, but the apex of the cone wandered over the surface of the electrode and sometimes left it altogether. This did not always make the end come down, but it caused irregularities in the yarn. Yarns produced with this device were weak and irregular; fibre alignment was inadequate.

Occasionally, the leading edges of fibres travelling down the tube struck either the mass of fibres within the electric field or one of the electrodes. When this happened, loops were formed, causing irregularities in the yarn, leading to the formation of slubs.

TOP ELECTRODE

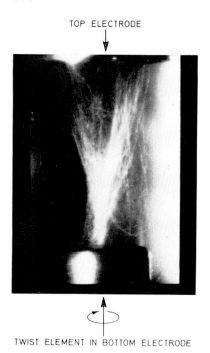

Fig. 9.5 Fibres in a Shirley/ Arshinov spinner whilst spinning.

TWIST ELEMENT IN BOTTOM ELECTRODE

Attempts were made to stabilise the yarn formation process by progressively changing the shape of the electrodes. When the device was spinning, it was still possible to see a concentration of fibres at one point, and this point wandered about on the electrode. The device shown in Fig. 9.6 was developed eventually to the form in which a curved prong projected from the right hand side of the top electrode. The function of this prong was to concentrate the electric field and to stabilise the fibre assembly. Considering the number of fibres present, and the relatively large mechanical forces in operation, fibre alignment was good when the device was stationary (see Fig. 9.6). Also, the device helped to separate

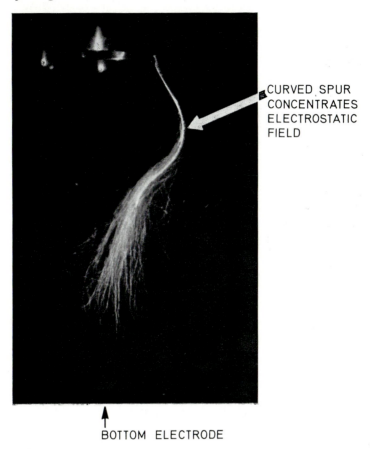

CURVED SPUR
CONCENTRATES
ELECTROSTATIC
FIELD

BOTTOM ELECTRODE

Fig. 9.6   Fibres in a modified Shirley/Arshinov spinner. N.B.: No twist is being inserted.

the fibre assembly zone from the zone of fibre alignment. This gave sufficient time for the fibres to re-arrange themselves before becoming attached to the forming yarn.

Fig. 9.7 shows the system under dynamic conditions. The differences between this and Fig. 9.6 illustrate the problems

caused by fibre movement through the system. In Fig. 9.7
it is possible to see a mass of fibre which was thicker than
elsewhere; such irregularities caused difficulties. Nevertheless, the mechanism was more stable than before, and fibres
no longer wandered about the top electrode. Without doubt,
this arrangement of the electrode was superior to the original
one. Fig. 9.8 is a flash photograph of the new system caught
in one of its moments of instability. The fibres have been
pulled off the electrode, and there is considerable loss of
fibre order, sufficient to produce a slub or end break.

Future Prospects

Yarns spun at Shirley Institute using these electrostatic
devices were too inferior to warrant testing, and could not be
considered seriously as competitors to ring spun yarn. They
provide an example of the way in which an elegant concept
can meet practical obstacles; in this case, difficulties arose
from the need to insert twist rapidly, resulting in increased
mechanical forces.

None of the processes considered in this survey were able
to reconcile the conflict between mechanical and electrical
forces. A balance is difficult to achieve because of the smallness of the electrical forces available to align the fibres. These
devices will need to undergo further development with the
aim of separating the alignment and twist insertion functions,
or of making the different forces applied to the fibres support
one another.

To meet the requirements of break spinning, it is necessary
for the fibre mass to be adequately opened (possibly by
mechanical means), and for the number of fibres in a
transverse section to be small enough. If these conditions
can be met, it may be possible to utilise electrostatic forces
to align and straighten fibres at the required rate. A low
fibre flux demands a high fibre velocity; fibres entering the
electrostatic field, therefore, have sufficient momentum
to carry them out of the field. The problem then arises of

Fig. 9.7 Modified Shirley/Arshinov spinner in action.

FIBRES

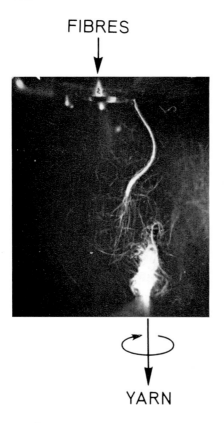

Fig. 9.8 Modified Shir-
ley/Arshinov spinner at a
moment of instability.

YARN

condensing the fibres to the required linear density before
twisting them into yarn. It seems necessary, therefore, to
provide a mechanical collecting surface; this could perhaps
be a combination of the Pavek needle device and the electrostatic system.

With further development, these electrostatic devices
could form the basis of processes with commercially
attractive features. Only a very small twister is needed to
rotate the yarn end, for example, so that high speeds should
be attainable with small power consumption. There are few

moving parts; the construction is simple and the amount of air required is low. The electrostatic method was developed during the late 1960s by the Electrospin Corporation of U.S.A., and an electrostatic device could play a significant role in spinning during the '70s.

AIR VORTEX SPINNERS

(A) Shirley Institute

Considered superficially, the fluid vortex appears to be the simplest system of break spinning. The staple fibre is dispersed in a fluid medium in which a rotating vortex is created. The priming yarn is introduced into this vortex and then withdrawn slowly. Fibres are assembled onto the yarn whilst the end is rotated by the vortex; twist is inserted and yarn is formed, on which further fibres assemble. In this way, the essential requirements of any break-spinning system are satisfied, i.e., fibres are dispersed to give the necessary break, they are then transported across the break and assembled on to the forming yarn. Coincident with the assembly of the fibres, the yarn end is rotated to insert twist.

Two obvious choices of fluid are water and air, both of which are cheap and abundant. At Shirley Institute attempts to make water devices produce yarn were unsuccessful, and it was considered unlikely that the water system would be developed into a successful process. Air, on the other hand, is a most convenient fluid for this purpose, and is already used widely in the textile industry for manipulating and transporting fibres.

Götzfried-type Spinning Tube

Fig. 9.9 shows a Shirley version of a Götzfried spinning tube; it illustrates difficulties inherent in many air vortex devices. A conventional drafting system with a very high front roller speed supplied fibres into the air stream entering

F

the main vortex tube. The surrounding tube provided a
means of applying suction which created the airflow into
and within the vortex tube. Götzfried [22] favoured the use
of compressed air, but in the Shirley Institute experiments
suction was found to be convenient. The Shirley Institute
vortex tube was of 1 in. diameter at one end, tapering through
a perforated section to $\frac{1}{2}$ in. internal diameter at the other
end. The vortex was used merely to assemble fibres on to
the forming yarn; a mechanical twister inserted the twist.
Twist created by the tube itself was caused by yarn rolling
on the internal surface of the tube; the mechanical twister
therefore had to rotate in a direction opposite to that of the
air vortex, so that the two twist insertion mechanisms were
not in opposition. (When the mechanical twister rotated in
the same direction as the air vortex, spinning was extremely
difficult.)

Powerful suction was needed to generate high vortex

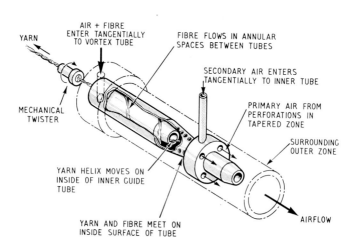

Fig. 9.9   The Shirley/Götzfried Mark 2 air-vortex spinner.

speeds, and this caused substantial fibre losses; many fibres failed to assemble on to the yarn and were carried into the suction device. There are advantages in keeping the vortex speed fairly low to minimise this fibre loss.

A fibre shield was used in an attempt to prevent fibres becoming attached to the outer surface of the yarn instead of being built into the body of the yarn. It was hoped that this technique would minimise production of hairy, weak yarns, in which many fibres make little contribution to the yarn strength. The fibre shield was located in many different positions, but it appeared to be generally ineffective.

Perforations

The perforations in the vortex tube were meant to slow down the vortex, making the relative velocity between air and yarn tail as large as possible. It was hoped that this would increase the pick-up of fibres by increasing the number of times the fibres passed the yarn, so giving fibres greater opportunity of becoming attached to the yarn. To intensify the effect, the speed of the yarn tail was maintained by a secondary airstream which entered the vortex tube tangentially at a point downstream of the perforated section. Thus, although air passed through the perforations and the vortex was slowed down in that region, the yarn tail speed was maintained by the secondary vortex. The main difficulty with this device was that the perforations in the tapered section quickly became choked with fibres; it was necessary for the device to be stripped down after each test to remove the fibres from the perforations.

A simpler device was examined, which included a fibre shield as shown in Fig. 9.10; this served to maintain a high vortex velocity in the upstream section. A mechanical twister was used. The fibre shield was of $\frac{3}{4}$ in. external diameter and 4 in. long with a $\frac{1}{8}$ in. bore; the vortex tube was of 1 in. internal diameter. Fig. 9.11 shows a photograph of the tube, with some of the inserts used. A 20s c.c. (30 tex)

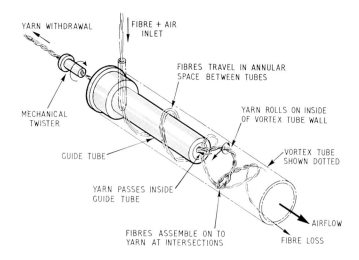

Fig. 9.10   The Shirley/Götzfried Mark 2-1 air-vortex spinner.

yarn was spun with this device from cotton of $1\frac{7}{16}$ in. effective length at some 500 inches/min., using nominal twist factors in the range of 8 to 12.4. The twist insertion efficiency was about 60%, the actual twist factor thus being in the region of 5 to 7. There was little correlation between tenacity and twist factor, the tenacity varying between 7 and 10.5 gf/tex.

Fibre Loss

The fibre loss in these experiments ranged from about 27% to 36%, the figure depending on the suction applied to the device. Fig. 9.12 shows the effect of varying the suction in a similar device. Fibre loss increases with the suction; this is characteristic of devices of this type. Yarn tenacity was also affected by the suction; it deteriorated as the suction increased. A 5s c.c. (120 tex) yarn was spun on this device

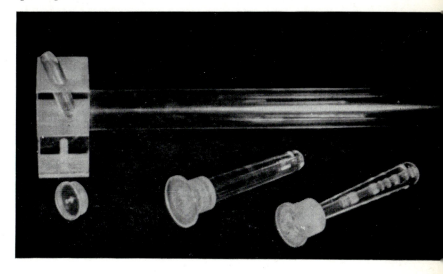

Fig. 9.11   The Shirley/Götzfried Mark 2-1 vortex tube with alternative inserts.

at about 500 inches/min. from a $\frac{7}{8}$ in. Strict Middling American cotton, with twist factors similar to those used for the longer cotton. The yarn was very irregular and weak; there was a marked deterioration in tenacity with the shorter staple length.

Man-Made Fibres

As the device was more successful with the longer staples in the coarser count ranges, it was used for spinning man-made fibres. Yarns were spun using $1\frac{7}{16}$ in. viscose rayon, $1\frac{9}{16}$ in. acrylic, $1\frac{1}{2}$ in. polyester and $1\frac{1}{2}$ in. polyamide fibres. All yarns were 8s count (74 tex); they were produced at speeds up to 2000 inches/min. An air suction of 14 to 16 inches of water was used and the fibre loss was between 20% and 25%. In general, the faster yarn was produced, the worse was its quality; in practice, it would seem that yarn quality

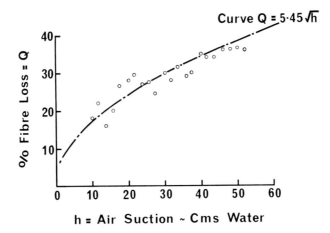

Fig. 9.12 Simple air-vortex spinner. Mechanical twister speed=21,000 rev/min. 1 7/16 inch cotton. 10s c.c. (60 tex) yarn.

must be balanced against production rate. An unsuccessful attempt was made to spin a polynosic rayon fibre.

The poor regularity of some of the yarns was probably due to instability in the yarn-forming process. Flash photographs of yarn in the second vortex tube showed how the length of the yarn tail varied during spinning; these changes in yarn tail length are associated with variations in the yarn structure along its length.

Fig. 9.13 shows an interesting phenomenon which may explain the sudden shortening of the yarn tail. An aggregate of fibres is loosely connected to the yarn tail, and seems about to break off (which is probably what happened). This phenomenon was observed on many occasions, and it was concluded that the tail sometimes picked up a larger aggregate of fibres than usual, causing the end of the tail to break off. Such an occurrence would affect the regularity of the yarn.

Analysis of the fibres which had failed to assemble on to

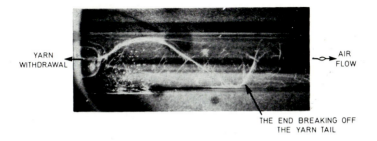

YARN WITHDRAWAL

AIR FLOW

THE END BREAKING OFF THE YARN TAIL

Fig. 9.13   Flash photograph of the fibres and yarn in a vortex tube.

the yarn showed no predominance of shorter fibres. It should therefore be possible to recirculate them to reduce fibre wastage.

Future Prospects

The devices described were simple to make, and power requirements were modest, but the yarns produced were of only limited value. They were of poor quality and limited to the coarser counts, and reliable spinning was achieved only by using longer staple fibres. Despite these limitations, further development of the devices may yield worthwhile results. Break-spun yarns of this sort may eventually displace condenser-spun yarns for some purposes, and a device similar to those described might become of commercial value for the production of this type of yarn.*

* This section is based on work which is fully described in the Shirley Break Spinning Report available from Shirley Developments Ltd., P.O. Box 6, 856 Wilmslow Road, Didsbury, Manchester M20 85A, England.

(B) University of Manchester Institute of Science and Technology, U.K.

by M. S. Sadasivam* and P. R. Lord

The air vortex spinner is potentially a cheap device, but the twist insertion rate is limited. As the capital cost of the break spinner is reduced, so is the running speed needed to yield minimum yarn production cost (see Fig. 10.19†). There are thus two obvious lines to follow in development of the air vortex spinner. On the one hand, attempts may be made to improve the twist insertion rate at the expense of additional capital cost. On the other hand, development could be concentrated on the production of a simple, low-cost device with a modest twist insertion rate. At U.M.I.S.T., the latter course was adopted.

Many points of interest were noted during early development work. One, for example, concerned the spinning draft ratio, which is the ratio of the yarn withdrawal speed to the fibre supply speed at the front rollers of the mechanical drafting system. The product of the mechanical draft ratio and spinning draft ratio gives the overall draft ratio. The spinning draft ratio itself comprises a pneumatic drafting stage and a condensation stage as explained in the previous chapter.

In early tests, a spinning draft ratio of about 3.5 was used, with unsatisfactory results. When the ratio was reduced to about 1.0., spinning was greatly improved; it was possible to spin continuous lengths of fairly reasonable yarn.

The positioning of the fibre entry tube was another important factor. Fig. 9.14 shows a diagram of the tubes eventually developed. In the early designs, however, the fibre entry duct was located downstream of that shown in

* Research Assistant, University of Manchester Institute of Science & Technology, U.K.
† page 208

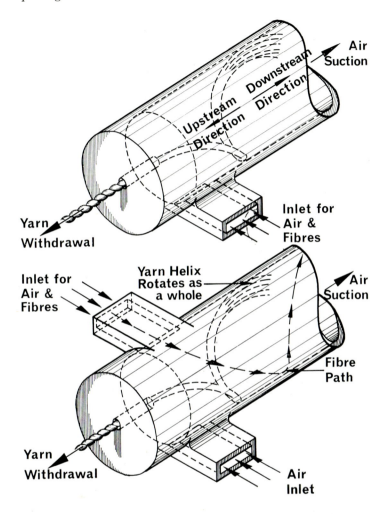

Fig. 9.14   Simple air-vortex tubes as developed at U.M.I.S.T. *Note:* no mechanical twisters were used.

F*

Fig. 9.14. Periodic slubs appeared on the yarn due to sub-sidiary vortices formed between the fibre entry and the yarn exit hole. Fibres caught in these vortices did not pass down the tube until the accumulation of fibre became so large as to be caught by the main air stream. These accumulations were assembled on the yarn to form slubs. When the fibre entry tube was moved upstream as far as possible, this trouble disappeared. One of the main lessons learned from this work was the necessity of avoiding any discontinuities in the air flow within the tube. In an early design, for example, a step in diameter at the junction between the nozzle block and the tube itself caused a considerable deterioration in performance.

"Perspex" Tube

In the earlier part of this chapter, an account has been given of the inadequacy of electrostatic forces and the predominance of mechanical and pneumatic forces. Almost the reverse was found to be the case with vortex tubes of "Perspex". When the device was running in a dry atmos-phere, the "Perspex" rapidly acquired an electric charge, which adversely affected spinning. Some improvement was obtained by using a high relative humidity. A metal vortex tube also eliminated unwanted charges, but it was quite ineffective as a spinner; it appeared that a degree of electric charge had a beneficial effect. It is possible that each fibre became an electrical dipole, one end being attracted to the tube surface and the other repelled, making it easier for the forming yarn to pick up projecting fibres. When the charge was too great, fibres were decelerated too rapidly on the tube surface; the resulting telescopic condensation made fibres bunch together and become entangled with each other. It seems desirable, therefore, to control the electro-static charge rather than to eliminate it.

Of all the tube materials tested, "Perspex" proved best, despite its tendency to acquire a charge. Anti-static coatings provided a temporary solution, but the most effective solution lay in the use of a Shirley high-voltage static eliminator which ionised the air stream entering the tube. Significant improvement in yarn quality resulted from the use of the eliminator.

Stripping from Card

In the work so far described, a conventional roller drafting system supplied fibres to the inlet tube. A stage was reached at which fairly good yarns were produced, comparable with good condenser spun yarns. Further improvement was sought by gathering the fibres from an earlier stage in the process. In a conventional process, the main cylinder of the card is the only place where fibres are sufficiently well opened to be used directly in a break-spinning machine. An attempt was made, therefore, to spin direct from the card and fibre was sucked from the card cylinder, which was stripped almost clean. When a lap feed was used, the resulting yarn was of poor quality, because the carding action was much reduced; fibres passed only once under the flats, and there was no bed of fibres below the surface of the wire to keep the tufts within range of the flats. Under these circumstances, the card web had many more neps and tufts than usual. When card sliver was fed to the card taker-in, providing a double carding action, good yarns were produced. Regularity was improved and there was little difference between yarns produced from similar vortex tubes fed with fibres in the two different ways (i.e. from the roller drafting system and from the card cylinder).

The size of tube was not a critical factor, but test results indicated that the optimum tube diameter was a function of staple length. For example, the best size for $1\frac{7}{16}$ in. staple was about 1 in. diameter, whereas a $\frac{1}{2}$ in. diameter tube produced better yarn when spinning short staple material. A $1\frac{1}{4}$ in. tube (the largest used) gave the best results with 4 in. staple; even better results might have been obtained with a

PROPERTIES OF SOME CLOTH WOVEN USING AIR VORTEX SPUN FIBRO WEFT

	Conventional Weft	Air Vortex Spun Weft
Drape Coefficient	45%	65%
Bending Length		
Warpwise	1.51 cm.	1.20 cm.
Weftwise	1.41 cm.	1.12 cm.
Flexural Rigidity		
Warpwise	0.044×10^3 mg./cm.	0.022×10^3 mg./cm.
Weftwise	0.036×10^3 mg./cm.	0.018×10^3 mg./cm.
Bursting Pressure (4 in. dia.)	30 p.s.i.	22 p.s.i.
Tensile Strength		
Warpwise	50.0 kg.	50.0 kg. $\left(\begin{smallmatrix}\text{Test piece}\\ \text{2 in. wide}\end{smallmatrix}\right)$
Weftwise	33.6 kg.	18.0 kg.

Table 9.1

larger tube. The longest staple spun was jute of some 18 in. staple length; the shortest was asbestos (with 15% rayon as a carrier). Both were spun in a 1 in. tube; this illustrates the flexibility of the device. In general, yarn tenacity was about 60% of that of equivalent conventionally spun material.

It was possible to spin the asbestos/rayon mixture to a finer and more even yarn than the normal asbestos yarn, which is rather coarse and uneven. Other fibre mixtures were therefore examined, including combinations of cotton, rayon, nylon and polyester. The results were disappointing, the strength of yarn produced from a mixture being inferior to that of yarns from individual fibre components. A factor which may have contributed to this was the different extensibility of the fibre components, resulting in uneven distribution of load. The fibre waste contained component fibres in almost the same proportions as the original supply, indicating that the device does not tend to segregate the materials.

In general, fine staple fibres produced better yarn than coarse fibres; yarn quality varied directly with fibre flexibility. Very coarse fibres yielded poor yarns. Highly crimped fibres did not spin well, but the resultant yarn was highly extensible. When wool fibres were used, extremely poor

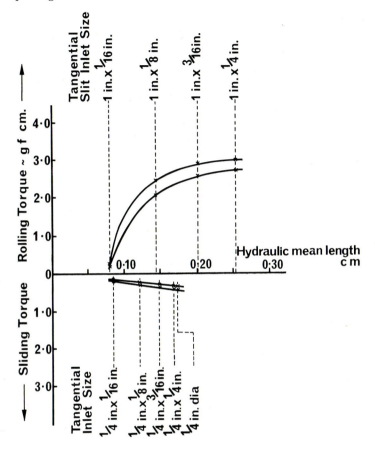

Fig. 9.15 Relationship between hydraulic mean length and torque (sliding and rolling). Cotton yarn=245 tex. Yarn length constant=20 cm. Air pressure=25 in water and 30 in water.

results were obtained. With unscoured wool, grease and dirt accumulated rapidly, and it was apparent that the air vortex spinner was not suitable for such material. Rayon proved most successful; it was spun at relatively high speed

for extended periods, providing sufficient material to be made
into garments. The characteristics of woven cloth are listed
in Table 9.1.

In early experimental work, fibres entered the tubes
through a cylindrical duct of about $\frac{1}{4}$ in. diameter. When
working from the card, it was necessary to use a slit entry
similar to that shown in Fig. 9.14 because a $\frac{1}{4}$ in. wide strip
of card web from the cylinder did not contain sufficient fibres
to give an adequate output. The slit entry was effective, but
it resulted in an important side-effect. When viscose rayon
was fed through the rectangular fibre supply duct, twist
was inserted in the opposite direction to the rotation of the
vortex; when cotton was used, the twist was in the same
direction as the rotation of the vortex. By varying the
proportions of the fibre entry duct, the amount and sometimes the direction of twist could be altered. Measurements
of the torque on a seed yarn rotated by an air vortex within
the tube confirmed this effect, showing that the geometry of
the fibre inlet duct is of considerable importance (see
Fig. 9.15). When spinning rayon, (taking into account the
necessity to conserve airflow to minimise power costs) the
optimum dimensions of the entry duct were $\frac{7}{8}$ in. $\times \frac{1}{8}$ in.
With other fibres, optimum dimensions were different.

Torque

The amount of torque that could be introduced was
limited by the torsional stiffness of the yarn tail. Excessive
torque made the yarn tail snarl despite the effects of centrifugal forces and elements of the yarn moved radially inwards
where they could no longer pick up fibres (see Fig. 9.16). It
is difficult to analyse the forces acting, as there were three-
dimensional changes in air velocity. The yarn did not always
travel at the surface of the tube and the position of any
element of yarn could not readily be determined; in consequence it was impossible to identify the forces involved.
It was apparent, however, that a stiff yarn behaves differently

from a flexible one. In the latter case, under a certain set of critical conditions, there was occasionally a sudden change in torque; this was almost certainly due to an element of yarn moving radially to or from the tube walls. When the yarn helix collapsed inwards, there was an increase in torque. This was of little value, however, as it was obtained at the expense of the assembly efficiency because the elements of yarn not in contact with the tube walls had less chance of picking up fibres.

Length of Yarn Tail

A characteristic of these tubes is that yarn strength and regularity, as well as fibre assembly efficiency (i.e. 100% − percentage fibre loss), deteriorate together. This deterioration is associated with an increase in length of the yarn tail in the vortex tube. The fibre assembly efficiency depends upon the number of intersections of the yarn helix with the fibre

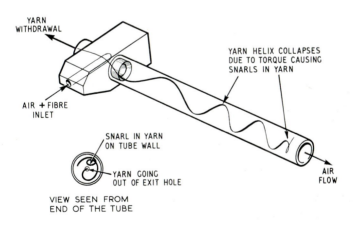

Fig. 9.16   Instability of yarn helix.

path, and upon the efficiency with which fibres are picked up at each intersection.

If x% of the arriving fibres are picked up at each intersection, (100–x)% will carry on after the first intersection and $\frac{x}{100}$ (100–x)% will be picked up at the second intersection; the remainder will carry on to the next, and so on. Such a process continues, with the population of the fibre stream dwindling and the thickness of the yarn tail decreasing, until fibres can no longer assemble on the yarn tail. A situation may be considered, for example, in which assembly cannot be maintained after the fibre population is reduced to 10% of its original value. If x = 30%, fibres will be picked up at some seven intersections; if x is increased to 60%, however, the number of useful intersections is reduced to three, and the desirable end point is apparently a single intersection with x = 100%. Since the number of intersections is related to the yarn tail length, a short yarn tail is indicative of a high value of x and a good overall fibre assembly efficiency. Retardation of the fibres sliding on the tube walls tends to produce undesirable telescopic condensation; Fig. 9.13 shows how fibre alignment also suffers after fibre has slid for some distance. These two factors are responsible for the weak, irregular nature of the yarns.

There is thus a qualitative explanation of the observed phenomena. Only a portion of the yarn tail, however, can be in contact with the tube wall. The portion nearest the withdrawal point balloons freely, and this portion suffers the most force from the air vortex; for this reason, it has been called the drive portion. As it is essential that there should be a useful drive portion, the yarn tail length cannot be reduced below a certain value (which implies that some imperfections must remain). The total torque input into the yarn is mainly that derived from the drive element less that lost due to friction. Frictional loss is caused by the downstream portions of the yarn tail rubbing the surface; too

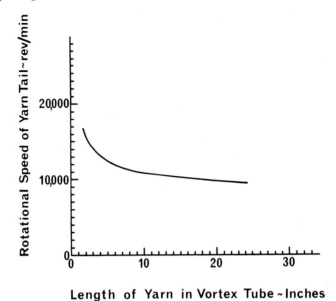

Length of Yarn in Vortex Tube ~ Inches

Fig. 9.17 A typical speed characteristic of a yarn in a simple unassisted air-vortex tube. N.B.: the net twist-insertion rate is less than the rotational speed of the yarn tail because of twist leakage.

long a tail thus reduces the effective torque, and this in turn reduces the twist insertion rate (see Fig. 9.17) unless a mechanical twister is used. Also, the layer of slowly moving air adjacent to the tube walls increases in extent downstream; the remote portions of yarn do not suffer so much propulsive force. It seems desirable, therefore, to keep the yarn tail as short as possible; this is largely a matter of tube design.

The rectangular fibre entry duct gave the required short yarn tail when spinning rayon. It also had advantages other than those indicated. The helical fibre stream round the inside wall of the vortex tube was tape-like rather than rope-like. The yarn tail passing over this stream had access to a

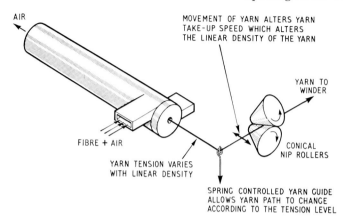

Fig. 9.18   A simple autoleveller for use with an air-vortex tube.
U.S Pat. 3,469,388

greater proportion of the fibres in that stream because of its
flatness; in consequence, the fibre assembly efficiency
improved (best recorded was 96%, i.e. 4% loss; more
generally a figure of about 85%, i.e. 15% loss, was obtained).
Also, fibres were able to spread out more, reducing the risk of
entanglement. The length of the fibre inlet duct should be
about one fibre length to ensure that suction is carried to the
source of fibres, and to prevent the creation of drafting
waves in the fibre stream entering the spinner.

Long Term Irregularity

Working from the card increased the chances of long term
irregularity. There was no conventional method of dealing
with this, so a new technique was devised. Wide variations
in yarn take-off rate had little effect on the twist insertion
rate (i.e. the number of turns per inch in the yarn did not
vary greatly), but an increase in take-off rate reduced the
linear density of the yarn, and vice versa. Yarn tension was

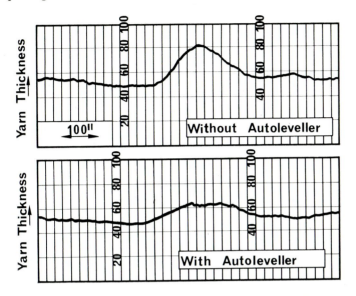

Fig. 9.19 The effect of passing a thick slub in the fibre supply through a vortex spinner.

a simple function of the linear density of the yarn; this tension could be used to control the take-up rate, and thus the linear density of the yarn, without significantly affecting the twist factor. To reduce the inertia of the control system, a pair of constant speed conical rollers was used to withdraw the yarn (see Fig. 9.18); only the yarn had to be moved along the nip line to secure a change in speed. As the yarn position was varied, so the yarn withdrawal rate and the linear density were altered. A lightweight yarn guide was used for this purpose; yarn tension acting against a light spring determined its position according to need. Although the device was not perfected, it produced good results, and proved capable of dealing with large variations in linear density of the supply material (see Fig. 9.19). The only

YARNS SPUN DIRECT FROM THE CARD USING AN AIR VORTEX SPINNER

Fibre	Nozzle	Air Pressure cm. H$_2$O	Fibre Assembly Efficiency	Linear Density tex	Evenness p.m.d. %	Tenacity gf/tex	Twist Factor	Take-off Rate m./min. in./min.	
1$\frac{7}{16}$ in. Egyptian	1	50	89.8	91	11.7	8.1	2.8	5.5	215
		75	93.0	100	10.7	9.2	3.3	5.5	215
		68	92.2	88	11.7	7.9	2.8	7.1	280
1$\frac{1}{4}$ in. American	1	70	89.1	72	16.2	7.1	—	5.5	215
		70	94.9	140	17.8	4.9	—	5.5	215
		70	95.3	144	17.9	4.3	—	5.5	215
1$\frac{7}{16}$ in. Fibro	2	64	85.7	93	14.5	6.1	4.0	7.1	280
		60	80.0	46	16.5	7.5	3.9	11.1	440
		50	90.0	46	16.8	8.1	3.6	18.4	720

Table 9.2

practical difficulty was that the yarn winder had to follow the speed variations; this was overcome in the prototype unit by driving the winder by a slipping wire belt drive similar to those used in ciné projectors.

In general, cotton could only be spun at some 300 to 400 inches/min., whereas rayon could be spun without mechanical help up to about 1,600 inches/min. With cotton, the strongest yarn with the most twist was spun with a $\frac{1}{4}$ in. diameter fibre inlet duct, the twist being in the same direction as the vortex. When a rectangular fibre inlet was used with cotton, the yarn tended to be soft and weak, irrespective of whether the dimensions were arranged to give co-incident or reversed twist. With rayon, the $\frac{7}{8}$ in. $\times$ $\frac{1}{8}$ in. rectangular fibre inlet duct was used, and the twist was reversed. Table 9.2 includes results obtained using this method; viscose rayon yielded a reasonably strong yarn with a remarkably low fibre waste and a satisfactory take-off rate.

In the production of heavier yarns spun at the highest speed, outputs approaching $\frac{1}{4}$ lb./hr. were achieved. With some 40 vortex tubes working from a card, it should be possible to work the card, with rayon, at about 10 lb./hr. This is still too low to be commercially attractive, but with development it might be possible to increase the rate to a satisfactory level.

10

The Drum Spinner

by P. A. Smith* and P. R. Lord**

The drum spinner is the most highly developed type of break spinner, and it forms the basis of most commercial systems. This chapter discusses the results of experiments carried out at the Universities of Leeds and Manchester. The operation of the device is explained, and the requirements for successful operation are described. Economic and technical factors are taken into account.

YARN CHARACTER

Analysis of break-spun yarn shows that it differs from ring-spun yarn in several respects. Externally, break-spun yarn is more even; it is often more extensible, but the average strength is lower than that of ring-spun yarn. Internally, the two types are of different structure. The fibres in break-spun yarn are not uniformly packed, and twist varies from one radius to another. Fibre migration in break-spun yarn does not exist in the same way as in ring-spun yarns, and the shape of the fibres as assembled in the yarn varies from the ideal. All these factors tend to weaken the yarn and to increase its bulk. Increased bulkiness tends to reduce the inter-fibre contact forces and for this reason higher twist factors are usually required for optimum results.

A poor yarn made from badly orientated and hooked (or entangled) fibres will be generally very bulky, extensible and

* Conference author. Dept. of Textile Industries, University of Leeds, U.K.

** Conference author. Associate Professor, North Carolina State University at Raleigh, U.S.A., formerly of the University of Manchester (U.M.I.S.T.)

weak. Yarn failure will be due partially to fibre slippage, and a strained yarn will not recover its original structure. On the other hand, a good strong yarn will be made from well-orientated fibres existing mainly as pure helices, with just sufficient of the fibre ends migrating to give the required cohesion. The load will be more evenly distributed amongst the fibres and the fibres will be well organised, so that the yarn will be strong without being bulky. On average, a greater component of the load will act along the fibre length, and for this reason there will be less fibre bending and torsion; the yarn will thus be less extensible. In practice, yarns fall between these two extremes.

An indication of the position of a real yarn within this spectrum is given by considering the fibre shape in the assembled yarn. For simplicity, the fibre helices may be regarded as geometrically developed, such that a perfect helix becomes a straight line. In this way, the so-called straight fibre may be considered as the ideal, and an entangled fibre as the least desirable condition.

YARN CHARACTERISTICS
Results obtained by SENTURK at UMIST

FIBRE SHAPE	TYPE OF SPINNER			
	Air Vortex	Radial fed drum	Tangentially fed drum	Ring frame
————————	11·4%	21·4%	37·2%	49·9%
⌐————————	11·5%	16·8%	17·4%	21·8%
⊂————————	16·1%	20·5%	18·8%	7·2%
⊂————————	19·2%	13·0%	10·6%	8·6%
⊂————————	12·0%	9·0%	3·9%	4·1%
Entangled	29·8%	19·3%	12·1%	8·4%
TWIST FACTOR	3·9	5·0	5·9	4·5
BREAKING TENACITY gf/tex	5·8	8·9	11·8	14·5

Table 10.1

Table 10.1 shows the results of an investigation using the tracer-fibre technique. Several sorts of spinning device were used, ranging from the air vortex spinner to the ring spindle. As discussed earlier, the air vortex spinner produces a weak, bulky yarn whereas the ring spindle can produce a strong, lean yarn, It is evident from Table 10.1 that strength is associated with the high number of straight fibres and the low number of badly hooked and entangled fibres. Bulk has an inverse relationship with these factors.

From these results it may be deduced that fibre straightness and orientation are important factors, and every attempt should be made at all stages to preserve them. In the air-vortex tube this is difficult, because the fibres slide along a stationary surface. Deceleration causes the fibres to buckle; air velocity gradients and static electricity both create strange effects. Similarly, in the radial-feed drum machine, the fibres change direction abruptly in at least two places. The momentum of fibres in motion causes them to move out of the air-stream at these points of directional change. When the fibres collide with a surface, order and straightness suffer. It is not surprising, therefore, that tests rate the devices in the order shown.

The design of radial- and tangential-fed drum spinners may be considered in the light of these factors. The machine consists of a number of elements which may or may not be mechanically separate. As discussed earlier, break spinning includes the following phases:

1. Drafting of fibres down to groups of ones and twos.
2. Transport of these fibres without disturbance.
3. Condensation of the fibres to give the necessary linear density of yarn.
4. Removal of the fibre assembly.
5. Insertion of twist.
6. Winding of the newly manufactured yarn.

Each stage will be considered in turn, with particular reference to the research carried out at U.M.I.S.T. and Leeds University, England.

1. DRAFTING

Ideally, it is necessary to draft the supply sliver to such an extent that fibres travel into the spinning drum in single file. In practice, it is sufficient to ensure that there is no mechanical connection between the fibres flowing into the spinner. In other words, the fibres should flow in very open order and should be straight. Any hooks, entanglements or crimp in the fibre lead to a greater space requirement by that fibre; in general, the non-straight fibres can flow only in less dense fibre streams. Since the duct through which the fibre flows is of restricted size, it follows that the degree of drafting required depends on the straightness of the fibre entering the transport system.

At present, there are two main methods of drafting fibres for break spinning: (1) the Czech "taker-in" device, and (2) an adaptation of conventional roller drafting.

(a) Czech "Taker-in" Device. Sliver is fed to the device, and the teeth attack the advancing fringe of fibres from the sliver. Due to the high surface speed of the "taker-in" rotor, the fibres should be caught by the teeth in ones and twos (which is satisfactory) but they are, in fact, likely to be hooked round the teeth (which is unsatisfactory). A short duct, which permits an airflow, is arranged tangential to the "taker-in" rotor; fibres which are thrown off are carried up this duct to the spinner. Doubtless some fibre straightening takes place in this duct, but its adequacy under extreme conditions is unknown. The system is flexible, but under some circumstances it can cause fibre damage. It has the advantage that stop motions can be fitted more easily, but it has the disadvantage of consuming more power than a conventional system.

(b) Adaptation of Conventional Roller Drafting. The roller drafting system on its own is probably incapable of meeting the requirements of break spinning (see Chapter 8); on the one hand, the front roller speed would be excessive, and on the other hand the nip might have difficulty in dealing with single fibres. Fortunately, most short staple drum spinners are self-pumping, and correct design can ensure sufficient air-flow into the spinner. The use of a pneumatic stage, for example, has been found very effective. The air-flow over the emerging fibres tends to straighten them and to remove them as soon as they become free. A substantial number of fibres can exist in the front nip of the mechanical drafting system, and the front roller speed may be modest. This pneumatic drafting stage has been found remarkably effective. If care is taken in the transport stage, it is possible to run with as many as twelve fibres in the cross-section of the duct into the spinner. As will be seen later, this is an important result; the departure from the ideal concept of fibres flowing in single file removes a serious limitation to break spinning.

2. FIBRE TRANSPORT

It is important that fibre straightness and order should not be destroyed in the transport phase. This may be overlooked because the actual transport system is, or should be, very simple indeed. The best possible system is a straight tube disposed on the ideal fibre flow path, which is a line drawn tangentially to both drafting rollers (or rotor) and spinning drum. The straight path is essential, as any deviation causes the fibres to touch the side of the tube. When this happens, the fibre is decelerated; it may buckle and impede the flow of other fibres. Under bad conditions, entanglements are caused and the drafting apparatus must work at a higher draft ratio than would otherwise be the case.

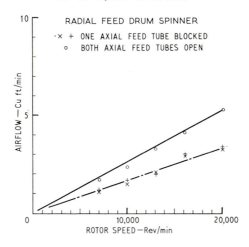

AIRFLOW CHARACTERISTICS
OF A DRUM SPINNER

Fig. 10.1

The Radial Feed Machine

In the radial drum spinner, the fibre supply tube is disposed axially with respect to the drum. Fibres travel along the tube and are taken, partly by the air-stream and partly by centrifugal force, to the collecting surface at the periphery of the drum. For short-staple spinning, a self-pumping device may be used. The radial length of the pumping holes will determine the pumping pressure for a given drum speed; the number, size and attitude of these holes will be the main factors controlling air-flow. The self-pumping action causes a sub-atmospheric pressure inside the drum; this may be used to inhale the fibres through the feed tube and, when necessary, to inhale a yarn end for the purposes of piecing up.*

With such a drum, the pressure head $\propto$ speed^2 and also to airflow^2; therefore, the airflow $\propto$ speed. Results which demonstrate this are shown in Fig. 10.1. Experiments at Leeds University showed that an airspeed of 160 ft./sec. could be obtained in the feed tube, but it is probable that this may be increased, perhaps to about 300 ft./sec. This could not produce the ideal fibre flux of 1.0 (see Chapter 9) but, as already indicated, higher fluxes can be tolerated under certain conditions. With too low an airspeed, however, the straightening effect will be less efficient, and the separation may be poor. The Leeds experiment used high speed photography to observe the effects; at the velocity used (160 ft./sec.), the fibres were shown to travel down the centre of the tube, many of the hooks (especially the leading ones) being removed by the air-stream. It was found in general that fibres travelled down the supply tube in the straight condition desirable for efficient spinning. The Manchester experience confirms these results, the conclusion in this case being drawn by examining fibre webs deposited on the drum surface.

Air Stream Velocity

A fibre moving in a uniform air-stream will be accelerated until it reaches the air velocity; it should thereafter continue to move at uniform speed. When a fibre is in a uniform air-stream all portions of the fibre will be accelerated by about the same amount and no fibre straightening will occur. If, however, a fibre flows into an air-stream of ever-increasing velocity, it will be subjected to a larger force acting on the leading end than on the trailing end. This will tend to

* The method of piecing is very simple. A yarn end is inserted into the yarn-withdrawal tube; as soon as an increase in tension is felt, the yarn is steadily withdrawn and threaded into the moving yarn take-up mechanism. Spinning should continue automatically from that point.

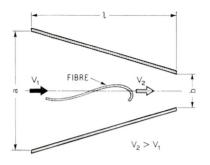

EDBERG VENTURI

Fig. 10.2

straighten the fibres, as was shown by Edberg [12]. A condition of this sort is produced by using a tapered tube or Venturi as shown in Fig. 10.2. Results obtained with such a rig confirm that the number of hooked fibres diminishes and the number of straight fibres increases as the Venturi effect is strengthened (see Table 10.2). In other words, it is desirable for the fibres to go through an accelerating air-stream, rather than through a decelerating one. Deceleration acting on the leading end of the fibre has the undesirable effect of making the fibre crumple. A fibre moving from a high speed air-stream into a low speed air-stream, for example, will crumple; contact with a solid object will have the same effect. Unfortunately, using the central method of feed, this is precisely what happens. In a radial feed machine, fibres undergo two abrupt changes of direction, and their momentum tends to carry them out of the air-stream into contact with the walls of the drum. This may cause fibre crumpling and hook formation.

Fig. 10.3 shows estimates of air speed within the drum. The tangential air velocity is considerably lower than that which might be inferred from drum speed. The minimum air speed will reduce probably to a value around 25 ft./sec. Thus the

FIBRE STRAIGHTENING CAUSED BY AN
ACCELERATING AIRFLOW

	Case 1		Case 2		Case 3	
	Entry	Exit	Entry	Exit	Entry	Exit
Dimension a mm	30	—	30	—	30	—
Dimension b mm	—	25	—	15	—	7
Dimension ℓ mm	150		150		150	
Relative exit area	—	0·83	—	0·50	—	0·23
Fibre Category						
Hooked	15%	10%	16%	4%	10%	1%
Parallel	36%	45%	49%	75%	80%	94%
Oblique	49%	45%	35%	21%	10%	0%

Table 10.2   Note: the dimensions a, b and 1 refer to Fig. 10.2.

fibres must decelerate from a fairly high velocity to a fairly low one as they emerge from the supply tube.

A second ciné film, taken under similar conditions, followed the behaviour of fibres as they emerged from the supply tube. The fibres hovered in a zone half way between the tube exit and the collecting surface; there was evidence of local vortex motion and fibres were seen to form into hooks and tangles. Some fibres were blown directly on to the out-going yarn without reaching the collecting surface. All these phenomena are obviously undesirable.

Drum Speed

Table 10.3 shows that with increasing drum speed, other things being equal, the number of straight fibres decreased significantly and the number of hooked fibres remained fairly constant. On the other hand, the number of tangled fibres increased very significantly. This means, probably, that turbulence within the drum was linked with

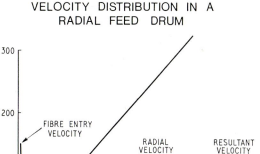

Fig. 10.3

the drum speed. It is known that turbulence exists within such a drum, caused probably by rapid deceleration of the air-stream coming from the fibre-feed and yarn-withdrawal tubes. The inevitable sudden expansion and the reaction between the two jets of air are bound to produce such turbulence. A system of this sort is thus unsatisfactory, and prospects of the successful development of a radial flow system are poor.

The Tangential-Feed Machine

In the tangential-feed machine, the fibre supply tube discharges its air at a velocity and in a direction which do not differ significantly from those of the air with which it comes into contact. Under these conditions, a smooth

EFFECT OF DRUM SPEED ON FIBRE SHAPE
ON THE COLLECTING SURFACE OF AN
SACM TYPE RADIAL FEED MACHINE

Drum Speed (rev/min)	10,000	15,000	20,000
Fibre Category			
Straight	49%	46%	35%
Hooked	35%	40%	31%
Tangled	16%	14%	34%

Note: Front roller speed = 1000 rev/min

Table 10.3

transfer of fibre is much more likely than in the case of the radial-flow system.

It is desirable that the fibre should be accelerated at every stage up to its arrival on the collecting surface; the air velocity in the transit tube must therefore be higher than the surface speed of the thinning rotor or front roller of the drafting system and less than the speed of the collecting surface inside the drum. The amount of air which can be pumped by a drum is limited, even if only by power requirements, and this limits the diameter of the transit tube. If the tube is too small, however, the fibres will be unable to flow freely through it. In the U.M.I.S.T. spinner a $\frac{3}{8}$ in. dia. tube was found to be successful.

It is not possible for the transit tube to be truly tangential to the collecting surface (see Fig. 10.4); as will be seen later, this has some repercussions. Velocity differences exist in practice, and the sudden increase in the air-stream from the tube causes turbulent flow which affects the emerging fibres. If the tube protrudes into the drum it also affects the airflow; this too makes the fibres deviate from the preferred path. Despite these shortcomings, which will no doubt yield to

THE SPINNING DRUM AND FEED TUBE

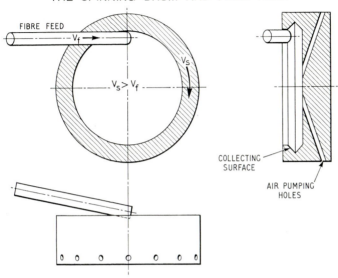

Fig. 10.4

experimental work now in progress, the tangential-feed system shows much greater promise than the radial system.

In addition to the smoother velocity transition obtainable with a tangential-feed machine, there is a further advantage in that the fibre entry point to the drum is closer to the collecting surface. There is thus less opportunity for hooks and tangles to form, and there is less likelihood of the short circuiting which causes wrapper fibres to be laid on to the emerging yarn.

The improvement resulting from use of the tangential configuration is shown in Table 10.1; the number of straight fibres has increased significantly, the numbers of both hooked and tangled fibres have diminished. It is probable that further improvement would result from modifications of

G

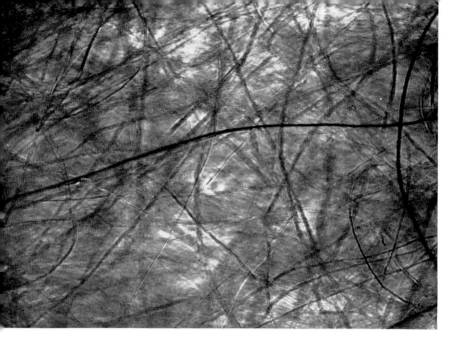

Fig. 10.5 Fibres deposited on a U-shaped collecting surface.

technique; a tapered fibre supply tube, for example, would accelerate the air-stream as it moves down the tube, and alteration of the inclination of the inlet tube with respect to the true tangent might affect the proportion of hooked and tangled fibres.

3. FIBRE CONDENSATION ON THE COLLECTING SURFACE

When the collecting surface inside the drum moves faster than an approaching fibre, and both move in the same direction, there is a tendency for the fibre to be straightened. If the velocity difference is too great, the approaching fibre may skid and disrupt the orderliness of fibres already there. If the fibre approach is oblique, there is a component force which, in combination with the turbulence already described, can destroy the orderliness of the web laid on the collecting surface. A web so deposited on a cylindrical collecting

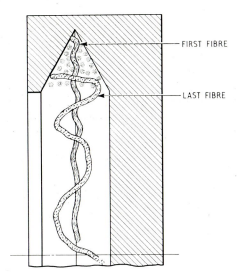

FIRST FIBRE

LAST FIBRE

DIAGRAM SHOWING THE MANNER
IN WHICH FIBRES LIE ON THE
COLLECTING SURFACE

Fig. 10.6

surface resembles a random-laid web consisting of a discrete
number of layers (Fig. 10.5). This difficulty may be overcome by machining a deep vee-shaped groove on the
inside of the drum to act as a collecting surface as shown
in Fig. 10.4. Centrifugal forces press the fibre into the vee
and the fibre tends to be straightened. If there is a sharp
apex to the vee, the first fibre may be completely
straightened. Later fibres will be incompletely straightened
(see Fig. 10.6); coarser yarns will thus contain more bent
fibres. As already stated, this will affect the quality of the
yarn. The overall effect of the vee, however, is to cause a
very significant straightening of the fibres in the yarn.

   The obliquity of the transit tube has an interesting effect.
The momentum of the fibres carries them to the remote wall
of the collecting surface, where a build-up is caused. The
close packing of these fibres encourages straightening;
photomicrographs of the cross-section of the web (Fig. 10.7)
show a dense, well-organised layer of fibre. In the remainder
of the collection zone, the fibres are disposed in layers which
have the sort of disorganisation shown in Fig. 10.6.

CROSS-SECTION OF FIBRES LYING ON
COLLECTING SURFACE

Fig. 10.7

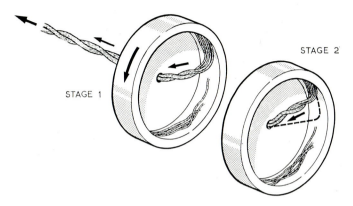

DIAGRAM SHOWING MOVEMENT OF PEELING POINT

Fig. 10.8

The asymmetrical nature of the fibre cross-section has an important influence on the nature of the yarn; this is discussed later in this chapter.

Piecing-Up

To piece up a broken end, the seed or priming yarn is allowed to be inhaled into the yarn withdrawal tube. The forced air-vortex within the drum drags the seed yarn end round with it, and centrifugal force carries the yarn to the collecting surface. When it reaches the collecting surface, the yarn is pulled round faster; it is possible to feel a stronger pull caused by the higher centrifugal force acting on the yarn. As soon as the yarn is caught in this way, there is a rapid twist insertion which (if normal spinning is not commenced) will cause the yarn to over-twist and break. If, however, the fibre feed and the yarn-withdrawal systems are both started when the yarn end makes contact with the collecting

surface, all will be well and spinning will commence. With
a little skill, the piecing thus made is almost undetectable,
partly because the increase in yarn diameter is small, and
partly because the piecing is elongated.

4. REMOVAL OF THE FIBRE ASSEMBLY FROM THE COLLECTING SURFACE

The full thickness of web is peeled off the collecting surface
and is taken radially inwards to be withdrawn as shown in
Fig. 10.8. Rotation of the drum inserts twist; this is en-
couraged to run back to the collecting surface to give the
radial portion sufficient strength to hold together. Immediately behind the place from which the web has been
removed, the collecting surface is bare. At other points round
the circumference, the thickness of the web will be proportional to the time which has elapsed since the peeling
point last passed. Thus, the web lying on the surface is
tapered.

The peeling point moves with respect to the surface; if it
moves in the same direction as the surface (which is preferable), the twist insertion rate will be slightly higher than
the rotational speed of the drum (by a fraction of a per cent).
There is, therefore, a differential action; one layer of fibres
is deposited per revolution of the drum and during this time
the peeling point moves around the surface by $\dfrac{1}{\text{t.p.i.}}$ inches
(this is a close approximation). By the time that the peeling
point has moved πD inches round the surface, the drum will
have rotated very nearly $\pi D(\text{t.p.i.})$ times and this number
of layers will have been deposited. This factor, known as the
doubling factor, is usually of the order of 100. Multiple
doubling accounts for the good evenness obtainable with this
device, and for its use as an efficient blender.

The peeling point may move in either of two ways

relative to the drum; the yarn tail may thus move at a speed which is fractionally faster or slower than the drum itself. The twist insertion rate is related to the speed of the yarn tail, but in practice the twist insertion is commonly taken as being the same as the drum speed.

It is preferable for the yarn tail to move faster than the drum, as the yarn tail will assume a shape which assists in peeling the web from the collecting surface. In practice, better yarn is produced and there are fewer end breaks than when the yarn tail moves slower than the drum. Ripka [23] has shown that the combination of the centrifugal, pneumatic and other forces will determine the shape of the radial portion of the yarn. His mathematical model showed that under certain circumstances, when the yarn tail was travelling more slowly than the drum there was a discontinuity which produced a shape as shown in Fig. 10.9. With a shape of this sort, fibres could bridge across and become attached to

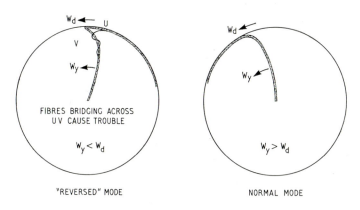

THE TWO WAYS OF PEELING FIBRES FROM
THE COLLECTING SURFACE

Fig. 10.9

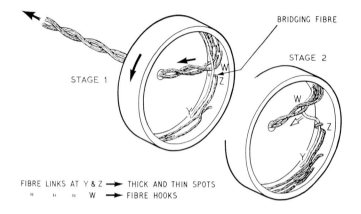

FIBRE LINKS AT Y & Z ➡ THICK AND THIN SPOTS
    "   "   "   W ➡ FIBRE HOOKS

THE EFFECT OF BRIDGING FIBRES

Fig. 10.10

two places on the yarn as shown in the same figure. When this portion of the yarn is withdrawn, the fibre either breaks loose or accepts more than its fair share of the load on the yarn. In the one case, a tuft of fibres may be removed, leading to unevenness. In the other case, the fibres in the main body of the yarn do not take their share of the load and the yarn is weakened. In either case, there is a deterioration in quality, and it is therefore preferable for the yarn tail to move faster than the drum.

Bridging Fibres

Fibres arrive randomly at the collection surface and there is thus a possibility that fibres will be laid across the gap behind the peeling point (see Fig. 10.10). These bridging fibres, for several reasons, may cause deterioration in the yarn. If the fibre becomes attached to the forming yarn at W it will be carried radially inward to form a hook with a whip-lash tail. If the bridging fibre also becomes attached to other fibres at Z, these fibres will be carried inwards and become assembled out of their correct sequence. If a tuft of fibres is carried forward because of interconnections such as at Y and Z, the yarn will have a thick spot followed by a thin spot. Furthermore, these fibres will be wrapped around the parent yarn to give an undesirable layer which is incapable of carrying much load.

The chance of a fibre bridging the gap depends on the ratio of the staple length to the circumference of the collecting surface. Clearly, the larger the drum (or shorter the staple), the less is the chance of a fibre bridging the gap. When an entangled tuft is fed to the spinner, however, it is the tuft length that determines the chance. A tuft of, say, 5 fibres could theoretically have a tuft length of five times the staple length; this would require an unacceptably large drum to deal with it. The number of fibres per layer and the probability of obtaining tufts are determined by the drafting system. Using a bad feed system, it would be necessary to limit the number of fibres per layer in order to spin with a reasonably small drum. With a good feed system, such tufts as may be present are not tangled, and it is possible for the bridging tuft to be separated into components at the peeling point.

In practice, by taking great care in the preceding stages, it has been found possible to spin with as many as 12 fibres per layer. If a mechanical drafting device capable of handling a larger amount of fibre had been available, even thicker layers could have been used.

It can be shown that the percentage of bridging fibres $= \dfrac{100L}{\pi D}$, where L is the mean fibre length and D is the diameter of the drum. It follows, therefore, that it is advantageous for the drum diameter to be large in comparison with the staple length. In the case of a 3 in. diameter drum working with $1\frac{1}{2}$ in. fibres, the number of hooks created by bridging fibres might be expected to be about

G*

16%. Not all bridging fibres are caught by the outgoing yarn, however, and the actual percentage could be less than this figure. On the other hand, if the fibre supply is tangled and tufty, the percentage could be higher.

Hooked Fibres

Table 10.4 shows results from Leeds which suggest that, on average, some 14% of the fibres were changed from straight to hooked by the action of yarn withdrawal. It might be possible, from these results, to assess what happens to an already hooked fibre on the collecting surface. Disregarding the effects of tangles, the effective fibre length is shortened and the chance of a hooked fibre bridging the gap is thus reduced. However, this is difficult to establish, as those hooked fibres which do form a bridge will still show up as hooked or tangled fibres in the yarn.

EFFECT OF FRONT ROLLER SPEED ON FIBRE STRAIGHTNESS (TANGENTIAL FEED)

On Collecting Surface

Fibre Category	Front roller speed rev/min		
	280	1,000	2,850
Straight	46%	47%	53%
Hooked	33%	34%	25%
Tangled	21%	19%	22%

In Yarn

Fibre Category	Front roller speed rev/min		
	280	1,000	2,850
Straight	30%	37%	34%
Hooked	48%	44%	43%
Tangled	22%	19%	23%

Table 10.4

CHANGE IN PERCENTAGE HOOKS FROM COLLECTING
SURFACE TO YARN

	Front roller speed rev/min	Leading Hooks		Trailing Hooks	
		Observed (%)	Expected (%)	Observed (%)	Expected (%)
Large drum	270	+5·1	+3·9	−7·0	Nil
	1,000	+11·7	+3·6	−1·8	Nil
	2,850	+1·2	+3·3	−11·2	Nil
	Mean	+6·0	+3·8	−5·3	Nil
Small drum	290	+9·1	+6·0	−2·0	Nil
	1,000	+6·9	+6·4	−0·7	Nil
	2,850	+11·0	+7·2	−4·6	Nil
	Mean	+9·0	+6·5	−2·4	Nil

Table 10.5

The simplest approach is to consider what happens to straight fibres, disregarding the effects of already hooked fibres. This enables measurements to be made and correlated with a reasonable theory. In addition, both web and yarn may be analysed in terms of trailing and leading hooks. The bridging fibres would not be expected to produce trailing hooks and any changes here will therefore be of interest. Table 10.5 shows the differences actually measured in another experiment; it gives an indication of the actual number of hooks arising from bridging fibres. In columns 3 and 5, theoretical values based on the total number of straight fibres are calculated. The observed changes in the number of leading hooks are always larger than expected and there is a decrease in the number of trailing hooks. These changes may be due to frictional effects (both pneumatic and mechanical) during the yarn withdrawal.

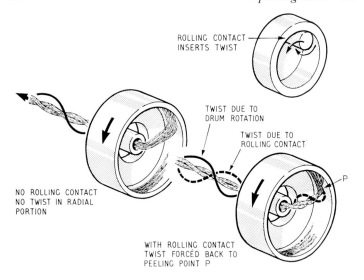

TWIST FLOW

Fig. 10.11

5. TWIST INSERTION

Rotation of the drum causes twist to be inserted in the yarn at a point near its axis. The existence of a twist trap at that point would cause the radial portion of the fibre assembly to be twistless and weak. To strengthen the fibre assembly and enable it to withstand the centrifugal forces, twist must be forced back to the peeling point. This may be done by allowing the yarn to roll on a stationary circular surface as shown in Fig. 10.11. If too much twist is forced back, the free end of the yarn will rotate and twist is lost. As an intermediate stage, if the torque acting at the peeling point is just too large, it may result in uncontrolled drafting in parts of the yarn, leading to irregularity. Generally, failure occurs at the peeling point rather than elsewhere and

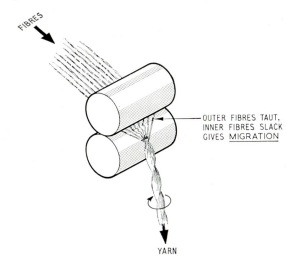

FIBRES

OUTER FIBRES TAUT,
INNER FIBRES SLACK
GIVES MIGRATION

YARN

CONVENTIONAL SPINNING

Fig. 10.12

the extent to which the twist is forced back affects the end breakage rate. It is easier to spin at high twist factors than low ones, as the torque generated by the twisted yarn determines the rate at which twist is forced back.

Peeling Zone

To investigate what happens in more detail, it is necessary to consider the peeling zone more closely. As in ring spinning, there is a delta zone in which the untwisted fibre assembly merges into the twisted yarn. In ring spinning, the fibre assembly is more or less flat, but in break spinning it is prismatic. Thus in ring spinning the delta is more or less two-dimensional; in break spinning it is three-dimensional. If little twist runs back, the delta will be elongated and fibres will travel a considerable distance before becoming trapped

NORMAL FIBRE MIGRATION

Fig. 10.13

in the twisted structure. During this transit period, the centrifugal force acting on that part of the fibre which has left the collecting surface will be opposed only by the forces of cohesion. The cohesive forces available in a well-aligned web are very small, but the centrifugal acceleration is of the order of 10^4g, sufficient to generate a force of a fraction of a gramme on each fibre. In a long delta, a large portion of the fibre could be in the transit zone, and it would be subjected to sufficient force to cause a break. In a short delta, only a small portion of the fibre would be affected, the remaining portions being supported by the collecting surface or by the twisted yarn. When low twist factors are used, or design is poor, the amount of twist forced back is insufficient to keep the delta short and frequent end breaks occur.

In ring spinning, the fibres are restrained at the nip of the front rollers and the insertion of twist creates a variety of fibre tensions in the delta zone. The fibres with lower tensions tend to move towards the outer surface of the yarn (Fig. 10.12). Under these circumstances, a fibre does not exist as a perfect helix at an unvarying radius from the yarn axis; on the contrary, its radial position changes along its length as shown in Fig. 10.13. The intertwining of these fibres enables the yarn to hold together.

In drum-spun yarn, fibre migration is greatly diminished, as fibres in the delta zone are force restrained rather than position restrained. A fibre can move without causing a significant change in its tension; a slack fibre is therefore

(A) Long Delta gives some migration. Yarn formed at low tension.

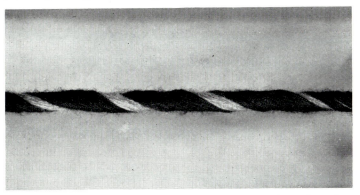

(B) Short Delta gives dense core and migration. Yarn formed at relatively high tension.

Fig. 10.14 Twisted woollen strands showing migration in break-spun yarns. *Note:* light strands represent the densely-packed fibres on the collecting surface. Dark strands represent the less-densely-packed fibres on the collecting surface.

rare and tension differences are small. Some migration does, however, take place. The triangular section has to change to a circular one, necessitating some collapse at the corners which leads to local migration. In the case of an

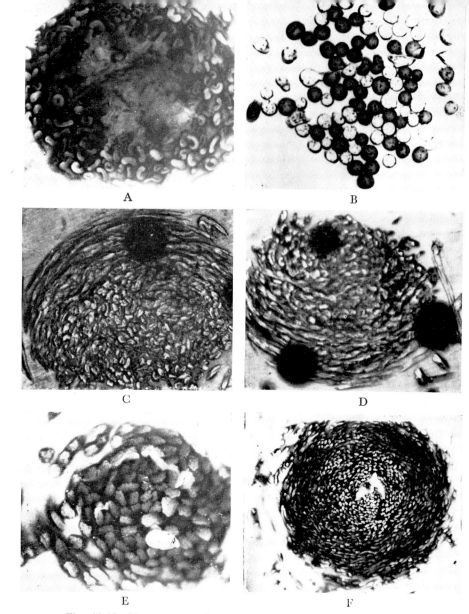

Fig. 10.15 Yarn cross-sections produced by various drum spinners.
(a) A commercial prototype machine. (b) Prototype MS 400 machine.
(c) U.M.I.S.T. experimental machine. (d) U.M.I.S.T. experimental
machine. (e) BD 200 commercial machine. (f) Experimental SACM-type
machine.

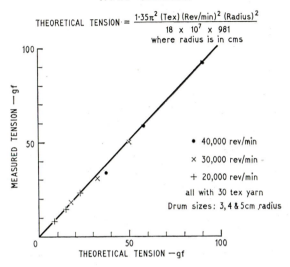

Fig. 10.16

asymmetrical cross-section, such as that shown in Fig. 10.7*, the centroid is moved causing an increased amount of migration.

Yarn Structure

The above effect may be demonstrated by using a model in which woollen strands represent the individual fibres. When such a system is twisted, the dense, well-organised portion tends to move to the centre, and the less dense, poorly-organised material is wrapped round this core in a helical fashion. Since such a helix consumes more length, the wrapped portion is presumably stretched, helping to straighten the fibres there. A photograph of the strands in a model of this sort is shown in Fig. 10.14. The light strands (50% of the total) represent the dense portion of the system.

* See page 188

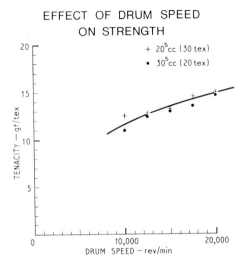

Fig. 10.17

Variations in the rotor design can have a marked effect on the fibre behaviour at that point and it is possible for quite large differences to show in the cross-section micrographs of yarn from various break-spinning machines (Fig. 10.15).

The migration which occurs in break spinning is an important factor in yarn quality. The migration pattern is, however, different from that of a ring-spun yarn, and the characteristics of the two types of yarn are different too. Generally, the migration is more local in break-spun yarn with one layer being interlocked with adjacent ones rather than being locked through the whole structure. The increased abrasion resistance of break-spun yarn, for example, may be associated with this effect; a fibre removed from the yarn surface would not affect the internal structure of the yarn to any great extent.

SOME RESULTS FROM THE U.M.I.S.T. SPINNER

Material	Spinner	Twist Factor	Linear Density Tex	Tenacity gf/Tex
$1\frac{7}{16}''$ Egyptian Cotton	Ring	3·3	29	21·1
	3″ Drum	5·2	34	18·7
	2″ Drum	5·9	40	14·3
$1\frac{7}{16}''$ Viscose Rayon	Ring	3·5	30	12·5
	3″ Drum	3·9	31	10·0
	2″ Drum	5·5	37	8·5
$1\frac{7}{16}''$ Polyester	2″ Drum	7·0	36	14·3

Table 10.6

Tension and Yarn Strength

The tension in the yarn being withdrawn from the drum may be calculated from the centrifugal force acting on the radial portion of yarn. Its magnitude will depend on the yarn count, the drum radius and the square of the drum speed. Experiments have shown a close correlation with theory (Fig. 10.16) and it is apparent that increased tensions are associated with some improvements in strength. The actual measured tension may be merely symptomatic of the true causes, and therefore almost irrelevant. The increased centrifugal force acting on the yarn formation zone (i.e. the delta zone) is probably more important; this and the yarn tension are directly linked. The increased fibre tensions during assembly and the increased fibre tension *differences* are probably direct causes of changes in the yarn structure. Spinning at higher speeds appears to produce stronger yarns (see Fig. 10.17).

Experience with the U.M.I.S.T. spinner suggests that the loss in average strength need only be very small, especially when a larger drum is used (see Table 10.6). The excellent results with this machine are probably due to the care taken in designing the fibre feed system.

Regularity

Table 10.7 gives irregularity figures from the Leeds experiments in which the drum speed was varied from 15,000 to 20,000 rev./min. and the front roller speed of the drafting system from 1,000 to about 3,000 rev./min. Increase in drum speed improved yarn regularity to some extent, but variation in front roller speed was found to be more significant. Air currents produced by the high operating speed of the front roller may play a major role in regularity deterioration at high speeds.

When spinning with a radially-fed drum machine, asymmetry in the air flow (such as that caused by blocking some of the air pumping holes) caused a marked deterioration in evenness, but with a tangentially-fed drum machine similar conditions caused only a slight deterioration.

Wrapper Fibres

Wrapper fibres arise from premature capture of fibres by the outgoing yarn (see page 256). The inclusion of a separator plate influences the formation of wrapper fibres, and yarn hairiness is much decreased (Fig. 10.18). As might

EFFECT OF DRUM SPEED AND FRONT ROLLER SPEED

	COEFFICIENT OF VARIATION				IRREGULARITY INDEX			
Drum speed (rev/min)	15,000		20,000		15,000		20,000	
Front roller speed (rev/min)	1,000	2,850	1,000	2,850	1,000	2,850	1,000	2,850
Linear density (tex)								
30	13·1%	14·7%	12·2%	12·0%	1·67	1·88	1·61	1·59
20	14·4%	16·4%	13·9%	15·8%	1·41	1·60	1·39	1·58
15	17·2%	18·5%	15·8%	18·6%	1·46	1·57	1·49	1·76

Table 10.7

be expected, reduction in the number of non load-bearing wrapper fibres increases the load carrying capacity of the yarn. The use of a separator can also reduce yarn tension, enabling yarn to be spun at a lower twist factor.

LIMITATIONS OF THE SYSTEM

In the flow of fibres through the system, mass flow must be conserved and the product of the number of fibres in the flow cross-section and the fibre velocity must always be constant. Consider two positions, viz., the yarn withdrawal point and the point where fibres are deposited on the collecting surface:

$$V_s K_s = V_y K_y \quad \text{......(Eq. 10.1)}$$

but $V_s = \pi DN$ inches/min. where $D =$ drum diameter in inches

$N =$ drum speed in rev./min.

$K_s =$ number of fibres per layer deposited on collecting surface.

$V_y = \dfrac{N}{\text{t.p.i.}}$ inches/min. where t.p.i. = twist per inch in yarn.

$K_y = \dfrac{n_y}{n_f}$ where $n_y =$ linear density of yarn in tex.

where $n_f =$ linear density of fibre in tex.

Assuming $n_f = 0.2$ tex and re-arranging:

$$(\text{t.p.i.}) = \frac{5 N n_y}{DK_s} \quad \text{......(Eq. 10.2)}$$

In the English cotton count system this may be expressed:

$$(\text{t.p.i.}) \simeq \frac{1000}{DK_s(\text{c.c.})} \quad \text{......(Eq. 10.3)}$$

and twist factor $\simeq \dfrac{1000}{DK_s(\text{c.c.})^{1.5}} \quad \text{......(Eq. 10.4)}$

where (c.c.) = yarn count.

Thus for a given drum operating at a constant twist factor, $K_s(\text{c.c.})^{1.5}$ must remain constant. In other words, it is possible to alter the count being spun only by changing the number of fibres in the layer approaching the collecting surface, or by altering the twist factor. Assuming the latter alteration to be undesirable, any limitation in the number of fibres per layer on the supply side will also limit the count which can be spun. Hence, a break-spinning machine with a poor fibre supply system will be unable to spin coarse counts except at a high twist factor. The pattern can be seen in Table 10.8 where, for instance, if no more than 3 fibres/layer are permitted in the entry duct, it will not be possible to spin coarser than about 10s c.c. at a reasonable twist factor. On the other hand, to spin 2s c.c. it is necessary to be able to handle 12 fibres /layer (this is possible: see page 178). The use of a larger diameter drum eases the situation.

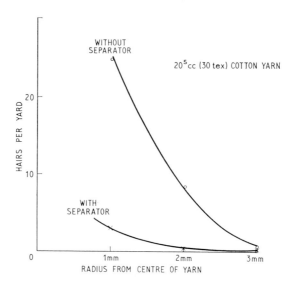

Fig. 10.18

Because of the relationship between the yarn count and Ks, the doubling factor does not alter in the way that might be expected. For very coarse counts, the doubling factor is reduced rather than increased; Table 10.9 shows how it varies.

For the finest yarn, the doubling factor is between 100 and 200; with the coarsest yarns, the doubling factor declines to between 50 and 100. This means that the coarser yarns are not likely to have such a low index of irregularity.

ECONOMICS

The foregoing has shown that as far as quality is concerned, it is desirable to use as large a drum as possible. With a large drum, the doubling factor is increased, coarser yarns can be spun, and the percentage of bridging fibres is smaller; as a result, the number of fibre hooks and the unevenness are reduced. In every respect except economy and safety, the larger the drum the better.

The bursting speed of a rotor is inversely proportional to its

Fibres/layer of entering fibres	$= K_s \longrightarrow$	1	3	6	12	
English c.c.	tex					
30^S	20	2·9				
15^S	40	8·2	2·7			
7^S	80	23.	7·7	3·9		Twist
5^S	120		14.	7·1	3·5	Factor
3^S	200			12.	7·5	
2^S	300				14.	

Diameter of collecting surface = 2 inches

Table 10.8

Fibres/layer of entering fibres	$= K_s \longrightarrow$	1	3	6	12	
English c.c.	tex					
30^S	20	100				
15^S	40	200	67			⎫
7^S	80	400	133	67		⎬ Doubling
5^S	120		200	100	50	⎱ Factor
3^S	200			167	83	⎭
2^S	300				125	

Diameter of collecting surface = 2 inches

◄ Line of
Reasonable
Twist
Factor

Table 10.9

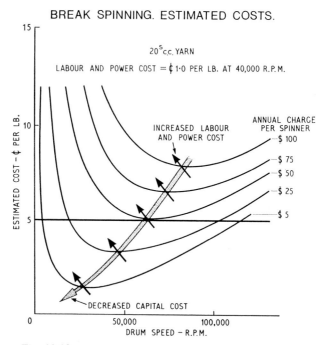

Fig. 10.19

BREAK SPINNING. ESTIMATED COSTS.

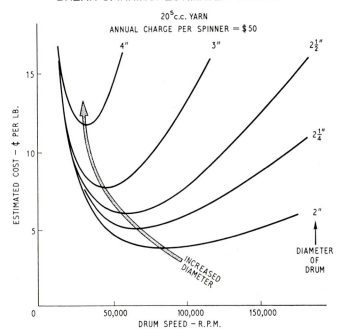

Fig. 10.20

diameter; this sets a limit on the size of drum. The drum must be larger for long staple than for short staple fibres; the speed of the long staple spinner must therefore be reduced to within safe limits.

The costs of converting sliver or roving into yarn derive in the main from three components viz., capital, labour and power costs. At present, the capital costs of break-spinning machines are high; with continued development and competition, these costs will fall. In general terms, the annual cost of this capital element per pound of yarn will reduce hyperbolically with machine speed, but the power cost will increase as (machine speed) [2.6]. Power cost will also increase as (rotor diameter) [3.8] and a large high speed rotor will consume an appreciable amount of power. Since the gains in respect of reduced labour costs are offset by high annual charges, power consumption could be a critical factor. The effect of an increase in drum diameter is shown in Fig. 10.20; not only is the cost per lb. of yarn increased but the optimum speed is reduced. The figures shown are estimated, but they suggest that an increase in drum diameter from $2\frac{1}{4}$ in. to 3 in. would increase the cost at optimum speeds by about 55%

Fig. 10.19 shows how optimum speeds are likely to move as the capital, labour and power costs are varied. In the future, labour cost will probably increase and the capital cost of the machines will fall. Both trends will reduce the optimum speed at which the machines should run; it is likely, therefore, that in the future they will run at speeds less than those technologically possible. The situation will not be dissimilar to that already existing in ring spinning, and production levels will be much higher.

11

The BD 200 Break-spinning Machine

The Czech B.D.200 machine is the first break spinner to enter commercial use, and data relating to its performance are now available. In this chapter, evidence from a number of sources is brought together to show how the machine performs in practice. The types of material produced are described and their characteristics are considered.

1. CZECHOSLOVAKIAN COTTON INDUSTRY RESEARCH INSTITUTE*

Introduction

By 1967, the initial development phase in break spinning was coming to an end. In that year, textile experts from many parts of the world attended the opening of the first break-spinning pilot plant in Czechoslovakia. Break-spinning machines have since come into operation in various countries, and by the end of 1968 a new break-spinning mill equipped with BD 200 machines, produced under licence by the Toyoda Co., was opened in Japan by the Daiwa Co. In England, BD 200 machines are operated by Courtaulds Ltd.

* Part 1 of this chapter is based on the lectures given by Z. Pospíšil, Deputy Director of the Czechoslovakian Cotton Industry Research Institute (V.U.B.) and J. V. Kasparek of the same Institute at U.M.I.S.T. in April 1969.

211

YARNS MADE ON THE BD 200 MACHINE
by J. V. Kasparek

Yarns made on BD 200 machines differ from ring-spun carded yarns, particularly in terms of variations in weight/unit length. This assessment is based on test results obtained from the V.U.B. mill in Czechoslovakia, measurements being made largely on Uster Laboratory equipment. The tested yarns ranged from 15 to 50 tex and the mean irregularity of the break-spun yarns has been compared with Uster world standards. The linear evenness of break-spun yarns down to 25 tex is below the line denoting the 5% level of world production; it is closer to the ideal curve than that of conventional carded yarns, as shown in Fig. 11.1.

Imperfections

Imperfections were studied by means of an Uster indicator, which counts thick and thin places, as well as neps, on a yarn running between condenser plates. The small number of thick and thin places in yarns from the BD 200 machine showed that it produced far fewer imperfections than the ring frame. Also, the number of neps was low as compared with the world standard for cotton carded yarns. In establishing the regularity of break-spun yarns, Uster spectrograms were made, showing the relationship between yarn irregularity and error wavelength. It was noted that the position of maximum amplitude was shifted towards the shorter wavelength region of the spectrum as compared to the theoretical curve; this is thought to be due to the internal structure of these yarns. The improved evenness and the reduced number of imperfections of these yarns result in an even, pleasant appearance in the final products.

Shape

One of the characteristics of a yarn is its external shape. A photometric measuring device was used to determine the

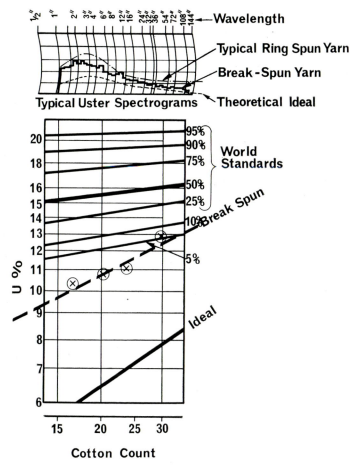

Fig. 11.1 Comparison of regularity of break-spun yarn with the Uster standards.

shape of ring- and break-spun yarns. Kasparek [24] reported that a sample of yarn 2 cm. long was fastened between two clips having a common axis of rotation, forming a holder capable of being turned bodily to any required angle. An

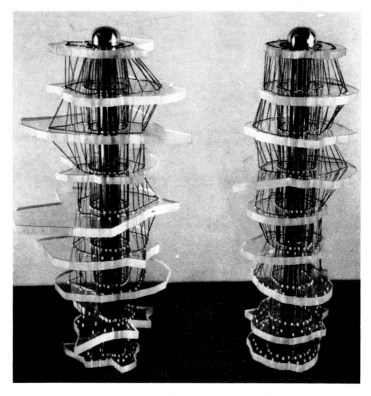

Fig. 11.2   Geometrical model of yarn structure. *Left:* Ring-spun yarn.
Right: Break-spun yarn.

enlarged shadow of the yarn sample was projected on to a
slit, behind which a photocell was placed. This enabled a
photometric measurement to be made of the light passing
through and around the yarn. A piece of yarn of 29.4 tex
was turned gradually about its axis and measurements were
made perpendicular to that axis. The shapes of the yarn
core and of the fibres surrounding it were determined and
this information was used in creating a geometrical model

as shown in Fig. 11.2. Comparison of the two models shows differences in the spacial arrangement of the fibres in the two cases. The cross-sectional shape of the ring-spun yarn was approximately circular, but the break-spun samples were roughly oval. This is a parameter which can be changed by the design of the machine.

Structure

The core of the BD 200 yarn contained between 75% and 87% of all the fibres. Despite the higher twist of the break-spun yarn, fibres were not so densely packed as in the ring-spun yarn. In fact, the break-spun yarn was bulkier than an equivalent ring-spun yarn. In the model, the individually-measured yarn sections were represented by shaped plates, and the zones were outlined by coloured threads; the sections were each separated by 2 mm. and the distance apart of the plates was scaled accordingly. Kasparek's model shows how the appearance of the yarn changes from one section to another, and it is clear that the break-spun yarn has a generally smoother appearance.

Some features of break-spun yarn appear to be in contradiction to normal mill experience. Compared with ring-spun yarns, they are more even, and despite the higher twist factor, they are not so strong. Break-spun yarns are bulkier, but they reach about the same number of cycles in fatigue tests as equivalent ring-spun carded yarns. The internal structure of the yarns was studied in the hope of finding an explanation of these facts. The parallelism and extent of hooking of the fibres in the yarn were assessed, using a method similar to that of Urano[25].

The yarn was cut into lengths which were a fraction of the staple length, and comb-sorter diagrams were made and analysed. If all the fibres were straight and perfectly aligned, a diagram similar to that shown in Fig. 11.3(a) would be obtained. If, however, some of the fibres were disposed obliquely, such fibres when cut and combed parallel would

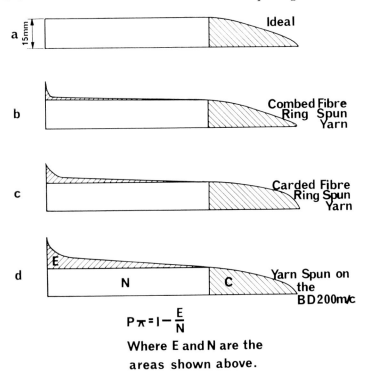

Fig. 11.3   Staple diagrams from cut sections of cotton yarns 15 mm long.

be longer than the majority. Similarly, if the knee of a hook occurred between the cutting planes, these hooked fibres would be considerably longer than the majority. Also, any departure from straightness of a fibre in the cut zone would cause some overlength fibres to be produced. Urano analysed such comb-sorter diagrams by judging the amount of fibre overlength relative to the basic staple length.

Kasparek related the areas of the various parts of the diagrams as shown in Fig. 11.3(d). A length of 15 mm. was

SOME VALUES OF FIBRE PARALLELISM FACTOR FOR COTTON YARNS

Linear Density in Tex	20	30	36	
Combed/Ring Spun Yarn	0.92	0.92	—	
Carded/Ring Spun Yarn	0.90	0.88	0.89	$P\pi$
BD 200 Yarn	0.74	0.78	0.81	

Table 11.1

chosen because a 20 mm. cut did not give so much difference between the samples. A so-called fibre parallelism factor $P\pi$ was defined according to Lindsley by the relationship $P\pi = 1 - \dfrac{E}{N}$, where E was the area occupied by the excess fibre lengths in the staple diagram, and N was the basic area of the diagram without the short fibres C (all these areas are defined in Fig. 11.3(d)). The greater the value of $\dfrac{E}{N}$, the greater was the proportion of hooks and non-straight fibres, and the lower was the strength of the yarn, In other words, the strength of the yarn increased with $P\pi$.

The method was not exact; staple arrays prepared by skilled workers from the same stock showed differences in the effective length of up to $1\frac{1}{2}$ mm. Also, the analysis was laborious. Despite these disadvantages, however, the technique provided a method of comparing the various types of yarn, and it was found that $P\pi$ could be related to yarn strength. The lower three diagrams in Fig. 11.3 are drawn from actual diagrams from various yarns; differences can be noted which agree with the known characteristics of the yarns.

Break spun yarns contain a greater number of hooked fibres than ring-spun yarns, and fibre orientation is poorer

H

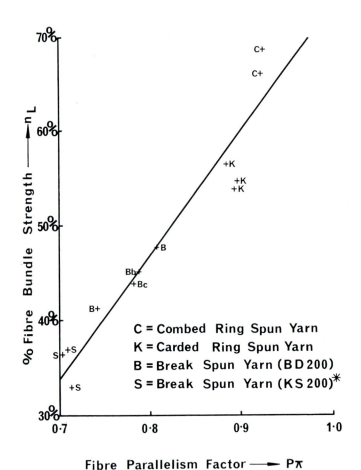

Fig. 11.4   Yarn strength as a function of fibre parallelism.

(see Table 11.1). This is consistent with the greater number of long fibres in the Urano staple diagram, and with the lower number found in combed yarns. An analysis of several yarns was made and the results showed that break-spun yarns were bulkier and weaker than the equivalent conventional yarn. In fact, a correlation between strength and the factor $P\pi$ showed how the relative strengths varied (see Fig. 11.4). In this case, the strength was expressed in a non-dimensional form which related the actual strength to that which could possibly be obtained (i.e. the total fibre strength). This expression was:—

$$n_L = \frac{\text{actual yarn tenacity}}{\Sigma \text{ single fibre tenacity}}$$

When n_L was plotted against $P\pi$, the coefficient of correlation was 0.959 ± 0.023 which proved a dependance. The relationship could be expressed in the form:—

$$n_L = 1.32P\pi - 0.59 \quad\text{................(Eq. 11.1)}$$

The difference in the structure of cotton yarns made by the various systems of spinning was thus explained in terms of the parallelism and "hookiness" of the fibres.

Properties

Differences in the properties of yarns spun on the two types of spinning frame became more apparent during processing. Due to their different structure, break-spun yarns were more sensitive to changes in tension, and care had to be exercised in subsequent processing. A study was made to compare the behaviour of the two kinds of yarn, particularly as regards changes in elongation and fatigue characteristics. Samples of yarn were tested at three stages, viz., after spinning, sizing and weaving; Fig. 11.5 shows the stress/strain diagrams of both sorts of yarn after each of these stages. The break-spun yarn behaved like a conventional yarn, but there were differences. The operation of sizing increased the yarn stiffness and it improved the yarn strength, but repeated straining during weaving reduced the

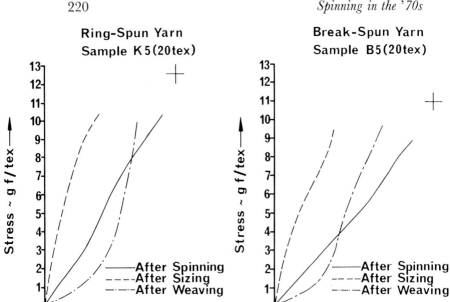

Fig. 11.5   The effect of processing spun yarns.

stiffness again. The latter effect was more noticeable with conventional yarns at strains below 5%. Many workers have shown that fatigue phenomena are related to the processing involved, the amount of working of the yarns being an important factor. Kasparek examined the resistance to cyclic strain by a Kukin pulsator type PK-3 at a frequency of 475 cycles/min with a test length of 500 mm. The results of this experiment showed that resistance of both kinds of yarn against cyclic strain was practically identical, although some results suggested a slight superiority in the break-spun yarns. This phenomenon was studied in greater detail, because of the anomaly that break-spun yarns have lower average

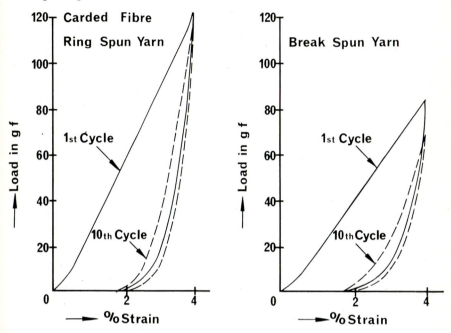

Fig. 11.6

strengths and yet show comparable resistance to repeated deformation. Experiments at V.U.B. showed that at higher values of cyclic deformation, break-spun yarn was more resistant to repeated deformation because its structure consisted of fewer aligned fibres. In break-spun yarn, a displacement of fibres occurred in the first deformation stage, but this was followed by partial alignment and stabilisation of the structure. In loading both the ring- and break-spun yarns to a constant tension of 5 gf/tex, the curve area of the break-spun yarn was greater than that of the conventional yarn. When tested at a constant elongation of 4%, the ring-spun yarn had the greater area, as shown in Fig. 11.6. Also, the ratio of areas was more or less main-

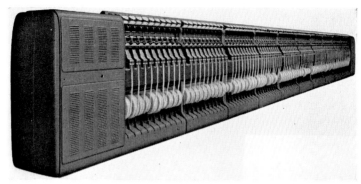

Fig. 11.7   *Above:* General view of the BD 200 break-spinning machine, and (*right*) a close-up view showing how access is gained to the spinning drum.

tained, at least over the first ten cycles. The constant extension behaviour is more typical of the treatment an actual yarn receives, and therefore deserves greater attention.

In a perfectly elastic yarn, the load-extension curve would be a single line, and the hysteresis area would be zero. In a real yarn, however, fibres move over one another, and frictional forces between the fibres play a part. The greater the friction, the greater is the area of the hysteresis curve; this area can be expressed in terms of energy lost per cycle. It is apparent from Fig. 11.6 that, at constant extension, the energy loss per cycle of the break-spun yarns was smaller. This infers that a superior performance could be expected during weaving.

During processing, these and other yarn characteristics— such as the enhanced resistance to surface abrasion—play a part in determining the behaviour of the yarn.

OPERATING THE BD 200 MACHINE
by Z. Pospíšil

In the V.U.B. mill in Czechoslovakia, ten BD 200 break-spinning machines were installed, operating at 30,000 rev./min. Sliver was prepared on S.A.C.M. Flocomat equipment and the mill produced a range of yarn counts from 15 to 50 tex, mainly from Russian cotton of grades I and II. The mill was provided with air conditioning to 22°C (72°F) and 55% relative humidity. The long-term end-breakage rate confirmed the first experience, end-breakage rate per pound of yarn being the same as with ring spinning [26]. A yarn breakage can be repaired in about 12 to 13 seconds, and a skilled spinner takes not more than four months to train.

A photograph of a machine is shown in Fig. 11.7 and its specification is given in Table 11.2. It will be noticed that the twist required was somewhat higher than normal; the coefficient of variation of twist, 4.3%, corresponds to the normal value. The bobbin-to-bobbin yarn evenness was

SOME TYPICAL RESULTS FROM VARIOUS SPINNING PROCESSES

Sample of Cotton Yarn	Ring-Spun Combed Yarn		Ring-Spun Carded Yarn		Break-Spun BD 200 Yarn		Break-Spun yarn, Old-Type Machine	
Yarn Count	18.4	31.4	18.5	32.2	19.8	31.3	20.5	29.9
Metric Twist Coefficient Qm.	68.8	74.7	66.8	76.7	87.6	86.5	100.5	101.0
Tenacity (gf/tex)	15.2	15.8	12.6	13.4	9.5	10.4	7.6	8.4
Uster Evenness (U%)	14.01	12.46	15.63	14.57	10.57	12.53	10.99	10.08

Table 11.2

BD 200 MACHINE SPECIFICATION

Total number of spinning heads	200 in ten sections of 20
Machine length	14.85 km....
,, height	1.64 km.... Floor area 10.4 sq. m.
,, width	0.70 km....
,, weight	7000 kg. (15000 lb.)
Pitch between spinning units	120 mm. (4.7 in.)
Power installed	
to spinning units	2 × 7.5 kW
to thinning units	2 × 2.2 kW
to feed and take-off	1.5 kW
Power consumed at 30,000 rev./min. spinning speed and 8,000 rev./min. thinning rotor speed	16 kW out of a total of 20.9 kW installed.
Staple length of fibres	25 mm. to 40 mm. (1 in. to 1.6 in.)
Linear density of slivers	4.0 to 22.2 k/tex.
Singles yarn linear density	15 to 50 tex
Yarn take-off rate	800 to 2160 inches/min.
Yarn package weight	1.2 kg. (2.6 lb.)
Spinning speed	25,000 and 30,000 rev./min.
Thinning rotor speed	7,000 and 8,000 rev./min.
Twist insertion rate	14 to 38 t.p.i.
Draft range in the thinning mechanism	25 to 440

within $\pm 2\%$, and the overall coefficient of variation of yarn evenness compared favourably with that of normal yarn. The mean strength of the yarn was no more than about 10% to 20% lower than the Czech standards. The frequency diagrams of conventional yarns exhibited practically the same quantity of thick and thin places as break-spun yarns. Thin places were no stronger than the corresponding places in break-spun yarns. This factor affected the breakage rates in further processing, such as weaving; evidence given elsewhere in this chapter suggests that other factors may also play a part.

The preservation of extensibility in short staple yarns

is of major importance in further processing; and in this respect break-spun yarns show to advantage [26]. A mill test was devised to show the effect of yarn tension on the character of finished fabric. Although it was difficult to maintain different constant tensions in the experimental sizing device, sufficient information was obtained to show that strength figures of the finished fabric varied with yarn tension during sizing. The strength of the fabric made from yarn sized under the lowest tension was 30% higher than that of fabric sized in the normal way.

A comparison of warp breakage rates during weaving showed that break-spun yarns suffered only 88% of the end breaks normally occurring in the weaving of combed cotton. 20 tex yarns of both types were processed under mill conditions into shirting fabric with a construction of 100 ends and 60 picks per inch. The yarns were sized on a Sucker sizing machine equipped with a device for accurately controlling yarn tension. Both the conventional and break-spun yarns were woven as warp and weft on the same Czech K58 loom. The warp breaks with the new yarn were 30% and the weft breaks 75% of those obtained using conventional yarn.

Since 1967, when the production of break-spun yarn began, some hundreds of thousands of yards of fabric of various sorts have been produced in the V.U.B. pilot plant and elsewhere in Czechoslovakia. During this time, critical observations were made and the following processing requirements were formulated.

Warping

During warping, the tubes on which yarn is wound must be held firmly; this may be done by using special inserts on the creel pins. In producing yarn cheeses of large diameter, it is recommended that the cheeses be creeled in such a way that the yarns unwind in one direction only; this eliminates the risk of yarn balloon entanglement. When these con-

H*

ditions were satisfied, good results were obtained, even on high-speed warpers. Pirns could be wound straight from the cheeses, providing the packages were firmly anchored and precisely positioned to ensure central unwinding. At all stages of processing, the yarn should be held under low stress; otherwise it may lose some of its valuable extensibility. The maintenance of extensibility was an essential requirement for satisfactory weaving, ensuring a neat appearance in the finished fabric.

Sizing

In the sizing of break-spun yarn, it was advantageous to use modern sizing machines capable of controlling the warp tension. Yarn tension was kept as low as possible, especially in the yarn immersion section, over the squeezing rollers and up to the first drying drum of the machine. Very good results were obtained by using modified starches in sizing; it was advantageous to use a concentration of fat auxiliaries in the sizing recipe higher than that normally used. Such sizes have low viscosity and penetrate easily into the yarn core. The open structure of the break-spun yarn ensures that size absorption is increased; the yarn is thus reinforced satisfactorily.

If good quality sliver was used, the processing of break-spun yarns, in general, presented no unusual problems.

Man-made Fibres

Yarns were spun from blends of 67% cotton/33% rayon and 67% polyester (2.5 den, 38 mm.)/33% rayon (2.8 den, 38 mm.). On the BD 200 machine the staple is limited to a maximum of 40 mm.

The following conditions were established as being essential to the satisfactory processing of man-made fibres:—

1. The loose stock must not incorporate "married" fibres which are difficult to separate and cause breakages.

2. The loose stock must not incorporate uncut fibres of greater than twice the nominal staple length.

3. The antistatic lubrication on the fibres should be sufficiently permanent to withstand the conditions involved in high speed break-spinning.

4. Careful attention should be paid to sliver preparation.

Any system adapted to process fibres up to 40 mm. ($1\frac{9}{16}$ in.) could be used for sliver preparation, including converter systems capable of producing staple of the correct length without a significant number of overlength fibres. The preparation of sliver was of vital importance, good quality sliver being essential. Joined fibres and impurities caused breakages in spinning. Long fibres caused lapping of the combing roller, leading to the formation of neps and the accumulation of fibres under the separator, which impaired yarn quality.

The sliver can be fed to the BD 200 machine from bobbins or cans; the type of feed used depends upon the material in use. Winding should be harder for fibres of lower elasticity. If winding is too hard, however, deformation of the sliver tends to become set, impairing the passage of sliver through the feeding device. Under such conditions, fibre clumps were sometimes torn out by the combing roller; these were likely to cause breakages. A loose sliver did not pass satisfactorily through the feeding device or through the combing zone where the fibre fringe was decomposed even out of reach of the combing roller. The sliver count should be 3.8 Ktex or less and the clothing wires should be chosen according to the material being processed. The same wires could be used for rayon and cotton, but it was preferable to use wires with a smaller filling capacity and a smaller tooth density when processing synthetic fibres.

The speed of the combing roller is an important factor in processing, and it is essential to find the optimum speed for particular fibres. In 1969, the recommended speed for viscose fibres was 5,000 to 7,000 rev./min., whereas for synthetic fibres it was 6,000 to 8,000 rev./min. With correct setting, a smooth passage of the sliver through the feeding device could be ensured. Under these conditions, satisfactory fibre combing, fibre delivery, and fibre deposition in the spinning rotor could be attained. A lower twist factor could be used for rayon fibres than for cotton.

Polyester/Viscose Blend

A 40s metric (26 tex) break-spun blended yarn was made from a mixture of 70% polyester and 30% viscose fibres, the polyester having a staple length of 38 mm. and fineness $2\frac{1}{4}$ denier and the rayon 40 mm. and 2.75 denier respectively. The yarn was spun to a twist factor of about 5 (9.9 t.p.c.) and it had a mean strength of 10.1 gf/tex and a breaking extension of 18.1%. This yarn was used as warp and weft in a weaving experiment. Further processing was carried out without difficulty and breakage rate was very low. The sett of the fabric using conventional yarn was 180 ends and 172 picks per 10 cm;. the warp strength was 74.8 kg. and weft strength was 66.4 kg. The sett of the fabric made from break-spun yarn was 182 ends and 184 picks per 10 cm.; the warp and weft strengths were 54.6 kg. and 54.7 kg. respectively. The pilling effects of the fabrics were different; fabric from the conventional yarn exhibited on average 50 pills per 25 sq. cm., and that from the break-spun yarns showed only 40 pills per 25 sq. cm. The size of the pills was about the same. The angle of recovery after 5 and 60 minutes indicated that conventional yarn tends to crease less than break-spun yarn.

These mill results indicated that there is wide scope for break-spun yarns in the textile industry. The high evenness of the yarns, in particular, makes for fabrics of excellent appearance. Important potential applications are to be found in the production of terry fabrics, dress materials, bedding, pile and decorative fabrics, napkin, twills and sateens.

2. COTTON SPINNING AND TWISTING RESEARCH CENTRE, KARL-MARX-STADT, GERMAN DEMOCRATIC REPUBLIC*

With cotton, fibre cleanliness was found to be of particular importance. A blowing plant produced cotton stock containing less than 0·3% impurities by weight, but this was unsatisfactory; the yarn breakage rate in spinning was very high. Great attention was paid to improving the blow room performance, and the impurities were reduced to 0.22% with some 10 hard particles and some 60 neps per gramme of carded web. The spinning performance was, in consequence, improved by 10% to 20% in terms of end breakage rate (to about 1.2 end breakages per lb. of spun yarn).

Heavy accumulations of dust affected the breaking tenacity of the yarn by up to $1\frac{1}{2}$ gf/tex, and deterioration of this order could take place after about 100 hours of running. It was apparent that great care is needed in preparing the sliver used in break spinning; extra cost incurred at this stage yields substantial benefits in later stages.

Cutting

Tests with man-made fibres showed that good cutting is essential; over-length fibres cause trouble, especially by collecting behind the separator. When spinning a 30 tex polyamide yarn, the addition of 1% of $2\frac{1}{2}$ in. fibres raised the breakage rate to 1.34/lb. of yarn. When the length of the added fibres was increased to about 4 in., the breakage rate remained unchanged. With a 20 tex yarn, however, the rate increased from about 2 to 3 breaks/lb. respectively. Without overlength fibres, the breakage rate was immeasurably small. This experience stresses the importance

* Part 2 of this chapter is based on a report of the paper given by S. Geissler of the Cotton Spinning and Twisting Research Centre, Karl-Marx-Stadt, German Democratic Republic in Prague in March 1969.

of good cutting in preparing man-made material for break-spinning.

Crimp

Other experiments were carried out using polyacrylic fibres with varying crimp. Uncrimped fibres were readily spun, the breakage rates being below 2.5/lb. even when spinning 20 tex yarn. When crimped fibres were used, however, the experiments had to be discontinued because of the high breakage rate. Coarse, uncrimped fibres of proper length (40 mm.) also gave excessive end breaks. These results are in line with those of other workers experimenting with break spinners, confirming that coarse and crimped fibres do not spin satisfactorily. It is clear that dirty, stiff or overlength fibres are likely to cause trouble.

Twist

Experiments showed that cotton needed 20%, polyacrylic fibres 100% and polyester/cotton up to 50% more twist than ring-spun yarn. On the other hand, rayon could be produced with about the same twist as ring-spun yarn. The measurement of twist in break-spun yarns is difficult, most forms of measurements giving a higher value than the true one. Nevertheless, the figures quoted are too high to be fully explained by this, and the reverse behaviour with rayon is significant. It is interesting to note that with some air vortex spinners, rayon can be spun in a given tube, and twist will be in the direction opposite to that of cotton spun in the same tube. The reason is to be found in the different frictional properties of rayon and cotton; it is possible that these differences also cause rayon and cotton to behave differently in the BD 200 machine. Since the frictional characteristics can be modified by finishes applied to the fibre, the spinning behaviour of fibres could possibly be controlled by suitable treatment.

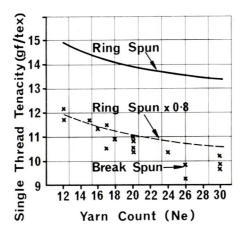

Fig. 11.8 Count/strength relationship for ring and break-spun yarns.

Fabrics

Break-spun yarns produced in the BD 200 machine were used in producing striped sateen, table cloths, shoe lining, stitching thread, night wear, diapers and plaster tapes. Knitted goods produced from the yarns were too hard to be entirely satisfactory. Spinning with lower twist factors could prove advantageous.

A disadvantage of the break-spinning technique lay in the extra care and cost involved in producing an acceptable sliver, but this was offset by the advantages derived from using break-spun yarns in weaving. As the economic advantage lies with the coarser counts, it is anticipated that heavier fabrics will provide a major outlet for break-spun yarns.

3. COURTAULDS LTD., U.K.*

BD 200 machines operated by Courtaulds Ltd., were the only break-spinning machines producing yarns commercially in the U.K. during 1969. Information in this section was derived from the operation of these machines, unless otherwise stated. Likewise, information concerning ring-spun yarns relates to commercial production from a mixing identical with that used for the break-spun yarns, unless otherwise stated. The BD 200 machine was designed for use with cotton, and the results relate only to this fibre.

The average tensile strength of a break-spun yarn is lower than that of an equivalent ring-spun yarn, as shown in Fig. 11.8. In this figure, the solid line represents averages for ring-spun yarn taken over a long period of time for the particular quality of cotton. The single points represent individual results representative of break-spinning production; the broken line illustrates the 80% level relative to the ring-spun control. It is apparent that the mean strength of a commercial break-spun yarn is about 20% lower than that of the ring-spun control, the precise difference depending upon count and twist. It has been suggested that the minimum breaking strength of break-spun yarn is as good as that of ring-spun yarn, because of the better coefficient of variation of the former. Evidence from commercially-produced yarn does not support this view, however, as is shown in Fig. 11.9; the histograms indicate the frequency of occurrence of various single thread breaking loads. The mean strength for the ring-spun yarn was 266 gf and the coefficient of variation 11.2%, whereas the mean strength of the break-spun yarn was 221 gf and the coefficient of variation 10.3%. Table 11.3 compares minimum strengths of the two types of yarn; it can be seen that, despite the better standard deviation, the minimum breaking load of

* Part 3 of this chapter is based on a lecture given by H. V. Shaw of Courtaulds Ltd., Manchester, U.K., at U.M.I.S.T. in April 1969.

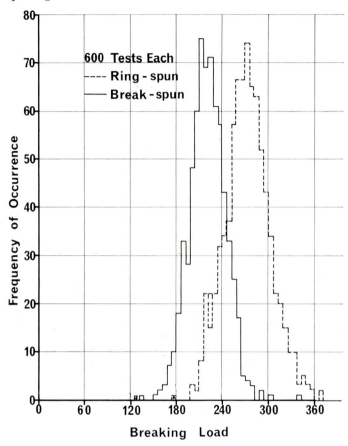

Fig.11.9 Histograms of single thread strength of 30s Ne (20 tex) ring- and break-spun yarns.

the break-spun yarn is some 15% lower than that of ring-spun yarn.

Fig. 11.10 shows the effect of twist on strength in both types of yarn. The count was 20s c.c. (30 tex) and the twist factor varied from 3.6 to 5.4; in this case the ring-spun controls were produced on a Shirley miniature spinning plant. With

COMPARISON OF MINIMUM STRENGTHS

Count c.c.	Linear Density Tex		Mean Breaking Load gf	Standard Dev- iation gf	Minimum Breaking Load gf
			a	b	a–3b
30s	20	RING SPUN	265.9	29.4	178
		BREAK SPUN	220.9	22.6	153
14s	43	RING SPUN	653	53.5	492
		BREAK SPUN	527	34.7	243

Table 11.3

a common twist factor of 4.4, the break-spun yarn strength was 80% of the control, but at the maximum strength for both sorts of yarn, the ratio was 85%. At a common twist factor of 5.1, the break-spun yarn had a strength similar to that of the ring-spun yarn. No data is available at a higher twist level, but the curves tend to converge; the difference in strength is likely to be insignificant at the higher twist values used in crepe and other high-twist yarns. There is evidence also of a difference in the ratios of lea to single end strength. Table 11.4 shows some lea and single end strengths brought to the same base for comparison. For ring-spun yarns, the ratio is almost constant at 0.76, but for break-spun yarns the values vary from 0.74 to 0.81. The reason for this is not known, but it may be due to differences in structure and frictional characteristics. Disregarding the results from 30s count yarn, it is apparent that break-spun yarns gain more from having external pressure applied to the outside of the yarn. Earlier tests with ring-spun man-made fibres indicated that regularity differences are not significant in this connection; it has been known for an irregular yarn to give a comparatively high lea strength,

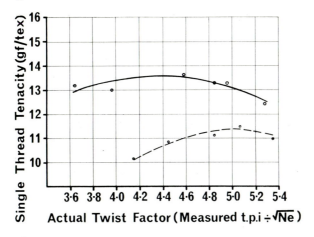

Fig. 11.10   Twist/strength relationship for 20s Ne ring- and break-spun yarns.

Another conclusion which may be drawn is that it is unwise to quote a single measure of strength for a yarn. For example, if lea strength had been plotted in Fig. 11.8 instead of single end strength, the relative balance would have been changed. In general, it is preferable to base judgement on the performance of the final product.

Neps

In addition to being more regular than ring-spun yarn, break-spun yarn is almost completely free from visible neps; it is also less hairy. Although neps are present in the sliver, they appear to remain embedded in the yarn and, in consequence, are rarely visible. Regularity curves typical of Courtaulds' production are given in Fig. 11.12, and blackboard wrappings are shown in Fig. 11.11. They demonstrate the superiority of the break-spun yarn.

COMPARISON OF LEA AND SINGLE THREAD
STRENGTHS

Count c.c.	RING SPUN			BREAK SPUN		
	Lea Strength gf/tex	Single Thread Strength gf/tex	Ratio	Lea Strength gf/tex	Single Thread Strength gf/tex	Ratio
12	11.5	14.9	0.77	9.3	12.0	0.77
15	11.0	14.4	0.76	8.9	11.6	0.76
17	10.8	14.1	0.765	8.9	11.0	0.81
20	10.6	13.9	0.76	8.5	10.6	0.80
24	10.3	13.7	0.75	8.2	10.3	0.80
30	10.1	13.4	0.75	7.3	9.9	0.74

Table 11.4

Extensibility; Strength

The failure of a yarn is caused by the applied load exceeding the yarn strength, and as the applied load is frequently a function of the extensibility of the yarn, extensibility is an important factor. Fig. 11.13 shows typical stress/strain curves obtained from an Instron tester. The non-linear behaviour of the break-spun yarn illustrates the possible dangers of overstraining the yarn. The differences in initial modulus are also significant. The breaking tenacity of break-spun yarn was only 73% of that of the ring-spun control yarn, whereas the initial modulus at 2% strain was about 84% of that of the ring-spun yarn. During weaving, therefore, a break-spun yarn would not suffer such a large load as the ring-spun equivalent; the end breakage rate would be much less than the 73% would indicate. It is probable that this factor contributes to the excellent weaving performance of break-spun yarns.

Fig. 11.11 Blackboard wrappings. *Left:* Break-spun yarn. *Right:* Ring-spun yarn.

Abrasion Resistance

The specific volume of break-spun yarns is approximately 10% greater than that of ring-spun yarns, despite the higher twist of the former. This is in conformity with the theory of a two-part yarn structure, which also influences the abrasion resistance of the yarn. Abrasion resistance was measured at a Courtaulds research laboratory, using a rig in which the yarn was threaded, looped around itself and then cycled until breaking point was reached. 12s c.c. (50 tex) yarns of both sorts were tested, in both the sized and unsized condition. Unsized ring-spun yarn broke after about 300 cycles. and sized yarn after about 750 cycles. In contrast, unsized break-spun yarn lasted for 4,900 cycles, and after sizing the figure *decreased* to about 1,700 cycles. These results have been confirmed by experiments carried out elsewhere, and there is no doubt that break-spun yarns are superior to conventional yarns in abrasion resistance. This is bound to have a significant effect on the performance of yarns during weaving or other processes.

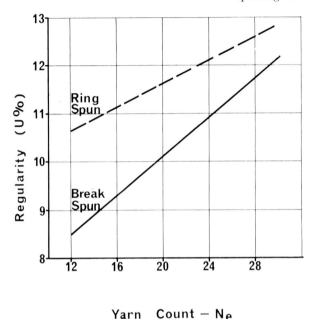

Fig.11.12   Measured regularity.

Sizing

The impairment of abrasion resistance of break-spun yarns by addition of size is further evidence of the characteristic structure of these yarns. The layered nature of break-spun yarn is probably responsible for much of the effect. Fibre migration is more localised in these yarns, and a surface fibre can be pulled away without greatly disturbing the core. Surface abrasion does not disintegrate a break-spun yarn to the extent that it does a ring-spun yarn. The addition of size restricts the freedom of the fibres, as does the interlacing of the yarns in a fabric, and some of the advantage is lost.

The differences in structure responsible for the greater

bulk of break-spun yarns also produce more voids in the yarn, break-spun yarns are able to absorb more liquid size than ring-spun yarns. It is necessary, therefore, to compensate by adjusting the concentration of size in the size bath, e.g. by a reduction of between 25% and 30%. Experience indicates that finer counts and high sett cloths are more critical in this respect; the effect of varying size concentration on coarser counts is less apparent in weaving. Stretch control in sizing is vitally important, and care must be taken to preserve the extensibility of yarns by limiting the stretch in sizing to about 1%; this ensures the maximum advantage in weaving. Providing this precaution is taken, the performance of break-spun yarns as warp is remarkably good.

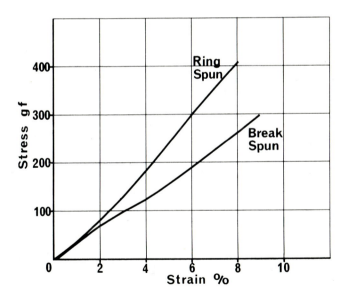

Fig. 11.13   Stress/strain relationship, 20s Ne ring- and break-spun yarn.

Breaks

The comparative performances of ring- and break-spun yarns may be expressed as the number of warp breaks per 10,000 picks per 1,000 ends, thus bringing them all to a comparable base. Results were obtained from the production of cloths of different widths in different weaving sheds; after bringing them to a common base, the degree of correlation was remarkably good. One of the weaving sheds was equipped with conventional looms, another with air-jet looms and a third with Sulzer weaving machines. The results are given in Table 11.5. The ratio between warp breaks when using the two sorts of yarn varied between 0.6 and 0.65 in favour of the break-spun yarn. The weft performance of break-spun yarn was also superior, the combined effect making it possible to increase the number of looms allocated to a weaver by as much as 50%. This improvement

WEAVING PERFORMANCE

Warp breaks per 10,000 picks per 1,000 ends.
Count-strength product shown in brackets.

Weaving Shed	Count in c.c.	Linear Density in tex	Warp Breaks/10,000 Picks/1,000 Ends Ring-Spun Yarn	Break-Spun Yarn
A	20's	30	0.198 (2200)	0.124 (1760)
B	24's	25	0.140 (2150)	0.093 (1700)
C	16's	37	0.153 (2250)	0.091 (1840)
	2/12's	2/50	0.365	0.232

Table 11.5

FABRIC

Group 1.	Group 2.	Group 3.	Group 4.
Satins	Denim	Filter cloths	Raised Fabrics
Sateens	Drills & Jeans	Backing	(Winceyette)
Poplins	Sheeting	Fabrics,	Crepe Fabrics,
Tablecloths	Printers	etc.	etc.
Filament	Drapes		
Warp/Spun	Brocades, etc.		
Weft, etc.			

Table 11.6

was effected in spite of the fact that the count strength product was only about 80% of that of the equivalent ring-spun yarns. Several factors contributed to the performance of the break-spun yarns, the high abrasion resistance being probably the most important.

Knitting

The established interlock fabric for underwear is produced mainly in counts of single 34s and single 38s in 100% cotton and blends. These counts were outside the range spun on break-spinning equipment in the U.K. in 1969, but satisfactory garments were made using coarser counts in fancy knit structures, and in eyelet or mesh constructions. Various constructions intended for outer-wear were also made from break-spun yarns with differing degrees of success. The structure of a knitted fabric tends to conceal small differences in yarn regularity; in fabrics where good quality carded yarns are used, the improved regularity of the break-spun yarn does not show to such advantage as in woven structures. This is particularly true of the eyelet or mesh type of construction.

The high twist factors used in break spinning can cause difficulties in knitting, but no problems are encountered on knitting machines equipped with positive feed devices. Allowance must be made in knitting for the additional bulk, either by adjusting the stitch length, or by using yarn of slightly finer count. If this is not done, the resulting fabric is stiff and boardy and unpleasant to handle. Plain constructions of knitted fabric are often used for casual shirtings, and yarn regularity is a more critical factor. For this reason, twofold yarns are commonly used in these structures, and a major price advantage results from replacement of these twofold yarns by single break-spun yarns. The high twist affects the tactile characteristics of the fabric, making the product more suitable for outer-wear than for under-wear. Knitting performance is good.

Woven Fabrics

Woven fabrics can be classified according to certain broad divisions as shown in Table 11.6. Group 1 represents fabrics for which appearance, evenness, regularity and cleanliness are of prime importance. Group 2 includes fabrics for which these characteristics are not of prime importance. Group 3 includes fabrics for which these characteristics are not at all important, the incentive to use break-spun yarns being purely one of cost. Group 4 includes those fabrics which use to advantage the special characteristics of break-spun yarns; a typical example is a crepe for which high-twist yarns are needed, the high-twist characteristics of break-spun yarns thus meeting the requirements.

All the fabrics listed under group 1 may be produced from break-spun yarns. The satins and sateens and the filament-warp spun-weft fabrics are made usually from combed yarns, which yield fabric of highly uniform appearance. The strength requirements of these fabrics are not critical, being secondary in importance to appearance. In the case of poplin constructions, however, resination in finishing may result in a reduction of strength of up to 50%; fabric strength is thus an important factor. The yarns

Fig. 11.14 A comparison of denim cloths. *Left:* Ring-spun weft. *Right:* Break-spun weft.

used for shirting poplins are at the fine end of the range spun on BD 200 machines. The fabric strength (after finishing) of poplins made from break-spun yarns in 1969 fell below the level of acceptability for this end use. This is therefore an example of an unsuitable use for break-spun yarns.

In the case of at least three of the fabrics listed in group 2 (where appearance is not of paramount importance), break-spun yarns improve the appearance of the product to such a degree that it enters a different field of potential use; the use of break-spun yarns thus upgrades the product.

In group 3, the introduction of break-spun yarns could change the pattern of use of different types of fabric. Denim, for example, was long regarded as a low quality functional fabric of poor appearance. The growing acceptance of denim as a fashion fabric stimulated interest in the improvement of its appearance. Fig. 11.14 is a photograph of two pieces of denim in which the warp, a ring-spun yarn dyed indigo blue, was common to both pieces of fabric. The fabric on the left has a ring-spun weft; the neps can be seen grinning through the surface of the warp and disturbing the smooth appearance. The fabric on the right had break-spun weft; the improved appearance is immediately apparent.

Similar results may be obtained in applications such as cotton sheeting, where improved appearance of the final product is an advantage. Domestic sheets have been produced from break-spun yarn with a 20s warp and weft construction; the tensile strength of the fabric averages only 76% of the normal ring-spun product, but the appearance is far superior. Several sets of these sheets were performing as well as ring-spun controls after being laundered 100 times.

Drill fabrics provide a third example of the effect of improved appearance due to the use of break-spun yarns. The regularity of the yarn and the absence of nep results in an extremely clear twill line, enabling drill fabrics to find novel end-uses. In the group 2 type of fabric, it is sometimes necessary to use a better cotton than that commonly used, but the improved results far outweigh the additional cost. The higher cost of yarn is offset by gains in weaving and winding performance, and by the increased fabric quality.

Fabrics made from break-spun yarns are particularly suitable for light raising during finishing. The raising process affects only the surface of the yarn which is easily disturbed; the dense core is not touched. As the surface fibres make little or no contribution to the strength of the yarn or fabric, the strength of the finished fabric is diminished, much less than it might otherwise have been. It must be stressed, however, that this advantage is restricted to lightly-raised fabrics. If a deep raise is required, such as that used for flannelette blankets, it is likely that the yarn core will be affected; deep raising is not successful. An experiment on two constructions of winceyette fabric showed that the weftwise strength loss due to raising was reduced from 48.5% to 27.5% by replacing ring-spun with break-spun yarn. The warpwise loss fell only from 15.3% to 13.8%, most of the raising being done in the weft. In the weft direction the difference was significant, suggesting that a raised break-spun fabric can be superior to the conventional product. In this particular case, the yarns used were not strictly comparable as it was difficult in commercial production to obtain the ideal conditions needed. The figures should be taken merely as a guide.

Conclusions

Courtaulds' experience conforms with that of Czech workers. The tensile and tear strengths of fabric from break-spun yarns were related to the tensile strengths of the yarns used. Abrasion resistance of the fabric was about the same as that of equivalent fabric from ring-spun yarn.

Established strength specifications have been built up on what was available in the past rather than on what is required in terms of use performance. Although differences in tensile strength may be disadvantageous where high performance characteristics are required of the product, this disadvantage may be over-emphasized. More often than not, it is freedom from end breaks during processing that is required, rather than a high breaking tenacity. Taking this into account, the balance of advantage may be in favour of the break-spun product. It is suggested that new standards should be established for most cloths, these standards being related to performance in use rather than to precedent.

Break-spun yarns are different from yarns produced by traditional methods of spinning, and the fabrics produced from them are likewise different. On balance, there are very real advantages to be gained by using break-spun yarns and the results described are extremely encouraging at such an early stage of development. Continued research will no doubt lead to higher yarn and fabric strengths, stimulating changes in the pattern of fabric end-uses.

12

Break Spinning of Synthetic Fibres using a Prototype MS400 Machine

by K. Susami*

Development work on break-spinning machines has been carried out in Japan, considerable attention being given to the spinning of synthetic fibres. The regularity of break-spun yarn is considered in some detail; as anticipated, regularity of such yarn is very good. The break spinner serves efficiently as a blender. Some of the difficulties encountered in spinning synthetic fibres are discussed. The market is assessed and requirements for future developments are outlined.

Introduction

In the manufacture of clothing, the cost of processes following the production of fibre is extremely high compared with the cost of the fibres themselves. This high cost of processing derives not only from spinning but from all the other processes, including weaving or knitting, dyeing, finishing and fabrication. It seems unlikely that mass production techniques will be applied to finishing and fabrication, at least in the foreseeable future. Spinning, however, is a process that may well be adapted effectively to mass production requirements.

Many novel techniques have been devised for spinning synthetic fibres. One of the most interesting is the process of tow spinning, especially the so-called "Direct Spinning System" in which yarn is formed in one step from a tow of 3,000 to 10,000 denier.

* Conference author. Toyo Rayon Co. Ltd., Japan.

246

During the 1940s, some 8,000 direct spinning spindles were established in Japan, and spun yarn was produced from viscose rayon tow. In Europe and America, various types of direct spinning machines were developed. Despite this promising beginning, however, direct spun yarn has not achieved real commercial success, and it is no longer in use to-day. The main reasons for the failure of direct spun yarns are as follows:— (1) tow costs were high compared with staple fibres, (2) uniform tow of high quality could not be obtained, (3) the draft-breaking process used produced a spun yarn with a high shrinkage, and its uses were limited on this account.

During recent years the uniformity of tow has improved, and production costs have fallen. If an adequate technique for cutting could be developed, it is probable that direct spinning could become of real importance in the synthetic fibre field.

At present, formidable difficulties remain, and several practical problems must be solved. In direct spinning, for example, a uniformly-blended yarn is seldom obtained; also, the ring and traveller system restricts spinning speed to less than 20 m/min.

In Japan, some ten million spindles are now operating on the cotton spinning system. About one third of these are used for spinning synthetic fibres and viscose rayon. The demand for synthetic spun yarn increases annually, yet the labour available diminishes every year. To meet the rising demand and bring about a substantial increase in the production of synthetic spun yarn, new techniques are required. The development of automatic and continuous spinning is an example of one such technique; break spinning is another. It seems probable that the production of break-spun yarn from synthetic fibres is destined to play a major role in the Japanese textile industry.

The Toyo Rayon Co., in co-operation with Howa Machinery Ltd., has been studying break spinning for several years, and considerable experience of this technique has been acquired. Some of the results of experimental work are described in this chapter.

The experiments were carried out with a drum-type spinning machine. The feeding mechanism consisted of a 4 line double apron drafting device, and the fibres were further opened and carried by an air stream. A 12 unit prototype machine was used in the experimental work, but a spinning machine of 200 "spindles" based on the same principles has already been in operation.

FIBRE MOTION IN DRAFTING AND ITS EFFECT ON THE QUALITY OF YARN

The drafting system was similar to that used in conventional ring spinning and will not be discussed.

In the conventional ring-spinning machine, the strand of fibre is drafted by passing it between successive pairs of rollers of different surface speeds. In this roller drafting system, fibres are accelerated when their leading ends approach the nip point of the front rollers. The position of the leading ends of fibres when acceleration takes place is called the velocity change position for the fibre leading end. Since this change position is distributed generally through the drafting zone, the distribution of the fibre leading ends and the thickness irregularity of a drafted sliver are different from those of the sliver before drafting. If the velocity change positions were stationary, the distribution of fibres in a sliver would be randomized; this would result in a greater regularity in thickness of the drafted sliver. If the distribution of the change positions varies with time, a drafting wave will appear; this reduces the regularity of thickness.

In the break-spinning machine, fibres are accelerated by the airflow, or by the mechanical action of a combing cylinder, when the trailing ends of the fibre leave the nip point of the feeding device. The position of the trailing ends of fibres at the point of acceleration may be called the velocity change position for fibre trailing ends. The distribution of these change positions for fibre trailing ends and its variance with time will have much the same effect as before on the thickness of the web collected on the inside wall of the drum. In the drafting operation of a break-spinning machine, however, the fibre trailing ends are controlled, whereas in roller drafting, the leading fibre ends are controlled.

In conventional roller drafting, uniform yarn is obtained when the velocity change position is stationary and individual fibres move independently. The same principle applies to the drafting in break spinning. The fibre bundle must be separated into single fibres and the velocity change position should be at a point near to the feeding device if a uniform yarn is to be obtained. Assuming all the fibres move in a cluster of K fibres, the relative variance (variance/(mean)^2) of the spun yarn will be K times as large as the relative variance when the clusters are separated into individual fibres. It is most important, therefore, that all the clusters should be separated into individual fibres. If this separation is perfect, any variation in the velocity change position will not significantly affect the yarn quality in break spinning.

If fibres in a cluster are to separate easily, interfibre cohesion should be low. Cohesion between fibres is related not only to the frictional properties of the fibres but also to their crimp. The relationship between inter-fibre cohesion and spinnability was investigated by carrying out tensile tests on slivers or rovings. The tensile strength of slivers or rovings provides a measure of the degree of cohesion between fibres. Table 12.3 shows the relationship between tenacity and the U% of the yarn spun. It is quite clear from Table 12.1 that the lower the strength of rovings, the fewer are the yarn breaks in spinning. It is also apparent that the higher the strength of rovings, the greater is the

I

SPINNABILITY

	Roving strength gf	Yarn break index
Rayon	24	1·0
Polypropylene	33	1·5
Acrylic	55	2·3
Rayon	60	2·1
Polyester	78	6·0
Polyester	118	14·0

Table 12.1

irregularity of the yarns. These results show that spinnability is greatly influenced by the cohesion between fibres. The spinnability of fibres in break spinning is related not only to the kind of fibres but also to their crimp, denier and length, and to oils or other substances which may have been applied to them.

When the fibres are carried away in the air flow and move to the inside of the drum, the distance between the fibre leading ends changes, but the relative position of fibres alters little. During this transport phase, entanglement and fibre bending may cause trouble. In experiments, the air resistance of fibres was measured, as this is one of the factors affecting fibre position. The tests were carried out on single fibres. A fibre was placed in the air flow in a lengthwise direction, one end of the fibre being connected to a strain meter. No significant correlations were observed between the air resistance of fibres and yarn breaks during spinning, nor between air resistance and yarn quality. The tensile strength of the roving and the cohesion between fibres have a more significant effect than air resistance on the yarn quality.

THE SELF-DOUBLING EFFECT

Fibres laid on the inside of the drum by the air flow are subjected to a form of doubling operation. The web on the drum is joined to the twisted yarn, which is then removed by the take-up roller. The surface speed of the inside wall of the drum is perhaps 100 to 300 times higher than that of the take-up roller. Thus, the draft ratio at this stage is fractional i.e. 1/100 to 1/300. A self-doubling effect is caused by the fractional draft ratios, resulting in an extremely uniform yarn.

The effect may be considered mathematically as follows, the following symbols being adopted:

U = Delivery speed of slivers from the feeding device.
V = Surface speed of the collecting surface of the rotating drum.
W = Surface speed of the take-up roller.
R = Radius of the drum.
Ψ = Rotational speed of the drum in revolutions per minute $= V.(2\pi R)^{-1}$

For simplicity, slivers delivered from the feeding device may be assumed to have a sinusoidal thickness irregularity of wave-length λ and relative amplitude a.

The thickness of sliver $S_i(x)$ at the position X taken on the lengthwise axis of the sliver is expressed in equation 12.1, wherein $\bar{S}_i$ refers to the average value of $S_i(x)$;

$$S_i(x) = \bar{S}_i \left(1 + a \operatorname{Sin} \frac{2\pi}{\lambda} X\right) \quad \text{(Eq. 12.1)}$$

The sliver is drafted between the feeding device and the collection surface of the drum at a draft ratio of V/U. The sliver after drafting, called a layer, will have a sinusoidal variance with a wave length of $\lambda V/U$ and relative amplitude of a. The average thickness of sliver after drafting is $\bar{S}_i\,U/V$. Denoting the thickness of the layer $S(x)$ we get equation 12.2.

$$S(x) = \bar{S}_i \frac{U}{V} \left\{ 1 + a \sin \frac{2\pi X}{\lambda_{\bar{U}}^{V}} \right\} \quad \text{...............} \quad \text{(Eq. 12.2)}$$

The layers, each with the thickness given by equation 12.2, are laid on top of one another on the internal collecting surface of the drum. The deposited multiple layers are peeled from the collecting surface and joined to the twisted yarn. The total number of layers is $Q = V/W$. Layers are accumulated on the inside wall of the drum successively at intervals of $k2\pi R$. The resultant thickness $S(x)$ of the fibre bundle removed (that is the thickness of spun yarn) is given by equation 12.3.

$$S(x) = \bar{S}_i \frac{U}{V} \sum_{k=0}^{k=Q-1} 1 + a \sin \frac{2\pi}{\lambda_{\bar{U}}^{V}} (X + k2\pi R) \quad \text{...........(Eq. 12.3)}$$

In the case where $\frac{\lambda V}{U}$ is large compared to $2\pi^2 R$, equation 12.3 can be expressed in approximate form as shown in equation 12.4. It will be noted that $\frac{\lambda V}{U}$ is the wavelength of error in the layer approaching the collecting surface and may be written λ'.

$$S(x) \simeq \bar{S}_i \frac{QU}{V} \left[1 + aA \sin \frac{2\pi}{\lambda'} \left\{ X + (Q-1)\pi R \right\} \right] \quad \text{......} \quad \text{(Eq. 12.4)}$$

This may be simplified further by expressing the equation solely in terms of error as shown in equation 12.5.

$$aA = \text{Max. \% error in yarn} = \left(\frac{a}{Z} \sin Z \right) 100\% \quad \text{......(Eq. 12.5)}$$

a = amplitude of sliver error[1]

$$Z = \frac{\pi^2 DQ}{\lambda'} = P\pi$$

λ' = wavelength of error in *layer*
   = wavelength of error in *yarn*
Q = doubling factor
D = drum diameter.

It might be noted that P is the number of error wavelengths in the total length of all the layers accumulated on the collecting surface just before they are converted into yarn, i.e.

$$P = \frac{Q \times \text{drum circumference}}{\text{Error wavelength of layer}}$$

Fig. 12.1 shows the relation between A and P and it can be seen that A decreases with an increase of P. This means that the amplitude of the periodic irregularity of the spun yarn decreases with the increase of P and that it becomes almost zero when P is greater than 4, i.e. when each layer has an error wavelength of less than $\frac{Q}{4}$ of the circumference of the collecting surface. This self-doubling effect is the most characteristic feature in break spinning.

In order to illustrate the effect of self-doubling as described

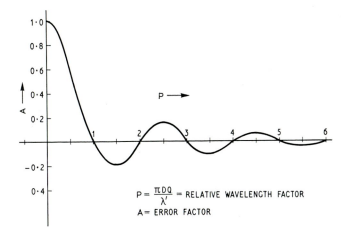

$P = \frac{\pi D Q}{\lambda'}$ = RELATIVE WAVELENGTH FACTOR

A = ERROR FACTOR

Fig. 12.1

above, a yarn of 24s (English cotton count) was spun in a break-spinning machine equipped with an eccentric roller drafting device. The same count yarn was also spun in a ring spinning machine equipped with the same drafting device. Fig. 12.2 shows the results. The fibre used was a polyester staple of $1\frac{1}{2}$ in. $\times$ 1.5 denier. The diameter of the front top roller was 1.15 in. with an eccentricity of 0.02 in., and the drafting ratio between the front and second rollers was 20.0. As can be seen from Fig. 12.2, a periodic amplitude irregularity of about 18% was observed in the ring spun yarn, whilst there was scarcely any in the yarn produced by the break-spinning machine. In this case the value of P was 1.75 and A was 0.14.

THE EFFECT OF USING AN ECCENTRIC FRONT DRAFTING ROLLER

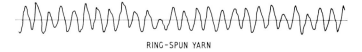

RING-SPUN YARN

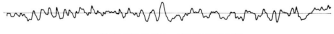

OPEN-END YARN i.e. BREAK-SPUN YARN

Fig. 12.2

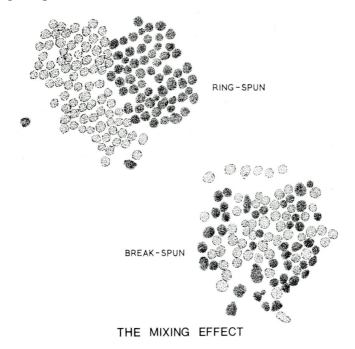

RING - SPUN

BREAK - SPUN

THE MIXING EFFECT

Fig. 12.3

THE DRUM AS A MIXER

Self-doubling is also very effective for making a uniform blend of fibres in the yarn. Because Q layers are deposited on the inside wall of the drum, this has the same effect as doubling Q slivers in roller drafting. When different fibres are blended, the greater the number of doublings, the more uniform the blend of fibres in the yarn. The theoretical number of total doublings necessary is more than the average number of fibres in the yarn cross section; even so, the doubling is sufficient to ensure that few fibres of the same sort remain together.

In conventional spinning, several separate doubling processes are necessary, but in break spinning this is not so. To demonstrate this effect, yarns of 26s cotton count were produced by feeding two rovings to both sorts of spinning machine. The two rovings were of polyester staple fibres, $1\frac{1}{2}$ in. $\times$ 1.5 denier, one roving being white and the other dyed black. Fig. 12.3. shows a photograph of the cross section of yarns produced by both methods; it is clear that the yarn produced by break spinning consists of an extremely uniform fibre blend. The value of Q in this experiment was about 140 and the number of fibres was 100.

Synthetic yarn and synthetic blended yarn are used largely for outer wear, and yarns must be more uniform than those needed generally in producing cotton fabrics. The effect of self-doubling is thus extremely important. Table 12.3 shows the quality of synthetic yarns and synthetic blended yarns produced; the U% and the variance of yarn strength

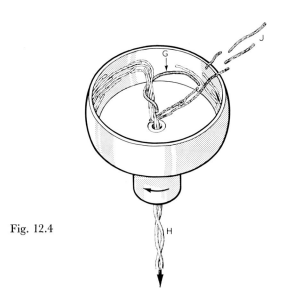

Fig. 12.4

Fig. 12.5   Good and bad break-spun yarn.

are small compared with those of yarn produced by ring spinning.

YARN CONSTRUCTION

The constituent fibres of break-spun yarn remain almost helical in shape. There is a constant deviation from the central axis of the yarn, which differs in this respect from ring-spun yarn. Also, the arrangement of fibres in a break-spun yarn affects its appearance, which is different from that of a ring-spun yarn. As shown in Fig. 12.4, some fibres may be taken off the thin end of the tail of fibres lying on the collecting surface, and some fibres may be blown against the radial portion of yarn already formed. These fibres form a coil of fine helical pitch around the parent yarn. The greater the number of these wrapped fibres, the worse is the quality of the yarn and the greater the number of yarn breaks during spinning. Fig. 12.5 shows good and bad yarns produced by this method. Good yarn has some resemblance to a ring-spun yarn; bad yarn is quite different in appearance, having many fibres coiled around the outer layers of the yarn.

Twist Construction

In break-spun yarn, the twist pitch of fibres in the centre differs from that in the outer layer of the yarn. It follows

K

ORIENTATION INDEX

Polypropylene	Break-spun		84·2%
Acrylic	''	''	80·2%
Polyester	''	''	82·9%
	Ring-spun		87·8%

Table 12.2

that the fibres in the yarn cannot all become parallel; even when the yarn is untwisted, the inner fibres are twisted in the opposite direction. A twist and untwist method may be used to test the twist of the yarn. Test results using this method show a twist lower by 5 to 20% than the calculated twist.

As in the case of cotton yarns, the strength of a synthetic break-spun yarn is low compared with that of an equivalent ring-spun yarn. Also, the optimum twist is higher and the bulkiness is greater. The torque in the yarn and the tendency to snarl are both small at a given twist. These features are a consequence of the peculiar twist construction of the yarn. The orientation index of fibres in a break-spun yarn, as measured by a combing method [25], is slightly worse than in a ring-spun yarn; caused partly by the twist construction of the yarn and partly by the bending of fibres. It is believed that fibres are bent as they are carried in the air flow to the collecting surface of the drum.* Table 12.2 shows test results for the orientation index of fibres in break-spun yarn.

The ratio of the diameter of drum to the length of fibres has a major influence on the twist construction of the yarn. The number of fibres coiled around the outer layer of the yarn increases as the fibre length increases (see Shimizu [27]). Further relationships have not yet been found between the properties of fibres and the twist construction of the yarn.

* Hooks and bends are caused by bridging fibres—see Chapter 10.

The design of the spinning mechanism (including opening device, conveying pipe and drum) has a greater effect than fibre properties on the yarn construction.

The transmission of twist at the twisting zone is an important factor in spinning. In ring spinning, the twist region is near the nip point of the front roller; in break spinning, the twist zone extends from the yarn outlet to the point at which fibre is taken from the inside wall of the drum. This may result in poor transmission of twist along the fibre bundle, causing yarn end breaks during spinning. As Ripka [23] suggested from his precise analysis of yarn shape inside the drum, important factors affecting the quality of yarn will be (1) yarn shape, (2) yarn tension on the inside of the drum, (3) cohesion between fibres, (4) friction between yarn and inside wall of the drum and (5) air resistance to the fibres. The shape, material and finish of the inside of the drum, the spinning finishes and the crimp characteristics of the fibre are important factors. Adhesion of fibre spinning finishes on the inside wall of the drum should be prevented, and air movement within the drum should be controlled.

BREAK-SPUN YARNS

Staple (1·5 den x 1½")	Tex	T.F.	gf/tex	Elongation %	U %
Acrylic	19·5	4·1	16·9	22	10·6
Polypropylene	20·0	3·9	26·2	18	11·6
Polyester	19·7	3·9	21·8	18	13·7
Rayon	20·0	4·0	13·0	11	12·8
Polyester (65) + Cotton (35)	19·7	4·1	13·5	17	13·1
Polyester (55) + Rayon (45)	14·9	4·2	16·7	11	13·1

Table 12.3

PROPERTIES OF SYNTHETIC AND BLENDED BREAK-SPUN YARN

Table 12.3 shows the results of tests carried out on various synthetic and blended yarns. Yarns of three different synthetic fibres of $1\frac{1}{2}$ in. $\times$ 1.5 denier were produced in both ring- and break-spinning machines. Table 12.4 shows the tensile strength, bulkiness, hairiness and abrasion resistance of these yarns expressed as ratios relating break- and ring-spun yarns. The results are similar to those obtained by Kasparek [24] in experiments with cotton yarns.

In the following paragraphs, the main properties of break-spun yarns will be discussed individually. Comparative figures are quoted which relate them to the properties of equivalent ring-spun yarns.

(1) Uniformity

The unevenness $(U\%)$ and the variance of single end strengths of synthetic and blended yarns were generally small (see Table 12.3).

(2) Single end strength

The single end strength was smaller by 5% to 20% (see Table 12.4)

PROPERTIES OF BREAK-SPUN YARNS
RELATIVE TO RING-SPUN YARNS

	Strength	Spec. vol.	Hairs/M	Abrasion Resistance
Polypropylene	0·86	1·14	0·33	0·79
Acrylic	0·94	1·12	0·26	1·00
Polyester	0·85	1·17	0·37	0·52
		Ratio $= \dfrac{\text{B-S}}{\text{Ring}}$		

Table 12.4

SIZING   CHARACTERISTICS

Size	Starch			Synth.
% Concentration	11·3	7·9	5·6	7·5
% Size on B-S Yarn	18·5	12·9	8·9	14·0
% Size on Ring Yarn	12·5	9·6	6·9	9·9

Table 12.5

(3) Bulkiness
The apparent volume per gramme of yarn was 10% to 20% greater.

(4) Hairiness
The hairs on a yarn of 1 m. length were counted. The number of hairs on break-spun yarn was found to be about one third of the number on a ring-spun yarn.

(5) Abrasion resistance
Yarns were abraded on the edge of a metal plate, using the flexing and abrasion method ASTM D 1175-64T, and the number of abrasions needed to break the yarn was counted. The twists of the two types of yarn were almost equal. Results are shown in Table 12.4. The abrasion resistance of break-spun polypropylene yarn was similar to that of ring-spun yarn; the abrasion resistance of break-spun polyester yarn, on the other hand, was very much lower than that of ring-spun yarn. The reason for the latter result lay in the peculiar twist construction of the outermost layers of and yarn, and in the inherent properties of polyester fibre.

The frictional properties of synthetic break-spun yarn change rapidly with twist.

(6) Affinity of the yarn to warp sizing
A 24s polyester cotton yarn (blend 65%/35%) was sized and the amount of size taken up by the yarn was measured.

Two kinds of size were used at three different concentrations, the main ingredients being either starch or synthetic size, and Table 12.5 shows the results. It is apparent that the amount of size placed on the break-spun yarn was from 1.3 to 1.5 times as much as on the ring-spun yarn; the concentration of size in the liquor used for break-spun yarn can thus be reduced by about 30%.

(7) Other properties of break-spun yarn

Bending rigidity of break-spun yarn is lower than that of ring-spun yarn, but the two types of yarn show little difference in the tendency to snarl.

SOME PROBLEMS IN COMMERCIAL PRODUCTION OF SYNTHETIC AND BLENDED BREAK-SPUN YARNS

Many kinds of woven and knitted fabrics have been manufactured from synthetic and blended break-spun yarns. The main features of these products may be summarised as follows:

(1) Yarn is uniform with little hairiness, and the appearance of fabric is good,

(2) Fabrics tend to be bulky and soft in handle,

(3) Pilling is slight,

(4) Strength is low.

The low number of yarn knots and high moisture absorption are advantageous properties in many applications.

The low strength of break-spun yarns is a disadvantage, particularly when yarns are used in the production of fabric for working clothes. The strength has been found adequate, however, for most clothing applications. Fabrics of excellent general quality have been made, and break-spun yarn is particularly suitable for use in underwear fabrics. The small amount of pilling is an important characteristic in synthetic fibre products.

The main advantages of break spinning lie in low spinning and labour costs. Calculations based on the spinning of 20s to 40s c.c. yarns have indicated that the number of operatives needed in the break spinning of man-made fibres is less than half the number needed in ring spinning; break spinning costs are 15 to 30% lower than ring spinning costs. In general, the finer the yarn count to be produced, the less is the difference in spinning costs between break and ring spinning. The critical yarn count depends upon machine cost, spinning speed, and cost of electric power consumed, but it is true to say that coarse yarns generally can be produced more cheaply by break spinning than by ring spinning. According to Catling's [28] calculations, the yarn count produced should not be finer than 50s at the present stage of development in break spinning.

In Japan, yarns of less than 40s count represent some 85% of the total production of synthetic yarns; 25s to 45s account for about 75% of total yarn production. Yarns coarser than 50s thus represent a considerable proportion of the market, and it is probable that a similar situation exists in other parts of the world.

Problems

If the commercial production of synthetic and blended break-spun yarns is to develop on a major scale, the following problems remain to be solved.

First, the technique must be adapted to make it suitable for spinning long fibres. This will mean using a large diameter drum which is costly to operate at very high speed. Also, it will be necessary to design an opening device suitable for long fibres. Synthetic fibres are used to a large extent in outer wear, shirting and domestic fabrics. For such end-uses, fibres of more than 2 denier are required, and the fibre length is commonly more than 2 inches. The number of ring spindles producing synthetic and blended yarn from fibre of less than $1\frac{1}{2}$ in. length is probably about 1/3 of the total number of spindles used for synthetic fibres. The development of break-spinning machines capable of spinning fibres longer than 2 in. will greatly extend the market for break-spun yarns.

The second problem which remains to be solved in break spinning is the prevalence of slubs on the yarn. The need for uniformity in thickness of synthetic and blended yarns is generally more critical than in the case of cotton yarns. In synthetic spun yarns, almost no slub defects can be tolerated, particularly when making union fabrics with filament yarn. As Kasparek [24] indicated, the number of slubs is usually less in break-spun yarn. Moreover, slubs can be removed without difficulty from ring-spun yarn, using virtually any type of slub catcher. The slub catchers in general use today, however, are not always effective in removing slubs from break-spun yarns. New ways of preventing slub formation in break-spun yarns are needed, and slub removers suitable for use with these yarns must be developed.

The third problem of break spinning is machine cost. The cost of break spinning is governed mainly by machine cost, delivery speed and power consumption. To make break spinning cheaper, it is necessary to decrease the machine cost and power consumption, and to increase the delivery speed. Increase in delivery speed, however, results in an increase in power consumption, and there are economic and technical factors which limit the extent to which delivery speed can be increased. The most promising line of attack on the problem of cost, therefore, is to reduce the capital cost of the machine.

At the present time, spindle speeds in ring spinning have reached 15,000 rev./min., and excellent auto-doffers and auto-winders have been developed. Ring spinning has reached a high state of efficiency, and the cost of the break-spinning machine will have to be reduced substantially if it

Fig. 12.6 An operator piecing-up an MS 400 machine.

K*

MS400

Cheese	200 mm. 1·7 kg
Sliver	14" diam. x 42" cans
Motor capacity	22 kW 16 kW at 30,000 rev/min
Drum speed	20,000 to 40,000 rev/min
Yarn count	10^S to 50^S c.c.
Staple length	0·8" to 2·0"

Table 12.6

is to compete effectively. It has been estimated that an economic figure for purchase cost should be less than about $140 per "spindle", assuming the drum speed to be 33,000 rev./min.

A photograph of the MS 400 machine is shown in Fig. 12.6 and the specification is given in Table 12.6.

13

Break Spinning of Long-staple Fibres

by C. J. Copple* and P. H. Challoner*

The technology of ring spinning long staple fibres in now very highly developed, and significant increases in processing speeds seem unlikely. Break-spinning techniques, however, have made it possible for semi-worsted type yarns to be produced at speeds at least three to four times higher, with the added advantage that yarn packages of almost un-limited size can be produced.

Break-spun yarns are generally more regular than ring-spun yarns, but they are weaker and require more twist than corresponding ring-spun yarns. Carpets produced from break-spun yarns appear to be as good in every respect as those produced from ring-spun yarns. Further applications are at present limited; in particular, the break spinner would seem to have little to offer to the woollen and fine-worsted sections of the textile trade.

In this chapter, arguments for and against break spinning of long staple fibres are outlined. A description is given of the production, properties and possible end uses of semi-worsted type yarns produced on a centrifugal drum spinning head.

Introduction

Long staple spinning is a specialised branch of the textile industry which makes use of well-established processes. Over the years, it has tended to resist major changes.

At the close of the '60s, practically all long staple spinning was based on the ring frame and the mule. In 1969, for example, there were still about 3.6 million woollen/worsted mule spindles in operation throughout the world (excluding

* Conference author. T.M.M. (Research) Ltd., Helmshore, Rossen-dale, U.K.

267

the Middle East, South American and East European countries), as compared with 9.1 million ring spindles.

Both the woollen and worsted spinning processes utilise long-staple fibres, but the characters of the yarns and the end uses are quite different. The viability of any alternative system will depend to a great extent on its capacity to produce yarns comparable with existing yarns made by these long-established process.

CONVENTIONAL SYSTEMS

(1) WOOLLEN SYSTEM

Woollen processing is basically a coarse/medium count system producing yarns in the range 650 to 50 tex. It has been described as the shortest commercially-accepted raw material-to-yarn textile process, and is capable of handling both natural and man-made fibres over a wide range of staple lengths and denier. The system consists of a series of carding operations, the number being determined by the raw material quality and the end-product. The final card web is divided into strips which are formed into slubbing by passing them through rubbing rollers reciprocating at 90° to the slubbing path. These are then wound on to bobbins which are deposited in the ring-frame creel.

Due to the method of draft and twist insertion at the ring frame, yarns of full soft handle can be produced which are unequalled by those produced by any other textile processes. The yarns, in general, tend to be low in strength but of good extensibility. Uses range from coarse carpet yarns to finer yarns for knitted, upholstery and dress goods. Typical production figures for a modern woollen ring frame with a 16 in. lift and $4\frac{1}{2}$ in. diameter ring when processing a 300 tex yarn would be 18 oz./spindle hour. Package weights vary from approximately 46 oz. for a 650 tex yarn down to 10 oz. for a 50 tex yarn.

(2) WORSTED SYSTEM

Worsted processing is concerned usually with yarns from a comber/gill preparation; it caters for the fine or quality end of the trade. Typical products are yarns for suitings, fine dress goods, knitted fabrics etc., in the range 70 to 11 tex. Only the finer wool fibres in the 3 in. to 8 in. mean fibre length range are used for this purpose. The yarns have a smooth round appearance with a well parallelised fibre structure.

In recent years, the heavy roving worsted system has come into its own, producing yarns in the 300 to 40 tex range. These yarns find applications in the heavy fabric, upholstery, apparel and hosiery trades. The processing of blends of wool and suitable man-made staple fibres to obtain improved wear, abrasion and strength characteristics is quite common, as is the processing of 100% synthetic fibres in various staple lengths and deniers. A modern heavy roving worsted ring frame would produce a 110 tex yarn at about 6 oz./spindle hour on a 14 in. lift × 4 in. diameter package. Package weights vary from 24 oz. for a 110 tex yarn to $3\frac{1}{4}$ oz. for a 11 tex yarn.

Semi-Worsted Processing

Semi-worsted processing is a relative newcomer to the long-staple industry. This system is a cross between the woollen and worsted processes. A typical modern semi-worsted installation would consist of an opening and blending plant, hopper feeder, card set with twin coilers, two or three passages of intersecting gills and double-apron drafting, sliver-fed ring frames. The yarns produced cover a range from 650 to 120 tex; in appearance and handle, they vary between woollen and worsted yarns. They have some of the fullness of woollen yarns, but their strengths approach those of worsted yarns. These yarns have been used primarily in tufted carpets, but they are extending into the hosiery, hand knitting and upholstery fields. Fibres used include rayon, modified rayon, polyamide, acrylic, wool and other materials of various deniers and staple lengths. Typical production figures for a semi-worsted ring frame with an 18 in. lift and 5 in. diameter ring when processing a 300 tex synthetic fibre yarn would be 18 oz./spindle hour. The net package weight would be 40 oz.

Break-spun yarn, as a general rule, cannot match the more exacting requirements of certain ring-spun yarns, and it is probable that the semi-worsted section of the trade offers the best chance for successful development of commercial long-staple break-spinning machines. Research and development in break spinning have been conducted intermittently for 100 years or more. Before any new process becomes commercially attractive, however, it must have well-defined operational, economic or aesthetic advantages over existing processes. In this respect, the ring frame is a formidable opponent, and the break spinner is competing with a highly developed technology. The ring frame is a versatile but relatively simple machine of surprisingly low capital cost capable of producing a wide range of either cheap or quality yarns. However, despite its present pre-eminence, the ring frame has limitations that justify attempts to develop an alternative staple yarn spinning process. The scope for further development of the ring frame is severely limited by these restrictions; this fact is highlighted by striking developments during the 1960s in the pre-preparation machinery used prior to the spinning process. There was comparatively little progress in ring spinning during this same period.

Consideration of the limitations of the ring frame throws light on the objectives of the break-spinning process. In ring spinning the package must be rotated to insert twist, the amount of twist being determined by the ratio of spindle speed to front roller speed. Of necessity, this requires high package rotational speeds, which impose limits on the maximum spinning speed. The factors involved may be summarised as:—

    (i) excessive power consumption,
   (ii) traveller wear and burning,
  (iii) high level of yarn tension required to control the yarn balloon,
  (iv) fibre loss, windage and lashing of broken ends,
   (v) difficulties in piecing up at high delivery speeds.

Because of these limitations, small package capacities have to be used. The ultimate limit for (say) a 16 in. lift × 5 in. diameter ring semi-worsted frame is about 6,000 to 7,000 rev./min., even when the balloon tension is reduced by using suppressed balloon spindles. In the case of worsted yarns, processed on a 8 in. lift × 2 in. diameter ring package, the spindle speed would be in the region of 15,000 to 17,000 rev./min., but yarn hairiness becomes a critical factor at such speeds. In break spinning, the package need be rotated only at the relatively low speed required to wind the yarn; therein lies the fundamental advantage of break spinning.

BREAK-SPINNING SYSTEMS FOR USE WITH LONG-STAPLE FIBRES

Unless some unforeseen major break-through occurs in the near future, only the electro-mechanical and the aero-mechanical types of break spinner need be considered as potentially viable devices for long staple spinning.

In the electro-mechanical system, electrostatic and mechanical forces are used to transport fibres to the yarn assembly point, and to hold them under control during the mechanical twisting action. In theory, this has the fundamental advantage that fibre parallelisation and control should be maintained during assembly of the yarn, and sufficient mechanical force should be available to impart twist. Yarn tensions are also low compared with those in ring spinning. In the field of long staple spinning, this system offers the greatest attraction to the worsted spinner, where generally fine counts of yarn of a highly parallelised fibre structure are required. Unfortunately, these characteristics can be achieved only at spinning speeds of the same order as those of the ring frame, and then only on an experimental basis with a cost disadvantage. At higher speeds, aerodynamic forces interfere with electrostatic forces, and the performance of the system falls off; these disadvantages might be overcome, however, by further development.

Another difficulty arises from the problem of obtaining an effective twist gripper that can be re-pieced conveniently. It is also necessary to have an extra high tension supply of about 20,000 volts upwards. Because it is the voltage gradient which is important, the system is restricted to the shorter end of the long-staple field, otherwise the absolute voltage becomes excessive. Despite the limitations of the electro-mechanical break spinning system, however, development will continue; the inherent advantages are sufficient to ensure this.

Aero-Mechanical Spinner

There are many variants of the aero-mechanical type of break spinner, the most highly developed being the use of the inner surface of a rotating cylinder to collect and twist the fibres. The system has been termed drum spinning, turbine spinning, pot spinning and, more recently, rotor spinning. The first of these terms will be used.

Basically there are two ways of supplying fibres to a spinning drum; either from a standard semi-worsted drafting system using a higher-than-normal front roller speed, or from a beater system with a pinned feed roller and a high speed large-diameter beater. Both systems have advantages and disadvantages. A drafting system feed can give the best presentation of fibres. The beater system is more compact and only the feed roller need be stopped when the supply of fibres has to be interrupted. This can be done by a clutch operated from the stop motion micro-switch. A disadvantage of a beater feed on the other hand, derives from the possibility of fibre breakage due to the large difference in surface speeds of feed roller and beater. Also, the large diameter beater requires considerable power to drive it at high speed.

The break in fibre flow is between the beater or front roller of the drafting system and the drum. An airflow carries the fibres across the break, the transport airflow being achieved in a variety of ways, using the pumping action of the rotor, an external source of suction or a combination of both. The transport airflow requirements of a long staple drum spinner are more exacting than those of the short staple version; the rotor speed must be variable over a wide range and for this reason it is impossible to rely solely on the rotor pumping action for satisfactory spinning.

In drum speed and diameter, the design requirements for a long-staple drum-spinner are more exacting than those of the short-staple spinner. The newly-formed yarn is subject to complex radial centrifugal and tangential drag forces as well as to the torque necessary to insert twist. The radial centrifugal forces may approach or even exceed yarn strength, causing an end break. For this reason the drum diameter and speed should be as small as possible, yet they must be large enough to generate sufficient tension to give a reasonable yarn strength. Also, they should be as small as possible in order to minimise power requirements, and to guard against mechanical failure of the drum. On the other hand, to ensure good fibre ring construction and regularity, the ratio of drum diameter to staple length should be as large as possible. The circumference of the drum must be considerably greater than the length of the longest fibre to be processed in it. A compromise must therefore be made, the balance differing from that reached in designing the short staple spinner. In the long-staple spinner, the drum speed must be reduced to compensate for the larger diameter needed.

A pair of rollers is required to pull the yarn out of the drum, the yarn being wound on to a package using either a grooved roller or a cam-operated traverse mechanism. The package may be a cheese or a cone, and it can be made to any required size, but there are problems in yarn tension compensation in cone winding from a constant delivery drum. A stop motion must be incorporated in the system, either between the drum and the delivery rollers or preferably between the delivery and take-up. This would normally be a micro-switch which would shut off the feed in the event of yarn breakage.

Problems

By the end of the '60s, drum spinning showed promise of finding limited application in the commercial long-staple field. But there were still problems to be solved, notably with respect to the count range, staple length and type of yarn which the system could produce. Mechanical speed limits and economic considerations of the system also had to be taken into account. Power consumption was a major factor in operating costs, particularly in view of the large diameter rotor needed for long-staple spinning. At rotor speeds of 20,000 rev./min., rotor power alone can account for 50% of the total machine power; at 25,000 rev./min., this may increase to 75%. Whilst processing power can be affected by the fibre being spun, it is insignificant compared with the power required merely to turn the rotor. Good mechanical design and good rotor bearings are vitally important factors in the development of a successful system.

DRUM SPINNING POSSIBILITIES IN THE LONG STAPLE FIELD

Woollen yarns are of relatively low twist, and therefore lack strength. This is one of the factors which precludes the use of drum spinning for the production of these yarns, as radial and tangential forces may exceed yarn strength, causing breaks. Furthermore, drum-spun yarns require higher twist factors than ring-spun yarns, and this alters the character of the yarn. Another problem is that woollen-type yarns require an oil treatment for the carding process, and oil or other additives tend to reduce the efficiency of the drum-spinning system. The additives contaminate the inner surface of the drum, and build up in the groove which constitutes the collecting surface, causing a break-down of the fibre ring lying on that surface. The processing of wool raises further difficulties due to natural grease, dead skin, mineral deposits and vegetable contaminants. Experimental work is continuing, however, in an attempt to improve the spinning performance of wool, alone and in blends with other fibres.

Worsted yarns are produced usually in the medium/fine count range; the fibres being parallelised, e.g. by combing before spinning. There are economic and technological considerations which limit the application of drum spinning in this field. Yarns processed on the heavy roving system are virtually fine semi-worsted yarns, and may be considered under that heading.

Taking all factors into account, it appears that long-staple break spinners will probably find their earliest applications in the semi-worsted field.

PROPERTIES OF LONG-STAPLE BREAK-SPUN YARNS

Long-staple break-spun yarns are considerably weaker than the corresponding ring-spun yarns, despite the greater amount of twist that has to be used. This effect is even more pronounced than in the case of short-staple yarns. Break-spun yarns are generally more regular than the ring-spun equivalents but in contrast to the short-staple yarns, long-staple break-spun yarns are less extensible than equivalent conventional yarns. Break-spun yarns usually have a better blackboard appearance; they appear to be fuller and less hairy.

Long-staple break-spun yarns have to be spun with higher twist factors than ring-spun yarns; for example, a blend of 50/50 "Courtelle"/"Evlan" of 6 in. staple length, 15 denier fibre fineness and 380 tex linear density was spun on a semi-worsted ring frame with 3.8 t.p.i., but it required 5.5 t.p.i. on a break-spinning rig to obtain a satisfactory yarn. The comparative strengths were 5.8 and 4.8 gf/tex respectively. Experience with a wide range of long-staple materials has shown that long fibres require more twist than short fibres; for example, yarns have been spun to 310 tex from 4 in., 5 in. and 6 in. staple lengths of 15 denier "Acrilan" under similar spinning conditions, and for satisfactory spinning the twists required were 5.5, 6.3 and 6.5 t.p.i. respectively. This illustrates the relative loss of fibre order in a break-spun yarn compared with a ring-spun yarn. On the other hand, a large quantity of $2\frac{1}{2}$ in. "Evlan" mixture of 50% 8 denier and 50% 15 denier has been spun to 400 tex with the same twist as would be used in a ring frame, viz., 4.6 t.p.i.

Airflow has an important effect on yarn properties. Yarns have been spun from a blend of 80/20 "Evlan"/nylon at airflows ranging from 30 c.f.m. down to an airflow too slight to be measured with the equipment available. The yarn breaking strength deteriorated from 5.2 to 3.6 gf/tex, extensibility from 13.4% to 11.1%, regularity from 10.1 to 10.7%U. The blackboard appearance also deteriorated. A compromise must be made between acceptable yarn quality and the cost of power needed to pump the air.

Tests have shown that the strengths of piecings of break-spun yarns were 86% of the mean yarn strength as compared with a normal value of 88% with ring-spun yarns. Piecings made on the break-spun yarn had a better appearance as they were less bulky and longer.

The major advantages of break spinning can be lost if the end breakage rate is too high. Some fibres (e.g. "Evlan") gave no trouble in this respect, but others, such as nylon or wool, caused problems. Twist level and the control of atmospheric conditions were significant factors.

Creel preparation is also important. A test was carried out in which several different slivers, ranging from card sliver to 3rd passage gill sliver with 84 doublings, were produced from 4 in. staple length 15 denier "Evlan"; they were all spun to 310 tex with 5.0 t.p.i. twist, and the properties of the yarns were compared. It was found that the best yarns were produced from slivers which had had three passages of gilling, using a total draft of between 125 and 200 with 25 to 40 doublings. Typical sliver weights used were between 3.8 and 4.8 Ktex. This again emphasises the importance of fibre assembly in long-staple spinning.

Allowing for the fact that break-spun yarns require more twist than ring-spun yarns, the much higher speed of the rotor makes possible a production rate several times that of a ring spindle. Assuming a rotor speed of 25,000 rev./min. against a spindle speed of 5,500 rev./min., and allowing 25% more twist in the break-spun yarn, the rate of production will be more than $3\frac{1}{2}$ times that obtained from a ring-frame. Another advantage of break spinning is that a large knotless package can be produced. In tufted carpet manufacture, this package can be creeled directly on the tufting machine, thus cutting out the intermediate winding process. These advantages are important in tufted carpet production, and the lower strength of the break-spun yarn is not a critical factor. The break-spun package will unwind satisfactorily during tufting at speeds up to 800 yards/min. The package can be made to almost any weight, 6 to 7 lb. being an acceptable size. The density of the package can be altered by changing the weighting on the package arm.

USES OF LONG STAPLE BREAK-SPUN YARNS

An obvious outlet for long staple break-spun yarn is the tufted carpet industry. Upholstery is a possible field in which the yarns could be used, but the lower strength might be a disadvantage. Most break-spun yarns are unsatisfactory for use as knitting yarns, as some of the apparent bulk may be lost during finishing. This is possibly due to the construction of the yarn, in which individual fibres are wrapped round the body of the yarn. This structure in long-staple yarns impedes the relative movement of individual fibres.

In carpets, the lower strength of break-spun yarns should not be a disadvantage, provided the yarn is strong enough to withstand the actual tufting process without breaking. A tenacity of 5 gf/tex is probably adequate in this respect. The cut tuft made from break-spun yarn is satisfactory, but differs in character from a ring-spun tuft. Abrasion tests carried out on samples of carpets produced from both sorts of yarn did not show any significant difference in abrasion resistance or weight loss. Loop pile carpets made from break-spun yarns are comparable in pattern definition and loop regularity with carpets made from semi-worsted yarns.

It seems probable, therefore, that long-staple break-spun yarns will find early applications in limited fields, such as carpet manufacture, where strength is not very important. In other fields, considerable development will be necessary before long-staple break-spun yarns are able to compete effectively with ring-spun yarns.

CONCLUSION

The pattern of progress within any industry is marked generally by periods of solid progress separated by periods of reduced activity. The textile industry is no exception.

During the present century, the textile industry has been affected by two world wars, by financial stringencies during international money crises, by unsatisfactory marketing conditions, and—in more modern times—by the competing attractions of more sophisticated industries. These and other influences playing on a vast international industry make the task of prophecy a difficult one.

Superimposed upon these swings of economic progress and recession we have the surges of activity that result from new inventions and discoveries. We live today in an age when an experiment carried out in a chemical laboratory can create a vast new industry almost overnight. The development of nylon, for example, brought revolutionary changes to the textile industry. For thousands of years, man had been making textiles from fibres provided by nature, and more recently from natural polymers modified in one way or another. Suddenly, he was presented with a fibre made from a polymer created from simple chemical raw materials.

A development of this type cannot be predicted before it happens, nor can the consequences be assessed with accuracy for some time after it has occurred. Nylon's discovery, for example, created a new branch of chemical and textile technology concerned with the production of the fibre itself. But the introduction of nylon into the textile industry was also to influence every aspect of textile manufacture. New machinery was needed to handle the fibre, and new techniques were devised which made use of its unique characteristics. New dyes were needed, and new finishes required.

Nylon itself was of enormous importance to the textile trade, but it was merely the first of many synthetic fibres which have appeared in post-war years. And as the synthetic fibre industry has grown, so has it stimulated research in the natural fibre field. Faced with competition from synthetic fibres with a range of novel and attractive properties, the producers of natural fibres fought back by developing new processes and techniques for the improvement of natural fibres.

The introduction of synthetic fibres in the years since World War II is an example of a development which brought rapid and revolutionary change to a vast modern industry. Other dramatic developments could occur in other aspects of the textile industry, including spinning, bringing sharp and unpredictable changes in the paths of progress.

In assessing the way in which spinning will develop during the '70s, it is impossible to take account of inventions which may bring such radical changes. It is possible, however, to try and foresee how newly-developed devices and techniques may influence the progress of spinning in the years ahead. This is what the contributors to this book have done.

The self-twist, twistless and break-spun yarns are obviously of outstanding interest in this respect. The productivity of the self-twist device approaches that of bulked filament machines. High speed in self-twisting has been achieved by reducing the rotating element to its minimum diameter, i.e. the diameter of the yarn. There are resemblances to the frictional types of false twisters used by throwsters. Production rates are in the same category as those of false twisters used on continuous filaments, and there seems to be little doubt that prospects for the commercial development of this type of device are good in the area of long staple yarn production. The yarns will probably find their main market in the worsted trade.

Break Spinning

Break spinning, likewise, is at the beginning of what could be a stage of rapid commercial development. The technique has advantages and disadvantages, and further development will no doubt be needed before the future of break spinning becomes clear. Production rates are higher than those of traditional spinning techniques, and this is a powerful spur to continued development.

Economics suggest that break spinning ought to make

headway particularly in the production of coarse yarns from the longer staples. Drum-type machines could well be producing carpet yarns on a significant scale during the early '70s. Such machines were producing traditional cotton yarns during the late 1960s, the economics being favourable except for the finer yarns. As capital costs fall and labour costs rise, the economic position of drum-type break spinning will improve further. As experience grows, the products will improve, new standards of quality will be attained and the ability to handle longer staple lengths will be developed. Thus in the '70s, break spinning will probably take over part of the short-staple market now held by ring spinning, and it is likely to expand into the medium length staple market especially in the area of carpet yarn manufacture.

REFERENCES

1. Williams, S., B.P. 3027, April 1807.
2. DeBarr, A. E. and Cateing, H., "The principles and theory of ring spinning", 1965, Vol. 5, Manual of Cotton Spinning, Textile Institute & Butterworths.
3. Henshaw, D. E., J.T.I., 1969, 60, No. 11, 443.
   Henshaw, D. E., (CSIRO) Australian Patent 260, 092, April 1964, B.P. 1, 121, 942, Oct. 1965.
4. Wray, G. R., "Techniques for the 70s," Textile Institute, 1969.
5. Ziegler, K., Makromole Chem, 1965, 18, 19, 186.
6. Natta, G., J. Poly. Sci., 1955, 16, 143.
7. Rasmussen, O. B., Text. Inst. & Ind., 1964, 2, 258.
8. Ford, J. E., Text. Rec., 1966, 43, 503, 26.
9. Volans, P., and Changani, P. D., "Studies in modern yarn production", Textile Institute, 1968, p. 1.
10. Lawrence, B., U.S.P. 2, 689, 813, Sept. 1954.
11. Meimberg, J., B.P. 828, 804 Feb., 1960; B.P. 969, 046, Sept. 1964; B.P. 1, 033, 074 June 1966.
12. Edberg, B., Textil, 1967, 22, No. 10, 380. "Studies in Modern Yarn Production", Textile Institute, 1968, p. 96.
13. Krause, H. W., "Studies in Modern Yarn Production", Textile Institute, 1968, p. 109.
14. Catling, H., "Studies in Modern Yarn Production", Textile Institute, 1968, p. 75. Text. Inst. & Ind., 1963, 1, No. 3, 12.
15. Lord, P. R., 11th Canadian Textile Seminar, Aug. 1968, p. 25.
16. Keller, H. A., Neue Zuricher Zeitung Technik Fernausgabe 155, June 1967.
17. Anon, I. T. S. Bull., Spinning, 3/1967, p. 1.
18. Jejurikar, G., M.Sc. Thesis, Manchester, 1962. Lord, P. R., Text. Manuf. Nov. 1962, p. 490.
19. Barker, A. F., B. P. 411, 862, June 1934. Text. World, 1962, 112, No. 5, 70.
20. Kyame, G. and Copeland, H., Text. World, 1964, 114, No. 3, 48. U.S.P. 3, 110, 150, Nov. 1963 and U.S.P. 3, 295, 307, 1967.
21. Arschinov, S. I., B.P. 979, 962, Dec. 1961.
22. Gotzfried, K., B.P. 825, 776, Dec. 1955; B.P. 880, 239, Dec. 1957, W. German P. 1, 146, 792, April 1961.
23. Ripka, J., Textil, 1965, 20, No. 8, 292. Textil, 1967, 22, No. 10, 369.
24. Kasparek, J. V., Text. Mfr., 1968, Dec., 484. Text. Mfr., 1966, 92, April, 134. Textil, 1966, 21, No. 6, 213; Textil, 1967, 22, No. 10, 370. Text. Industr., 1967, 131, No. 9, 147.
25. Urano, S., et. al., J. Text. Mach. Soc. Japan, 1963, 16, No. 10, 725. J. Text. Mach. Soc. Japan, 1964, 10, No. 4, 152. Text. Wkly. 1965, 65(1), Jan. 29, p. 172.
26. Rohlena, V., "Studies in Modern Yarn Production", Textile Inst., 1968, p. 130.
27. Shimizu, E., et al., J. Text. Mach. Soc. Japan, 1967, 20, No. 11, 845.
28. Catling, H., Text. Month, 1968, Jan, p. 66.

Index

SPINNING IN THE '70s